CULTURAL DIVERSITY

FRESH VISIONS & BREAKTHROUGH STRATEGIES FOR REVITALIZING THE WORKPLACE

Fieldbook

GEORGE F. SIMONS,
BOB ABRAMMS, &
L. ANN HOPKINS
WITH DIANE J. JOHNSON

PETERSON'S/PACESETTER BOOKS
PRINCETON, NEW JERSEY

Visit Peterson's at http://www.petersons.com

Library of Congress Cataloging-in-Publication Data

Cultural diversity fieldbook : fresh visions and breakthrough strategies for revitalizing the workplace / George F. Simons, Bob Abramms, L. Ann Hopkins, and Diane J. Johnson.
    p.   cm.
  ISBN 1-56079-602-2
  1. Pluralism (Social sciences)—United States. 2. Multiculturalism—United States.
3. Afro-Americans—Economic conditions. 4. United States—Ethnic relations.
5. Multicultural education—United States. I. Simons, George F.
HM276.C84   1996
305.8'00973—dc20   96-12615
                                                            CIP

Editorial direction by Andrea Pedolsky   Creative direction by Linda Huber
Production supervision by Bernadette Boylan   Interior design by Cynthia Boone
Composition by Gary Rozmierski

Printed in the United States of America

10 9 8 7 6 5 4 3 2

CONTENTS

Acknowledgments   vii
Preface   viii
How to Use This Book   xi

CLASS—THE HIDDEN SPOILER

Introduction   2
1. Struggling to Stay Even, *Missy Daniel*   3
2. Honor to the Working Stiffs, *Barbara Ehrenreich*   4
3. Who Is Moving Ahead?, *Share the Wealth*   7
4. Declining Wages, *Nancy Folbre*   8
5. Low Ranking for Poor American Children, *Keith Bradsher*   10
6. Real Populists Please Stand Up, *Ronnie Dugger*   12
7. Two Activities for a Class on Class, *Felice Yeskel*   13
8. Normalizing Poverty, *Celine-Marie Pascale*   15
9. Golden Rule, *Thomas Ferguson*   16
10. A Matter of Class, *Natasha Josefowitz*   17
11. Classism in Corporate Environments, *Frederick A. Miller with James M. Bradley*   18
12. Vandals in the Free Market Temple: The 200-Year-Old Hoax of the "Self-Regulating Market," *Marjorie Kelly*   20
13. Welfare: The System Provided a Way Out, *Rita Henley Jensen*   23
14. A Response to Jensen, *Dawn Marie Cook*   26
15. Millions of Persons In Poverty   27
16. Welfare: Facts and Fiction, *Ms. Magazine*   28
17. To Tell the Truth: The Proliferation of Really Big Lies—1990s Style, *Herbert Jacob*   30

RACE IN THE USA—EXORCISING OUR DEMONS

Introduction   34
18. Black Pride for White People, *Adrian Piper*   34
19. Treason to Whiteness is Loyalty to Humanity, *Noel Ignatiev*   37
20. Patterns of Behavior, *Bob Abramms Interviews Tom Kochman*   39
21. The Busy Citizens' Discussion Guide to Racism and Race Relations, *Studies Circles Resource Center*   42
22. Barney's in Bankruptcy, *Johnnie L. Roberts*   44
23. The Museum of Slavery, *Lance Morrow*   46
24. Color Blind, *Margaret L. Andersen and Patricia Hill Collins*   48
25. African-Americans and Automation, *Jeremy Rifkin*   48
26. Money Involved, *Don L. Dise*   49
27. Shades of Black, *Karen Grigsby Bates*   52
28. Guilty, *Jon Katz*   54

GENDER AND SEXUAL ORIENTATION—UNDERSTANDING AND RELEARNING OUR ROLES

Introduction   60
29. The Code of Honor: A Key to Including European-American Men, *George F. Simons*   61
30. Men Changing Men, *Robert L. Allen and Paul Kivel*   63
31. The "Born that Way" Trap, *Lindsy Van Gelder*   65
32. Homophobia—Counting the Costs, *Amy J. Zuckerman and George F. Simons*   69

CONTENTS

33. Management Women and the New Facts of Life, *Felice N. Schwartz*   72
34. Confronting Sexism in Black Life: The Struggle Continues, *bell hooks*   73
35. Teenage Pregnancy, *Rosemarie White-Starr*   74
36. Managing by Gender, *Judith C. Tingley*   76

DIVERSE AMERICA—ITS RICHES AND CHALLENGES
Introduction   82
37. Let's Make a Deal, *Deena Levine*   83
38. Inventory of Exposure to Various Cultures, *Dianne LaMountain*   84
39. The Manager in a Multicultural Organization, *Joy Bodzioch*   87
40. What Is Your Aging I.Q.?, *National Institute on Aging*   88
41. Diversity in Canada, *Lydia Phillips and Danielle Cécile*   90
42. Asian Americans: Common Stereotypes & Corresponding Cultural Explanations, *Toy-Ping Taira*   91
43. Asian Americans' Awkward Status: Some Feel Whites Use Them as "Racial Wedge" with Others, *Benjamin Pimental*   92
44. Marketing to Generation X, *Karen Ritchie*   94
45. Psychological Disability, the Workplace and the American Character, *George F. Simons Interviews Elizabeth Henry Power*   97
46. Blond Hair, Black Hair, *Roberto Rodriguez and Patrisia Gonzalez*   99
47. Bias Reduction Exercise, *Donna L. Goldstein*   101

DIVERSITY UNDER FIRE—RIGHT, LEFT, AND CENTER
Introduction   106
48. Our Common Citizenship, *David S. Bernstein*   107
49. White Men and Diversity, *Warren Farrell*   109

50. The Disuniting of America, *Arthur M. Schlesinger, Jr.*   112
51. Legacy of Slavery: A Conservative View, *Thomas Sowell*   113
52. Making Diversity A Way of Life, *George F. Simons Interviews Merlin Pope*   115
53. What If It Isn't Just Lousy Facilitators?, *Jack Gordon*   118
54. In Basket Memo, *Alan Richter*   121
55. Diversity and Organization Performance, *Jack Gordon*   122
56. Free Speech vs. Political Correctness, *Nat Hentoff*   123

NOURISHING THE HUMAN SPIRIT FOR THE DIVERSITY PILGRIMAGE
Introduction   126
57. Spirituality for Men, *George F. Simons*   127
58. A New Vision of Livelihood: Where Does Our Work Fit in the Cosmos?, *Matthew Fox*   131
59. Involving Culture: A Fieldworker's Guide to Culturally Appropriate Development, *Helgi Eyford*   132
60. Jewish Sources of Inspiration in Doing Diversity Work, *Ellen Hofheimer Bettmann*   134
61. Rúmí Poem, *Translated by John Moyne and Coleman Barks*   136
62. Islamic Universalism, *Rabia Terri Harris*   137
63. Work and Serenity, *Ralph G. H. Siu*   139
64. Dialogue with Myself: My Emotional, Intellectual, Spiritual, and Physical Selves, *Yu-Liang Huang*   141
65. The Peace Vision, *Elayna Reyna*   143
66. Norman, the Barking Dancing Pig, *Robert Fulghum*   144
67. Who's In a Name?, *Russell Means*   145

68. Affirmative Action and Racial Harmony, *Peter Gabel* 146
69. When Politics Fails, What Comes Next? The Case for Voluntarism, *James L. Payne* 150
70. What's In a Date?, *Amherst Educational Publishing* 151
71. Playing Straight with a Mixed Deck, *Bob Abramms and Diane Johns* 153

MODELS THAT WORK—ALTERNATIVE VIEWS AND BEST PRACTICES

Introduction 158
72. The Invisible Helping Hand: How Profit-Making Firms Help the Poor, *James L. Payne* 159
73. Multicultural Community Efforts—Tips for European Americans, *Bo Sears* 162
74. Becoming Allies, *Amy J. Zuckerman and George F. Simons* 166
75. Enhancing Diversity Fairness with the Multisource Assessment Approach, *Ann J. Ewen and Mark R. Edwards* 168
76. Diversity in Law, *Andrea Baker* 170
77. Take Back the Charter, *Paul Hawken* 171
78. A Model Prison, *Robert Worth* 173
79. Survival Styles, *Leonard Loomis* 173
80. Subject to Debate, *Katha Pollitt* 174
81. Diversity and Organizational Change, *Ginger Lapid-Bogda* 175
82. A Mentoring Dilemma, *H. Vincent Ford* 177
83. Health Care: 10 Communication Tips for Improving the Effectiveness of Interpreters, *Suzanne Salimbene and Jacek W. Graczykowski* 178
84. The Terminology of Diversity, *Niels Agger-Gupta* 179
85. Impetus to Awareness, *Ward L. Kaiser* 180

KEY DILEMMAS IN THE SEARCH FOR A WORKABLE FUTURE

Introduction 186
86. Assessing Diverse Employees: A Multicultural Quagmire, *Barbara Deane* 189
87. ¡Ya Basta! (Enough is Enough), *Chris Sandoval* 192
88. We say O.J. *sí*, They say O.J. *no!*, *Antonio Rey* 193
89. Jury Nullification, *Richard Moran* 194
90. Let the Dead Bury Their Dead, *Thomas Sowell* 195
91. The Farrakhan Phenomenon, *Ron Daniels* 197
92. ADR—Putting More Clout in Your Diversity, *Sybil Evans* 197
93. Immigration & Acculturation, *Carmen Vázquez and Diane Johns* 198
94. Immigrants In, Native Whites Out, *William H. Frey and Jonathan Tilove* 200
95. A Socially Engineered Head Start, *James S. Robb* 202
96. Immigrants, Memories, and Trash, *Andrew Lam* 203
97. The Subtle Forms of Bias, *Alan Weiss* 205
98. Seccession of the Successful, *Tim Vanderpool* 206
99. Government, of and by the People, *Walter E. Williams* 207

RECONSIDERING THE TOOLS OF JUSTICE— WHITHER AA/EEO?

Introduction 210
100. The Battle Over Affirmative Action, *John Bunzel* 211
101. A Vision Betrayed: Discrimination Is No Answer to Discrimination, *Doug Bandow* 214
102. Who Gets the Job: A Case Study, *Anita Rowe and Lee Gardenswartz* 217

CONTENTS

103. Alternative To Affirmative Action, *The American Enterprise*   220
104. Affirmative Action, Family Style, *Joan Steinau Lester*   221
105. The Color of Money, *Book Review*   222
106. Black Progress: A Conservative View, *Thomas Sowell*   224
107. "White" Losers, *D. Nico Swaan*   225
108. Hiring and Retention Goals for Men and Women, *Julie O'Mara and Lynda White*   226
109. Job Accommodations—Situations & Solutions, *Presidents' Committee on Employment of People with Disabilities*   227
110. Education: Doing Bad and Feeling Good, *Charles Krauthammer*   229
111. What's Fair?, *Karen Burstein Interviews Lani Guinier*   232

OUR COMMON FUTURE—SHAPING 21ST CENTURY PLURALISM

Introduction   238

112. Diversity Is A Business Issue, *Bob Abramms Interviews Roosevelt Thomas*   238
113. Choosing our Future, *Jeremy Rifkin*   242
114. Beyond the Tortilla Curtain: Welcome to the Borderless Society, *Guillermo Gómez-Peña*   243
115. My American Journey, *Colin Powell*   246
116. Beyond Black and White, *Manning Marable*   248
117. To Save Our Children, *Marian Wright Edelman*   249
118. People on the Move, *Philip Harris*   250
119. Vanishing Jobs, *Jeremy Rifkin*   251
120. The Disharmonic Convergence: The Far Left and Far Right as Strange Bedfellows, *Jay Kinney*   255

Making the Fieldbook Continue to Work for You   259
Contributors   261
About the Authors   272

ACKNOWLEDGMENTS AND DEDICATION

Our project has engaged a number of voices including and extending beyond those people whose names may appear in the table of contents.

Special thanks go to Amy Zuckerman, Noriko Takizawa, and Marta Kolodiejczak, at George Simons International, all of whom had a hand in the nitty-gritty work that put this book in shape, sometimes directly and often by getting done the things that freed the editors to be where they needed to be. Susan Bronstein provided support in the form of proofreading for the editors' own text. We found joy in Ineke de Raaff, Pam Fomalont, Melanie Jaynes, Karen Woodbeck, Steve Schulz, Ken Hockenbery, Don Pomroy, Bill Mahkovitz, Gene Millburn, Dennis Cruz, Jem Scanlan, Sarah Schley, the Grand River Group, and the Cyberguys. They showed up in person or online with good cheer to warm the days of despair when the fun of creativity turned to the drudgery of detail.

Thanks go also to our editor, Andrea Pedolsky, and the talented staff of Peterson's, who kept this volume relentlessly moving toward the light of day while they fought for quality each step of the way.

Our gratitude is extended also to Douglas Vickers, whose patience and dedication in facilitating our online exchanges from early morning to late at night diminished the sense that we were working across the continent.

We'd like to acknowledge the contribution of Howard Zinn, who guided the project with a number of excellent suggestions at an earlier stage of development. Many contributors to our other anthology (the *Cultural Diversity Sourcebook*), such as Robert Fulghum and Bo Sears, suggested ideas and provided us with imaginative pieces to include in this *Fieldbook*.

We appreciate the help and suggestions of a number of people with conservative organizations who helped network us to the best sources for expressing the conservative "voices" used in our anthology. These organizations include the Dartmouth Review, the Hoover Institution, Cato Institute, American Enterprise Institute, the Madison Center for Educational Affairs, and the Freedom Alliance. We appreciate the hard-hitting investigative journalism that came from the political left (*Ms.*, *Mother Jones*, and *Z Magazine*) as well as the political right (*National Review*, *American Enterprise*, and *The American Spectator*). We especially wish to credit Craig Cox of the *Utne Reader* for some excellent counsel on how to accomplish the formidable task of requesting over two hundred copyright permissions from authors near and far.

Thanks go to the hundreds of consultants, columnists, and cartoonists who submitted material for consideration in our book. While more than a thousand pieces were turned down, many of these had an impact on our thinking and our perspective on the field. It was incredibly valuable to have such a rich and far-flung network of people sharing their ideas, passions, values, and politics with us.

We'd like to thank Melinda McIntosh of the University of Massachusetts and the group of reference librarians there and others in the Santa Cruz, California Public Library who supported us by helping track down obscure references and locate authors via directories and databases that were inaccessible to us.

During our search for the best pieces we were privileged to work with assistants to our contributors, a number of whom shared their ideas as they were connecting us, arranging interviews, or preparing to send articles. Our thanks to Emma Oakley, Anna Awimbo, and those others we recognize by voice but not name.

Our deep gratitude goes to the contributors whose work is anthologized here. Your eloquent voices touched us personally as well as professionally with your wisdom and experience. We are pleased that you allowed yourselves to be enrolled into this diverse choir whose harmony and dissonance both contribute to a new world symphony for the next millennium.

We dedicate this book to our collegial partnership and all the loving partnerships we share, professionally, and personally. Dear reader, you hold in your hand evidence that much can be done when we human beings bring our diverse resources together in the pursuit of greater understanding.

PREFACE

*C*ultural diversity efforts in the United States tend to be seen as either promising the salvation of the nation or threatening its imminent destruction. Most material on the topic is radically polarized. Proponents expect others to agree with how essential diversity work is, while detractors expect their readers and listeners to see how absurd it all is. Each side characterizes the other as thoughtless, insensitive (or too sensitive), or, in many cases malicious or racist (anti-black or anti-white). Praising or stigmatizing the organizations and individuals that undertake or fail to undertake these efforts, they even label each other as traitors to the nation.

In some quarters it is an unquestioned assumption that diversity work is good, important, and necessary, and "all that separates us from success is that more of it needs to be done." This disturbs us, as does the contrary belief that any focus on diversity is inevitably divisive. The notion that individual Americans can solve all their problems by a change of heart and by private initiatives alone, without addressing systems and structures, strikes us as just plain naive.

Everyone brings bias to their work, including the editors of this book. At best we can attempt to make ours clearer to you by telling you who we are. Three of us are professional consultants. Two of us have done "diversity work" both internally (as staff) and externally (as consultants) for a major part of our professional careers. Of those two, one is a Euro American man who grew up in the 1950s, the other an African American woman who grew up as part of the '60s generation. All four of us are very familiar with the "pro-diversity" positions espoused by the dozens of books published on the topic in the last five years—we wrote a few of them ourselves.

We have been deeply engaged in continuous dialogue with each other about the meaning and inclusion of the material you find here. There were times when we disagreed with the positions expressed by our contributors, and even with each other. But we were committed to a full airing of a wide range of points of view. A sign of these times is that a few of us never met face-to-face during the

entire process and all of us struggled with the diversity of Apples and IBMs as we shot our work back and forth across the Net.

As we assembled the *Cultural Diversity Fieldbook*, we were forced to examine critically the "culture of diversity." We started to see ever more clearly the sets of assumptions, perspectives, established practices, and biases that are commonly accepted as part and parcel of the diversity enterprise.

Even leaving the straitjacket of "political correctness" aside, the diversity we encountered was not very diverse. While examining the undergirdings of public and private policy, assessment and measurement, and in the actual delivery of training and other interventions, we found a surprisingly monochromatic diversity culture. Even the most current literature from the field exhibits a narrow band of opinion.

Our editorial responsibilities led us to challenge everything we saw. We wanted to honestly address both the value added by diversity initiatives and the real problems that can result from these efforts. And so the *Fieldbook* airs widely differing perspectives on the value and purpose of diversity in North America. (The Canadian perspectives, represented here in more than token fashion, speak to a cultural diversity different from that of the United States.)

Seeking to break new ground we added a critical mass of leading-edge thinkers and practitioners from outside the diversity community to the project. We recruited a number of people whose perspectives are rarely looked at seriously by professionals who do diversity work—contributors from the edge of the traditional diversity opinion spectrum. We suspected that some of them might doubt our sincerity in including them in a volume such as this, but nearly all were surprisingly supportive. We soon began to think of these people (perhaps from an overdose of worship at our CRTs) as positions on a "screen." We had to scroll down and sideways to find contributors whose views had previously been "off our screens" (i.e., reflecting positions we hadn't even imagined existed).

A key task was to encourage people to be frank about what was working and what wasn't in the field of diversity. For example, the stresses and trauma of contemporary society on Euro-American men (still the largest single bloc) in an increasingly diverse workforce are often dismissed as trivial in diversity discussions where attention is largely focused on "targeted groups." Until now, most diversity efforts at best have focused on only two objectives for these men: 1) fix them, and 2) get them to share the power that they are, by definition, assumed to have. We have included several pieces about the dilemmas and perspectives of Euro-American men.

By speaking up, we do not imply that Euro-American men *should be* the dominant focus of diversity. Their inclusion in the diversity enterprise, however, is critical to understanding the dynamics of diversity at this point in its development. The enterprise will stall and fragment without them. This is only one example of the larger inclusion we have sought. Besides hearing strong voices from the political right, you will be introduced to other groups, such as workers with emotional disabilities and pregnant teenagers, rarely spoken about in diversity contexts.

Much of the *Cultural Diversity Fieldbook* consists of perspectives that have something constructive, and in many cases provocative, to say. We have edited our contributors' words carefully. Despite the need to shorten many pieces, we worked hard to preserve each person's unique voice. We acknowledge and appreciate the trust that each placed in us.

As we swelter in a hot political climate, our widely ranging contributors provide the cool breeze of perspective and open a hydrant of refreshing insights for the grumbling, stressed-out voter-in-the-street. Our authors rethink issues such as affirmative action and the place of spirit in commercial and organizational life. We need this diversity of vision and voice if we are to successfully redirect the course of our national agenda. Most people are tired of being squeezed harder and harder by political gridlock. This book suggests and guides meaningful conversations among people of widely varying perspectives and political affiliations.

We have taken this opportunity to include excerpts and resource reviews of classic materials (such as Malcolm X's "The ballot or the bullet" speech, page 45), which provide historical context for understanding the issues we now face. This is especially useful for readers under the age of 45 who did not experience the social turmoil of the 1960s civil rights movement and were not part of the revival of the women's movement at that time. These forces irrevocably altered the course of race and gender relations in North America. Those of us who did live through these times can revisit them for a fresh perspective.

How is the *Fieldbook* different from other books on diversity? It moves boldly into new territory, not just because it includes a broader spectrum of opinion, from left, right, and center: We hear from liberals, libertarians, anarchists, conservatives, and a host of other self-constructed identities and introduce you to previously unpublished or not-so-widely published thinkers and practitioners. Its principal difference is that it breaks with the traditional use of race, gender, and ethnicity as the central organizing schemes for understanding and dealing with our pluralism. It asserts that economic and social class—key and often overlooked dimensions of diversity—are omitted from our national conversations at great peril. Class does not stand alone, as the Marxists insisted to the point of bankruptcy, but honest consideration of class tells us much about what has been missing until now in how we have understood and handled the other dimensions.

A basic idea drives the content of the *Cultural Diversity Fieldbook*: The organization or society that benefits from the value that its diversity can add will be least susceptible to disintegration from within, best equipped to meet challenges from without, and most fully adapted to succeed in the emerging global marketplace. It is expressed in a model Bob Abramms and George Simons developed in collaboration with Baudouin Knaapen and drs. Guurt Kok of SYNACT (from the Netherlands), which they use as an analysis tool when assisting organizations to prioritize their diversity efforts. Simply called "The ABCD's of Diversity," it comprises a hierarchy of diversity challenges (see next page).

Managing diversity well requires meeting each of these challenges, and each challenge requires a different set of methods and activities. The technology of one level cannot do the tasks of the other levels. This means that

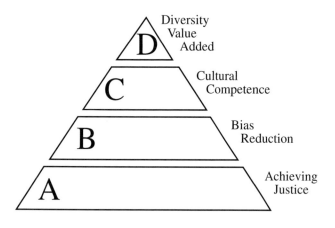

Diversity Value Added — Habitually managing differences as assets that contribute to the survival and success of the organization.

Cultural Competence — Learning how to work effectively with the specific values and behaviors of one's own and others' cultures.

Bias Reduction — Habitually recognizing and dealing with the biased thinking and behavior of one's own person or group.

Achieving Justice — Using legal and structural mechanisms to define and enforce fair access and treatment for all participants in a system.

The ABCD's of Diversity

although efforts made at each level can contribute to and support the work done at other levels, there is little point in attempting to meet higher-level needs if the lower-level needs are not also being addressed.

Having attempted a massive review of the field of diversity and visited its outlying districts and adjoining counties to bring you this *Fieldbook*, what prognosis can we make for the future? Whether the word *diversity* survives for long, at least in its present sense, is questionable. What will certainly outlive it are the issues it has raised in the North American workplace, in our communities, and in government and politics—and the polarities created as a result.

We are counting on the richness of our diverse society to synthesize these polarities and provide more effective solutions to our everyday problems.

As editors, we were called on to weigh and balance many seemingly contradictory points of view. We integrated and aligned the material to create the most useful guide possible for you, our reader. Many of our pet perspectives were dramatically changed by dialogue with our contributors and each other. We hope that this collection of ideas, perspectives, and activities stimulates you to discussion, discovery, and action as we grow together into a very pluralistic twenty-first century.

HOW TO USE THE CULTURAL DIVERSITY FIELDBOOK

Cultural [ˈkelch-(e)-rel], referring to the inner logic developed by a group of people in order to survive and succeed in their environment, and to the artifacts and constructs that result from this logic.

Diversity [de-ˈver-sat- ē], the sum total of the potential to be found in any group of people because of their differences.

Fieldbook [ˈfē(e)ld-buk] a notebook of practical ideas and tools for the understanding and successful practice of a discipline.

The *Cultural Diversity Fieldbook* is divided into ten sections. We introduce each with a "guidepost"—commentary about the material included. Most often we let authors speak for themselves, but we have added occasional guideposts to make your journey through this wealth of readings and activities a bit smoother. While we have written 98 percent of the guideposts, sometimes the words of our contributors serve the purpose best.

Lots of facts and data are included here too. But since information and opinions can be sterile without first-hand experience—and we expect many of our readers to be action-oriented—the *Fieldbook* includes some of the best ways to learn more about, and undertake diversity work. You will find more than forty activities, which vary from things you can do alone or with a partner to larger group exercises for corporate-training classrooms, organizational meetings, community gatherings, and church groups.

You'll find resources throughout the *Fieldbook*—annotations describing additional readings and/or organizations that can provide you with additional, relevant information on the topic at hand.

To facilitate your access to the materials, we've created icons that highlight most of the readings and resources:

Guidepost

Hands-On Activity

Data, Fact, Definition

Perspective or Opinion

Interview

First-Person Account

Resources

We have done our best to find, cite, and acknowledge the people who contributed to the *Fieldbook*. It is the nature of good ideas and effective activities to build upon each other and to move continuously toward improvement through many generations of active minds. It was not always possible to find the parentage of every piece that took hold of our imagination when we decided to include it. If you or someone you know has not received appropriate acknowledgment, please let us know and we will do our best to have future editions more accurately reflect their source.

We hope that the joy of interaction, learning about difference, and the imagination and creativity that we experienced in starting the *Fieldbook* process will be yours as you continue with it.

George Simons
Bob Abramms
Ann Hopkins
Diane Johnson

You may wonder why a book that deals with diversity opens with a section on class. The editors of this *Fieldbook* are not alone in seeing class distinctions as key to understanding diversity in North America. Our contributing authors, whether politically right or left, insist that ignoring class divisions will undermine the validity of a work that addresses other diversity factors, such as race, gender, immigration, regional culture, and creed. In this section they articulate the dire consequences of attempting to do otherwise.

The realities of class are addressed from a variety of perspectives. We have called class "the hidden spoiler" because we believe that rejecting the class perspective blinds both leaders and citizenry to the real consequences of inequity based on discrimination. This deliberate ignorance perverts diversity efforts in organizations and communities. Preaching diversity without listening to the pain of all the disenfranchised backfires and creates even more distrust, division, and anger among our people. Therefore, this section highlights what many do not know, do not like, or perhaps wish were not so about class in North America. The activities included pointedly bring home the contemporary realities of class distinctions. You will learn why systems such as welfare and entitlements, which once worked for both the poor and the rich, no longer do and may even contribute to the problems they were designed to solve. The contributors immerse us in the mood of anxiety that grips the continent in order to know and respond to our diverse fellow citizens more sensitively and creatively.

An economic class system has existed in North America since colonial times. It is the mercilessly widening gap between the richest and the poorest and the disappearance of a strong middle class that concern many Americans as we approach the new millennium. The U.S. social barometer—you can see it in the media and the polls, and hear about it on the street—indicates that national solidarity has fallen to the point where a hurricane of anger is ravaging places in the east such as Brooklyn, Quebec, and Miami. The discontented militia groups, like spring tornadoes, touch down to cause sudden violence in Oklahoma City and in the rural United States and Canadian midwest. Last but not least, communities are breaking apart along the fault lines of race and ethnicity in the west as shown in the debate over Proposition 187, the repeal of affirmative action legislation in California, and in resistance to immigration in western Canada.

As the title of Barbara Ehrenreich's new book suggests, "snarling citizens" abound, ready to take up words if not arms against the government and the people they see responsible for the ills of the economy. Sometimes this anger turns insidiously inward and is inflicted on a spouse or other family members. At times the rage blindly lashes out at fellow workers or the motorist who cuts in too close on the freeway. At the eye of this cyclone of violence is the isolated, disenfranchised individual—bereft of family, community, or cultural bonds.

When we turn to the detail of everyday life in organizations, an incongruity appears between the current fashionable language of organizational and personal empowerment—reengineering, total quality, effectiveness, core competencies, mastery, et al., and the fact that the fruits of these interventions reach fewer and fewer people. The "end of the boss" and the "end of the job" are touted as the wave of the future in managerial literature. But, within that future loom massive dislocations, underemployment, unemployment, and poverty. Being on one's own might be seen as a logical step in the evolution of the individualism of U.S. and Canadian culture.

Some might see this new individualism as a return to the principles of democracy or to an entrepreneurial frontier spirit. However, the "Common Good," the reason for our constitutional compacts, is rarely discussed in decisions about restructuring. "We the people," or, considering our present forms of diversity, "We the peoples," is no longer heard in such discussions. "We" becomes more difficult to say in our organizations, governments, neighborhoods, families, and in our relationships with others. When individuals are primarily "on their own," what is required is wider-reaching, more tightly woven social nets, rather than smaller ones, whether these be provided by family, government, or private interest groups. Successful pluralism in the new millennium must respond to this dilemma of the lone, disenfranchised individual with a formula for more equitable distribution of power, resources, and national wealth.

While the debate on affirmative action rages on, few recall that affirmative action efforts were originally designed to eliminate disparities of economic class in the United States. While it is, in part, useful to focus on factors such as race, gender, and disabilities, these characteristics are simply markers by which we commonly create class distinctions. Defining these attributes as sacred permanent categories of oppression defeats our commitment to fairness in U.S. society. Grappling with and understanding the debate on class here becomes absolutely necessary if one is to fully comprehend what our contributors have to say later in Section 9, Reconsidering the Tools of Justice (e.g., Affirmative Action, EEO, etc.).

Attacks on privileged classes—verbal, theoretical, sometimes even physical—have been a part of the struggle for fairness from before the very beginning of our nation. It is not surprising that we hear them today, when affluence at a level unimaginable in previous ages characterizes the privileged of North America.

1 ·   Struggling to Stay Even

MISSY DANIEL (*U.S. NEWS & WORLD REPORT*)

LORDSTOWN, OHIO—After 17 years on the line in a General Motors assembly plant, auto worker Tom Manley now builds car seats at Lear Seating Corp. factory a mile down the road. GM calls the move "strategic redeployment." But for Manley, 40, it symbolizes the waning strength of the United Auto Workers and the declining fortunes of America's working class.

"I've lost faith in my union," he laments at the bar of the Wooden Keg, where he comes for "lunch" during the night shift. "It's powerless on the issues that face me. The rich man goes to college, and the poor man goes to work. We are the people who make the country rich or poor, weak or strong. But we don't see the profits. I'm making $45,000, but it's not enough. We ought to live better than we do, and it's because of the way we are taxed. If you want prosperity, make the people who work the hardest prosper."

Prosperity and jobs are the issues that preoccupy "Populist Traditionalists" in this blue-collar stronghold in northeast Ohio. Unemployment in the area is 5.7 percent—far above the statewide rate of 4.5 percent. "It's always been a tradition to leave your kids a little better off than you were, but they say we'll be the first generation to leave ours in worse shape," says tool-and-die maker Arno Hill, 42, mayor of Lordstown.

Opportunities for what GM fabrication-plant quality controller Dick Armour calls "decent jobs—not hamburger jobs" are being lost to Third World countries. "At any time we could all be in a bread line," he says.

See Clifford Cobb, Ted Halstead, and Jonathon Rowe, "If the GDP is up, why is America down?" in *Atlantic Monthly*, October 1995, pp. 59-78F.

In *The Politics of Rich and Poor: Wealth and the American Electorate in the Reagan Aftermath*, by Kevin P. Phillips (New York: Harper, 1991, $11, ISBN 0-06-097396-X), Phillips documents the shift in wealth to the top one percent of the American population during the 1980s. He argues that such redistributive periods in American economic life historically have been followed by profound social and political transformations such as the Progressive Era and the New Deal.

2 · Honor to the Working Stiffs

BARBARA EHRENREICH

*P*ut another wienie on the fire for the working class. It's time for the annual barbecue in honor of the people who slaughtered the pigs, made the hot dog, trucked it to market, and bagged it for you. The little guy and gal, that is, the working stiffs. They could use a little honor these days. At the rate blue-collar wages are falling, the United States is going to reinvent slavery in the next few decades, only without any of its nice, redeeming features, such as room and board.

A job is supposed to be a ticket to self-respect and social betterment—at least that's what the pols tell us when the poor start clamoring for their welfare checks. But conditions in the low-wage end of the workforce are beginning to look like what Engels found in nineteenth-century Manchester and later described as "immiseration." Within 10 miles of my own suburban home, for example, there is a factory where (until they got a union contract a year ago) the workers slept in their cars and bathed in the ladies' room—because at the minimum wage, housing was not an option. A few miles in the other direction, Salvadoran refugees report getting $125 in cash for 60-hour weeks of heavy outdoor labor. For them, upward mobility would be a busboy's job at $2.90 an hour plus a cut of the tips.

Or I think of Jean-Paul, a Haitian-born janitor in one of the local schools. He's only a janitor at night. By day he works an 8-hour factory shift. On weekends he washes cars. That leaves 8 hours a day, on average, for sleeping, eating, commuting, washing, and brooding, as Jean-Paul often does, on the meaning of his life.

These are not isolated, exotic cases. Nationwide, the fraction of the workforce earning poverty-level wages rose from 25.7 percent in 1979 to 31.5 percent in 1987. During the eighties, the average hourly earnings of all blue-collar workers fell by $1.68, and those who were earning the least to start with tended to lose the most. In what some sociologists call the "new working class"—which is disproportionately minorities and the young and female of all races—work may be a fine ingredient for an "ethic." But it really doesn't pay.

Ask a tweed-suited member of the better-paid classes what's gone wrong, and you'll get a lot of chin stroking about vast impersonal forces such as declining productivity and global competition. But real wages fell faster in the eighties than in the seventies, although productivity *rose* faster in the eighties. And theories of the global economy may explain a lot of things, but they don't make it any easier for a U.S. worker to live on third-world wages.

Or go to Washington, and you'll find an administration that loves the working class—as a concept anyway. George Bush favored pork cracklings, and was probably munching on that well-known proletarian treat as he nixed the bill that would have extended unemployment benefits. Bill Clinton got labor's vote, then forgot his promise to raise the minimum wage. Labor is like motherhood to most of our political leaders: a calling so fine and noble that it would be sullied by talk of vulgar, mundane things like pay.

Even unions aren't much help anymore. Union workers earn 30 percent more, on average, than their nonunion counterparts, but there aren't many union workers left. Only 16.1 percent of the workforce is organized, and that number is falling fast. Union leaders complain that it's hard to organize under a government that doesn't adequately enforce the rights of workers (to join a union, for example,

Labor is like motherhood to most of our political leaders: a calling so fine and noble that it would be sullied by talk of vulgar, mundane things like pay.

THE FREE ENTERPRIZE SYSTEM SAILS ON...

GLOBOCORP

IN 1960 THE AVERAGE C.E.O. WAS PAID 41 TIMES MORE THAN THE AVERAGE WORKER. BY 1992 THE AVERAGE C.E.O. WAS PAID 157 TIMES MORE.

M.WUERKER WITH HOLLY SKLAR

ⓘ "What Will Rogers observed in 1931 is even more true today, 'Ten men in our country could buy the whole world and ten million can't buy enough to eat.'" Quoted from James W. Loewen, *Lies My Teacher Told Me* (New York: The New Press, 1995, $24.95, ISBN 1-56584-100-X), p. 194.

without risking being fired). But the unions haven't exactly been exerting themselves: according to the Labor Research Association, the number of organizing drives keeps declining from year to year, and when unions do go to war, it's too often with each other. In 1990, for example, four major unions spent an estimated $40 to $50 million battling each other to represent Indiana state employees—as if they were the last nonunion workers left on earth.

This isn't just a "labor problem." It hurts us all when hard work doesn't pay, and I'm talking about insidious, creeping, moral damage. Conservatives like to cite that ancient Puritan teaching: He who does not work, neither should he eat. But the flip side of that stern motto should be written in the social contract, too: He who *does* work does deserve a decent break. No footnotes about productivity, no disclaimers about global competition, no fine print about the rights of stockholders and CEOs—just a guarantee that hard work will be rewarded with some baseline of comfort, nutrition, and dignity. This was the principle behind the minimum wage, even if it's much too low: that survival cannot be left entirely to market forces or employer whim.

Take that guarantee away and despair sets in, followed swiftly by cynicism and eventually maybe rage. For a man like Jean-Paul, it's the despair of knowing that his work, his energy, his *life*, that is, are valued at five dollars and change an hour, less than it costs him to pay for lunch. For his children, the response may well be cynicism. The message from the Bureau of Labor Statistics is clear: Don't bother with a job. Go on welfare if you can. Rob a convenience store. Open up a cocaine dealership. Jobs are for chumps.

We need a little less talk about the "work ethic" and a little more ethics in relation to work. The president could set an example by expending some political capital to pass the union-backed bill that would prohibit the use of strikebreakers and give workers a fighting chance. Employers might think twice about spending more on union-busting "consultants" than a pay raise would have cost. The unions ought to lead the way, not just with a few scattered organizing drives here and there but with something far more evangelical—a national crusade, let's say, drawing on churches, communities, and campus idealists. And what could be more American? The way to honor work, which we all claim to do, is, first of all, to pay for it.

3 •   Who Is Moving Ahead?

SHARE THE WEALTH

*T*his activity shows where the income growth went during the 1980s. Set it up by telling a group that economists like to talk about the U.S. population in "quintiles" or "fifths" of the population. They imagine everyone in the U.S. lined up, from the lowest income to the highest. They then divide them into five equal population parts.

Have as many participants able and willing to stand in line up in the front of the room. At minimum, choose five individuals. Divide them into five equal parts with signs numbered one to five.

Tell them that they are going to take steps either forward or backward as you instruct them. Note that each step equals about 10 percent. This is a little like the childhood game, "Mother May I?"

PART ONE: GROWING APART

Explain that between 1977 and 1989, the lowest quintile took *two big steps backward.* (Have each group take their steps). Their income declined almost 17 percent. (Average income after taxes in 1990: $7,000.)

The second quintile takes *one step back.* Their income declined by 8 percent. (Average income after taxes: $16,000.)

The third quintile takes a *small step back.* Their income declined 3 percent. (Average income after taxes: $25,000.)

The fourth quintile takes a *half step forward.* Their income increased 5 percent. (After tax income: $35,000.)

The fifth quintile takes *two big steps forward.* Their income increased over 18 percent. (After tax income: $80,000.)

Note that within the fifth quintile—there is quite a disparity:

The top five percent takes *three big steps forward.* Their income increased over 25 percent (After-tax income: $150,000.)

The top one percent in the fifth quintile takes ten big steps forward. Their income increased over 110 percent. (After-tax average income: $400,000).

PART TWO: GROWING TOGETHER

Compare what has happened in the last 15 years to the postwar years: 1950–1978.

• First Quintile: Thirteen Steps Forward

Fighthing for control

of the past.

William Faulkner wrote,

"The past is never dead.

It's not even past."

- Second Quintile: Ten Steps Forward
- Third Quintile: Ten Steps Forward
- Fourth Quintile: Eleven Steps Forward
- Fifth Quintile: Ten Steps Forward

Note that federal tax and spending policies urged us to grow together—to lift people out of poverty into the middle class and share in the nation's growth.

PROPS: SIGNS SAYING:

First Quintile "Lowest Income"   Fifth Quintile
Second Quintile   Fifth Quintile-Top 5%
Third Quintile   Top 1%
Fourth Quintile

See *The End of Equality*, by Mickey Kaus (Basic Books, P.O. Box 588, Dunmore, PA 18512-0588, 1-800-331-3761). In this 1992 book, Kaus suggests that there are several ways to respond to the seemingly unavoidable growth in differences of income and wealth. Instead of what he calls "money liberalism"—a policy that seeks to reduce income inequality generated by the economy itself—he argues for "civic liberalism," in which the sphere of life in which money matters would be restricted while the civic sphere expands substantially in quality and influence.

America: Who Really Pays the Taxes?, by Donald L. Bartlett and James B. Steele (New York: Simon & Schuster, 1994); 1-800-223-2336. In this book, the authors of *America: What Went Wrong* document the economic side of Middle America's economic decline by focusing on the role of the tax system in detail.

4 · Declining Wages

NANCY FOLBRE

From 1950 to the mid-1970s, real average hourly earnings steadily increased, giving most ordinary people a sense of economic progress. After 1973, that progress ground to a halt.

Average hourly earnings, 1950–94
(private nonagricultural nonsupervisory or production workers, in $1992)

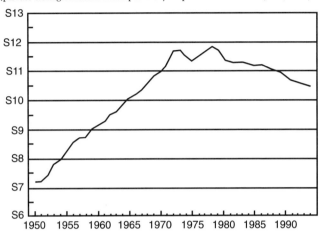

Source: Bureau of Labor Statistics, *Employment, Hours, and Earnings*, 1909–84, vol. 2 (Bulletin 1312-12). *EE* 41, no. 1 (Jan. 1994), p. 131, Table C-1. *EE* 41, no. 10 (Oct. 1994), p. 65, Table B-11. Note: 1994 based on Jan.-Sept. average. 1994 data are not perfectly comparable to earlier years.

ⓘ From *The New Field Guide to the U.S. Economy* by Nancy Folbre and the Center for Popular Economics. Published by The New Press and available from WW Norton at 800-223-4830. ISBN# 1-56584-153-0.

There is no doubt that the future of a nation lies in the hands of its children. Unfortunately, U.S. popular culture has created "childhood" as an extended stage of life where the adored child represents the lost innocence of adulthood. There are things many of us do for our children that we would not do for ourselves—a certain investment in the future. However, there is a paradox in this investment. The affluence that created "childhood" is disappearing. Education has deteriorated to unacceptable levels of ignorance. The resources and dollars that the United States dedicates to its children is far outspent by almost every nation in the world. If we are to provide for our children's future, we must provide them with: the skills they need to support themselves and others, the discipline and values they need to create a healthy social life, economic stability, and distributive justice. True and clear adult role models are essential. We must create these elements if we are to bequeath them to the next generation. The following piece deals with some of the facts about our children. Later, in Section 10, Our Common Future, contributors will discuss how we might address some of these issues.

ⓘ Poverty and Race Research Action Council (PRRAC) publishes a bi-monthly newsletter that offers articles on issues related to race, class, poverty, and public policy. The organization also awards grants to researchers exploring race and public policy issues. For further information contact: PRRAC, 1711 Connecticut Ave., NW, Suite 207, Washington, D.C. 20009, 202-387-9887. The American Enterprise Institute for Public Policy Research publishes the bi-monthly *American Enterprise*, which argues the conservative positions on politics, business, and culture. For further information contact *The American Enterprise*, 430 South Geneva St., Ithaca, NY 14850, 607-272-0909.

5 • Low Ranking for Poor American Children

KEITH BRADSHER (THE NEW YORK TIMES)

U.S. YOUTH AMONG WORST OFF IN STUDY OF 18 INDUSTRIALIZED NATIONS

The United States has proportionately more of its children in poverty than other affluent countries.

WASHINGTON, Aug. 13—Poor children in the United States are poorer than the children in most other Western industrialized nations, as young Americans suffer the brunt of several trends toward greater economic inequality, a new study shows. Only in Israel and Ireland are poor children worse off than poor American youths, according to the study, an analysis of 18 nations by the Luxembourg Income Study, a nonprofit group based in Walferdange, Luxembourg.

The results are the most comprehensive of several recent analyses, and are particularly striking because the United States has the second highest level of economic output per person of the countries examined, after Luxembourg itself, and has the most prosperous affluent children of any of the 18 nations.

It may not be surprising that childhood poverty is worse in the United States than in Scandinavia, where governments have racked up huge national debts while trying to maintain elaborate social safety nets. But the United States also ranks below countries like Italy, which has a considerably smaller economy per person and has less generous social policies than many northern European nations.

The United States appears to have sunk through the rankings over the last 30 years, although no conclusive data are available now, said Timothy M. Smeeding, one of the study's authors and director of the Luxembourg Income Study. The American lead in overall prosperity has dwindled since the 1960s, income inequality has risen briskly in the United States and child poverty spread here in the 1970s and 1980s, although it may have leveled off in the early part of this decade.

Some conservative economists have questioned the validity of studies that attempt to compare levels of income and distribution of wealth among nations with somewhat different economic systems and societies. There is general acceptance within the field, however, of the idea that the United States has proportionately more of its children in poverty than other affluent countries. The debate revolves instead around what to do about it.

The study comes as Congress is deciding whether to limit Federal spending on various welfare programs. President Clinton expressed strong concern about stagnant incomes, particularly for less affluent Americans. "We've got to grow the economy and raise incomes," he said. "That's why I want to raise the minimum wage, that's why I want to give every unemployed worker or underemployed worker the right to two years of education at the local community college, that's why I'm trying to have a tax cut that's focused on child rearing and education: to raise incomes."

Mr. Smeeding said there appeared to be several reasons why the United States had such extreme poverty among children. The United States has the widest gap between rich and poor, he said. The United States also has less generous social programs than the other 17 countries in the study, which [include] Australia, Canada, Israel, and 14 European countries: Austria, Belgium, Britain, Denmark, Finland, France, Germany, Ireland, Italy, Luxembourg, the Netherlands, Norway, Sweden, and Switzerland. The study did not include several Western European nations like Greece, Spain, and Portugal that have very poor children but limited data.

American households with children tend to be less affluent than the average American household, a pattern that is not true in many other countries. This trend may reflect that American mothers are less likely than European mothers to return to work quickly after childbirth, partly because inexpensive, high-quality child care is more widely available in Europe, said Lee Rainwater, the research director of the Luxembourg Income Study and the co-author with Mr. Smeeding of the latest report.

Some conservative analysts question whether international comparisons of prosperity should even be attempted. They point to the many differences among nations' economies and societies. There are more poor children in the United States than in many affluent countries, but that partly reflects the high number of poor immigrants and unwed teenage mothers here, said Douglas J. Besharov, a resident scholar at the American Economic Institute, a conservative research group here. "Is there more poverty in a big, diverse country like ours than in Western Europe?" he asked. "The answer is yes."

He and other conservative economists argue that the price the other countries pay for avoiding extremes of childhood poverty may be slower economic growth, which, they assert, leads to lower living standards for all. A large chunk of European social assistance to young families takes the form of generous unemployment benefits that have eroded incentives for people to work, Mr. Besharov said.

The study is critical of Republican efforts to cut American social spending now. It compares incomes of poor and affluent households with children. The figures include not only after-tax wages and other personal in-

	Poor household with children	Length of bars represent the gap between rich and poor children	Affluent households with children
Switzerland	$18,829		$59,502
Sweden	18,829		46,152
Finland	17,303		41,991
Denmark	17,268		46,326
Belgium	16,679		47,262
Norway	16,575		43,829
Luxembourg	15,396		50,071
Germany	15,257		51,874
Netherlands	14,529		42,616
Austria	14,321		39,911
Canada	13,662		56,174
France	13,003		44,835
Italy	12,552		44,280
Britian	11,581		43,933
Australia	11,512		49,863
United States	10,923		65,536
Israel	7,871		33,392
Ireland	6,692		27,185

$0 $20,000 $40,000 $60,000

come but also cash benefits from the government, like food stamps and the tax credit on earned income for low-income working parents with children. The calculations take into account differences among countries in the size of families and in the cost of living. The figures do not include free government services, like the free medical and child-care services available in many European countries.

Sheila B. Kamerman, a professor of social policy and planning at Columbia University, said that for this reason, the latest analyses may have underestimated the extent to which poor American children lag in income. "If you were looking at in-kind benefits as well as cash benefits, the situation in the U.S. would look even worse," she said.

6 ·   Real Populists Please Stand Up

RONNIE DUGGER *(THE NATION)*

*J*efferson wrote that what distinguished our new country from the Old World was the absence among us then of the fatal concentrations of private wealth that so deformed imperial Europe. Yet the gap between the very rich and the rest of us now is morally more obscene than anything Jefferson could have had in mind. Consider the following:

- One percent of the people among us own 40 percent of the national wealth.
- The after-tax income of the top 20 percent of U.S. families exceeds that of all other families combined.
- Between 1977 and 1989 the 1 percent of families with incomes over $350,000 received 72 percent of the country's income gains while the bottom 60 percent lost ground.
- In 1992 half of our families had net financial assets under $1,000. Debts exceeded assets for four out of ten of our families.
- In 1994, seventy American individuals and fifty-nine American families collectively owned $295 billion, an average of $2.3 billion. The top fifty-one individuals and families owned $197 billion, an average of $3.9 billion.

- The rate of child poverty in the United States is four times the rate in Western Europe.
- Although no democracy can work without a strong union movement, U.S. unions have been reduced to shadows, with 1 in 6 workers now belonging to a union, compared to 1 in 3 at their peak strength. If you exclude public employees, the figure is 1 in 9.
- Multinational corporations now employ about a fifth of the private American work force and are getting bigger and more powerful by the hour. Workers are falling into paycheck poverty— by the millions we are becoming expendable hired hands, interchangeable units of work, governed in what counts by entities that have abandoned the traditional quest for a loyal work force, much less a happy one.
- Corporations are extracting cuts in wages and benefits from their experienced workers, low-balling new workers in two-tier wage systems, requiring mandatory overtime and hiring temps to reduce the fringe benefits they have to pay, and letting hundreds of thousands of workers go while exporting their jobs to low-wage areas around the world.
- Young male workers with a high school education lost 30 percent of their real income in the twenty years ending in 1993, and the real wages of American production workers have dropped 20 percent in twenty years; average wage levels for men are now below the levels of the 1960s.
- As of 1993, 40 percent of women earned only about $15,000 a year.
- Among Hispanics 46 percent and among African-Americans 36 percent of workers do not earn an hourly wage sufficient to lift them out of poverty.

(i) "Twenty-five years ago, about 70 cents of every dollar spent on poor people went directly to them. Today 70 cents of every dollar spent goes to the poverty Pentagon, social workers, doctors, lawyers, all sorts of professionals who serve poor people. They ask not which problems are solvable, but which problems are fundable. So now [we] have a whole industry that's built on the backs of poor people. [Bureaucrats] don't get rewarded for reducing dependency. They get regarded based on the number of people they bring into a dependent relationship."—Robert Woodson, in *Diversity*, June/July, 1992.

7 · Two Activities for a Class on Class

FELICE YESKEL

ACTIVITY 1

Goal: To help participants understand how classism operates through our institutions.

Instructions: Hang large pieces of paper around the room with the name of a major institution in our society on each one. Depending upon the size of your group you may want to choose from 6 to 10 institutions such as the following:

health care	the political system
religion	the judicial system
employment/workplaces	education
military	the tax system

Break the group into the same number of small groups as you have institutions; there should be 4-6 people in each group. Give each group one institution to focus on, with some flip chart paper and magic markers. Ask the groups to write down their responses to the following questions:

- How is this institution classist now?
- How does it give privileges to some and limit access to others?
- What might it look like without classism?
- How would it be set up to be more equal for all class groups?

After about 20 minutes bring the small groups back together and have them put their responses under their institution around the room. Call on each team in turn and ask them to summarize their answers to the questions. If there was disagreement within a group, ask for the differing positions to be summarized, but not rehashed at length. You may also ask the group as a whole if there were any omissions that could be added.

ACTIVITY 2

Goal: To help participants understand how class stereotypes are conveyed through the popular media.

Materials: A large supply of magazines of different varieties, such as: *Newsweek, Home and Garden, Forbes, Ebony, Sports Illustrated, Architectural Digest, Readers Digest, Money, GQ*, etc.

Instructions: Spread the various magazines around the room; give participants about 20 minutes to look through the various magazines looking for things that strike them as classist; ask them to note the magazine in which it was found. You may suggest that this may be easiest and quickest to find in advertisements. After about 20 minutes or when everyone has found at least 2-3 examples, ask them to form small groups of 4-6 people each to share what they found. As a group they should focus on the following questions for each example:

- How is this example classist?

- What messages does it give to people of different classes?
- How does it reinforce stereotypes?
- What values does it hold up as the best?

After the small groups have had a chance to think about these questions, ask each group to collectively choose two examples that they thought were best to share with the whole group. Pay attention especially to the hidden (or not so hidden) messages conveyed. Make a list of these messages as each group reports back.

8 · Normalizing Poverty

CELINE-MARIE PASCALE (Z MAGAZINE)

*n*ot surprisingly, working- and middle-class borrowing has been steadily rising. During the early 1980s, 72.7 percent of all families fell into debt, according to *The Statistical Abstract of the United States.* Even grocery stores began to accept credit cards for food purchases. Household debt climbed to over $3 trillion and consumer installment credit more than tripled. By 1989, credit card debt claimed a greater percentage of household debt than mortgages. The government estimates that by the year 2000 credit card debt alone will be more than $432.9 billion dollars.

The number of pawn shops has doubled in the past decade to an estimated 10,000. Cash America, Jack Daugherty's chain of pawn shops is now on *Inc.* magazine's list of fastest growing companies. Today, its stock is traded on the New York Stock Exchange. C. Jensen and Project Censored reported on Cash America in their book, *Censored: The News That Didn't Make The News.* The average interest rate on loans at Cash America hovers at 200 percent, a common industry rate. In 1993, Cash America reported $13 million in profits on $186 million in revenues. With profits riding high, Daugherty claims to have tapped only one-sixth of the market—which he estimates to include 60 million people.

Pawn shops and check-cashing outlets serve low-income people, usually in urban ghettos who aren't served by mainstream banks. These services, now known as "fringe banking," are becoming a standard subsidiary of major banks. Fringe banking is one of the highest profit centers in the banking industry. There's no secret to their success. Check-cashing outlets charge as much as 10 percent of the

ⓘ See *The Changing Distribution of Income in an Open U.S. Economy,* by Jeffrey Bergstrand, Thomas F. Cosimano, John W. Houck, and Richard G. Sheehan, which documents the economic and demographic factors that have converged to slow the country's growth beginning in 1973 (New York: Elsevier, 1994, ISBN 0-444-81559-7).

check's value for their service. This means an individual would pay $5 to cash a $50 check and $10 to cash a $100 check.

The Consumer Federation of America and the U.S. Public Interest Research Group surveyed 300 large banks and discovered that the average annual cost of a regular checking account is rising at twice the rate of inflation. From 1990 to 1993, the cost of checking accounts increased 18.5 percent to $184; consequently, the portion of American families without a bank account is also rising. In 1993, 14 percent of all families could not afford a bank account. More and more families are being forced by economic necessity to use fringe banking services. Not surprisingly, the number of high-profit check-cashing outlets jumped from 2,000 in 1987 to nearly 5,000 in 1993.

A rapid growth in debt combined with an increase in the cost of living and a decrease in wages forces a new definition of middle class. While a strict definition of "middle class" includes only salaried white-collar workers, many Americans believe that middle class means middle income, regardless of whether or not the income is hourly or salaried, blue collar or white. The dramatic trend in downward mobility for both blue- and white-collar workers leaves very few people earning middle incomes regardless of their class. We need a perspective for understanding what this downward mobility means.

9 · Golden Rule

THOMAS FERGUSON (BOOK REVIEW)

 Golden Rule: The Investment Theory of Party Competition and the Logic of Money Driven Political Systems, by Thomas Ferguson (Chicago: University of Chicago Press 1995). ISBN: 0-226-24317-6, $17.95. 1-800-621-2736 or 312-568-1550.

To discover who rules, follow the gold." This is the argument of *Golden Rule*, a provocative, pungent history of modern American politics. Although the role big money plays in defining political outcomes has long been obvious to ordinary Americans, most pundits and scholars have virtually dismissed this assumption. Even in light of skyrocketing campaign costs, the belief that major financial interests primarily determine which parties nominate and where they stand on the issues—that, in effect, Democrats and Republicans are merely the left and right wings of the "Property Party"—has been ignored by most political scientists. Offering evidence ranging from the nineteenth century to the 1994 mid-term elections, *Golden Rule* shows that voters are "right on the money."

Thomas Ferguson breaks completely with traditional voter-centered accounts of party politics. In its place he outlines an "investment approach," in which powerful investors, not unorganized voters, dominate campaigns and elections. Because businesses "invest" in political parties and their candidates, changes in industrial structures—between large firms and sectors—can alter the agenda of party politics and the shape of public policy.

Ferguson analyzes how a changing world economy and other social developments broke up the New Deal system in our own time, through careful studies of the 1988 and 1992 elections. The essay on 1992 contains an extended analysis of the emergence of the Clinton coalition and Ross Perot's dramatic independent insurgency. A postscript on the 1994 elections demonstrates the controlling impact of money on several key campaigns.

This controversial work by the leading theorist of money and politics in the U.S. is valuable reading for anyone interested in campaign finance reform or the influence of class on politics and economics.

Like produces like. This tendency is certain to be projected into the process by which we choose the people we feel comfortable working with. It is what Natasha Josefowitz describes as the "clonal effect." We can also be fascinated by and attracted to difference, but this value tends to kick in only when we are feeling safe and secure in our culture or environment. The challenge to organizations, particularly when they are under the stress of competition, is partly a psychological one, which turns the fear of difference into viewing that difference as perhaps exactly what we need to address our organizations' environmental challenges more successfully.

10 • A Matter of Class

NATASHA JOSEFOWITZ

*R*ace, sex, and ethnic origins are often cited as bases for discrimination, but class is rarely mentioned. Yet class can be as much a factor in hiring, promotion, and selection as the more readily evident race, sex, ethnicity, or

The "clonal effect" refers to the tendency of people to hire and promote people that look, talk, and walk like themselves.

national origin. Because class is more difficult to define, the clues are more subtle. Discrimination is based on often minimal indicators of class that can be as tenuous as a manner of walking, a choice of words, a piece of clothing, a look, or a joke. The way a person enters the cafeteria, orders a meal, eats, relates with the staff, and pays the check often indicates his or her class. Of course, this prejudice lies not in the acknowledgment of the difference but in the preference of one way over the other; discrimination occurs when we act on this preference. Here again, we are seeking comfort by associating with the person who comes from a background similar to our own. We tend to place more trust in persons from our own social class. Thus, class becomes a factor in the clonal effect of hiring and promotion.

11 · Classism in Corporate Environments

FREDERICK A. MILLER WITH JAMES M. BRADLEY

*L*ike all social structures, the workplace becomes vulnerable to issues of class: social hierarchies that pigeonhole people and strain relations. The presence of class presents a distraction in the workplace which can be a source of great division and discord in the workforce. It subverts productivity and provides a breeding ground for greater problems, both personal and professional.

While many companies have sought to minimize effects of class by rethinking management structures, improving communication among all workers regardless of level, and minimizing physical boundaries in workspaces, the issue of compensation often remains unspoken and unaddressed.

Compensation is possibly the most sensitive indicator of class structure in the workplace, and its primary determinant. Often a matter of confidentiality, salaries, benefits, stock options, and bonuses lie at the core of privilege systems.

Obviously all people cannot be paid the same amount, nor should they be. But over the past decade, many organizations have called into question the size of the disparity in wages and benefits between the top and bottom earners and the means of distributing the organization's wealth. Several policies aimed at greater equity have resulted.

One is top-to-bottom ratios, which set the salary of the highest paid person as a multiple of that of the lowest. This ratio varies from company to company.

Herman Miller, for example, holds its CEO's salary and benefits (including stock options) to 20 times the compensation of the entry level worker, while Springfield Remanufacturing has long had a tighter 6-to-1 ratio. But the concept of checking the earnings of the CEO and keeping the entire organization moving upward together is what makes such plans successful at reducing class distinctions. While Ben & Jerry's—a company which in 1994 held a 7-to-1 ratio—acknowledged that the cap sometimes made it difficult to fill executive-level positions, they also felt it guaranteed that those who did rise to the upper echelons were committed to certain values, and not just chasing a larger paycheck.

Many argue that there is a problem in corporate United States regarding the compensation of top earners—if not in the amounts they earn, then in how such numbers are perceived by the rest of the workforce. The resentment is not mere jealousy; in times of financial restraint and downturning economies, of trimming staff in the name of efficiency, it is seen as inconsistent with the financial realities of the workforce and disproportionate to profitability. Recent studies have shown as much as a 964 percent disparity in comparisons of company size and performance with CEO compensation (base salary plus add-ons).

In discussing their book *The 100 Best Companies to Work for in America,* Robert Levering and Milton Moskowitz noted that issues of compensation are being tackled head-on in the model companies that made their list. "There are still perks at the top," says Moskowitz, "but there's also this sense now that you should cut all people in on those perks. There's a sense now that the salary differentials between the top and the bottom should not be that wide. And there's a sense that there should be more stock options—for everybody."

Many large U.S. companies, such as Hallmark, Avis, Polaroid, and Lowe's, have significant employee stock ownership and profit-sharing policies. After one year of service, Procter & Gamble invests 5 percent of a person's salary in P&G stock. This increases to over 20 percent in 20 years, providing people with retirement benefits well above the corporate norm. The plan also gives all people a greater sense of involvement in the success of the company, since their own fortunes are tied to it by more than just their daily job. Everyone reaps benefits when the company prospers; everyone takes a hit when the company falters.

ⓘ *TV Nation* is a news magazine show with a mission to expose the hypocrisy and humor of corporate upper-class America. It is currently airing on Fox TV. For more information, write Dog Eat Dog Films, P.O. Box 0831, Radio City Station, New York, NY 10101-0831; 212-977-2068, or address e-mail: TVNatFans@aol.com

See Tom Brown, "The 100 Best Companies: Do They Point the Way for All Business?" *Industry Week* 19, April 1993, pp. 15–18.

 In the following piece, Marjorie Kelly goes after one of the systemic sacred cows that has been quietly munching others' hay for a long time. At the heart of our diversity effort is uniting people of difference to shape a new socio-economic reality and a market economy that will make the world work for as many people as possible. We need a redefinition of work that enables all who can work to participate and be rewarded. The age-old question is, How can we do this in a hard-nosed but respectful way so that we do not get eaten by "the sharks"? How do we turn the sharks into something else? In a natural disaster, people of all kinds work side by side because they are aware of the common threats and the common goal of survival. The present socio-economic condition is a disaster, but there is no common perception of it as such. If an asteroid were hurtling toward earth, all resources would be focused on preventing an imminent disaster. When a socio-economic system is hurtling toward destruction, some people will profit—usually those with the advantages—and may even exacerbate the crisis.

12 • Vandals in the Free-Market Temple: The 200-Year-Old Hoax of the "Self-Regulating Market"

MARJORIE KELLY (BUSINESS ETHICS)

"Once a person has an internalized picture of reality, further experience tends to confirm that picture."
—Willis Harman, *Global Mind Change.*

I've been reading the most fascinating book recently—a book all the better because I picked it up for 25 cents from a bin at the Salvation Army (next to the luggage, across the aisle from Household Potpourri). It was a strange place to discover a 1944 paperback by an obscure economic historian—mingling with *Star Trek VI* and Danielle Steel—but there it was, *The Great Transformation*, by Karl Polanyi (still in print, by the way). The author's name caught my eye, for I'd seen references to Polanyi as one of the fathers of the free-market critique—considered as influential in some circles as John Maynard Keynes—and been meaning to look him up.

Polanyi puts a human face on free-market capitalism, and it's face of suffering—the suffering that has dogged the free market since the Industrial

Revolution. Reading Polanyi clarified something I'd always felt but never articulated—a suppressed rage about disparities of wealth. I as a businessperson do not, like many of my friends, think of business as an unalloyed evil. But I am alarmed that poverty is increasing steadily among people who work full-time. There's something seriously wrong, at the heart of capitalism. And it's time we faced it—not as social activists screaming over the fence at business, but as businesspeople looking ourselves full in the mirror.

It's a long-standing myth of capitalism, that competing self-interests work themselves out for the benefit of all, as though by an "invisible hand." But it's a fiction, Polanyi says. A hoax, I say.

As Polanyi explains, the myth of the self-regulating market turned human relations inside out.

Human beings and the natural environment became "commodities," with no intrinsic worth, only a price set by the market. Thus everything in the world—all people, all the Earth's resources—were to be used by the market for one purpose only: to increase profits. And to whom did profits flow? To the ownership class.

Pretty good scam, if you can get away with it: "Everything in the world exists to benefit us, the ownership class. This is the natural law. And if you let us get richer and richer, things eventually will work out to the benefit of all, as though by an invisible hand."

It's absurd, this bowing and scraping before the self-regulating market. We can with more truth say the body regulates and heals itself—but when Christian Scientists say that and their children die, we haul them into court. Because we know that the body heals even better with a little help, like splints on broken arms. Just as the market works better with help—like anti-trust laws, and food and drug regulations.

The market self-regulates, all right, just as the jungle does—allowing the strong to devour the weak. One would think our civilization had grown beyond that.

What's amazing is the recent resurgence of belief in the self-regulating market. One critic is Robert Kuttner, author of *The End of Laissez-Faire* (1991, Knopf). "My subject is in a sense the *second* end of laissez-faire," he writes, "for the ideal of a self-regulating economy seemingly had been dispatched once and for all after the bitter lessons of the global Great Depression, the ensuing World War II, and the explanatory power of Keynesian economics." But laissez-faire has risen repeatedly from the dead, he says—most recently in the wake of communism's collapse.

While free-market apologists worry that government will become a Frankenstein's monster, the market is the real monster. It's path through history is a path of human suffering. And as businesspeople, this is our burden of guilt—the

> The market self-regulates, all right, just as the jungle does—allowing the strong to devour the weak.

Blatant invocation of class has always made Americans uncomfortable, yet Todd Gilman, a writer with impeccable left wing credentials, is surely right that when a large majority of working Americans lose ground despite their best efforts, and when the gap between the richest and poorest Americans is as large as it was in the 1920s, there is ample reason to sound the alarm. "Throughout the wealthier nations, there is," as he says, "a need to shift energy and intelligence from the refining of differences to the composing of majorities." What makes that point even more important is that the right, understanding where its advantage lies, has been happy to play to those differences.

And so, unfortunately, have a great many of the nation's elites—corporations up to their eyeballs in diversity training whose main effect could well be reinforcing and exacerbating those differences; educational institutions more interested in multiculturalism and other methods of patronizing minorities than in fostering a common culture and national identity; media more concerned with niche marketing than community. Yet as long as the left is in the vanguard of this process, it has no reason to complain, much less to wonder, about why so few seem to be listening. It's because so few are being addressed.

—Peter Schrag

sins of the fathers being visited upon the sons and daughters. For even if we ourselves are good people, we are heirs to a frightening legacy. We must own up to it.

We might start by forgiving Adam Smith his blindness, for in 1776 when he published *The Wealth of Nations*, the effects of the free market were unknown. But within a decade it became clear that pauperism was rising with wealth. Rioting was growing more frequent. And by 1817 Robert Owen was lamenting that laborers were "infinitely more degraded and miserable than they were before the introduction of these manufactories."

It's worth lingering over these events, for nowhere can we find a market as unfettered. And it brought unmitigated suffering, for all but the ownership class. In Polanyi's terms, the free market created "Two Nations," one of which benefited enormously from the rise of industry, the other of which suffered.

Polanyi made this observation in 1944, yet it is more true today—in the wake of the Reagan-Bush era, when the hand of the market was again unfettered. The result is that *over half* of the additional income generated between 1977 and 1989 went—to the top *1 percent,* which is sinful. In that same period—the number of people who worked full-time, and fell below the poverty line climbed by an embarrassing 43 percent.

Note we're not talking here about street people. We're talking about people who work forty hours a week and can't feed their families. As businesspeople we ought to hang our heads: How can we allow this to happen?

And how *dare* we scream when Secretary of Labor Robert Reich talks about raising the minimum wage by a lousy 25 cents an hour. You know what that adds up to in a forty-hour week? $10. In an entire year? $520.

Business people say, "Let the market set wages." Translation: Let the people with power and wealth continue to take advantage of those who have nothing because they desperately need a job. That's the natural law of the market. Well, if that's the natural law we ought to change it. Like we changed the natural law that said most infants don't survive infancy.

We have to be willfully blind not to see the truth: that unfettered markets mean giving the wealthy a free hand to get wealthier. Because the Two Nations effect is built right in, maximizing profits means paying working people as little as possible, so that people who own and run the company can make as much as possible. That's the design of the system, to give as little as possible to one group, and as much as possible to another.

To call this natural law is like saying the divine right of kings is natural law. When we say the sole purpose of business is to enrich the ownership class, well, it's like saying the ownership class is the center of the universe. Which is like Ptolemy saying the Earth is the center of the solar system—a falsehood that people believed for fourteen centuries.

IDENTIFY THE BIGGEST WELFARE MOOCHER...

I GET A CHECK...

I GET A LUNCH...

I GET A SUBSIDY...

CORPORATE LOBBIES, INC.

© 1995 by Tribune Media Services. Courtesy of Jack Ohman, *The Oregonian*.

Belief in the self-regulating market is at two centuries and counting. We're overdue for a Copernican revolution—recognizing that enriching the rich really is not the center and purpose of capitalism. The real purpose of capitalism is to enrich all humanity.

See *Economic Insanity: How Growth-Driven Capitalism Is Devouring the American Dream*, by Roger Terry (San Francisco: Berrett-Koehler, 1995). 1-800-929-2929, Fax: 415-362-2512.

Tyranny of the Bottom Line: Why Corporations Make Good People Do Bad Things, by Ralph Estes (San Francisco: Berrett-Koehler, 1995). *Tyranny of the Bottom Line* tells the story of how the corporate system, originally created to serve the public interest, has acquired immense power over the public. Largely unconstrained by a captive regulatory bureaucracy, corporations today exercise a silent dominance over much of our society. This dominion can produce substantial good but can also bring injury and death to employees, financial and personal loss to customers, desolation to communities, and posionous pollution and hazardous waste to the nation. The book includes a practical, specific plan for creating more effective and humane companies, restoring the original public purpose of the corporate system, and allowing managers to make choices that effectively and ethically balance the interests of everyone.

13 • Welfare
The System Provided a Way Out

RITA HENLEY JENSEN (MS. MAGAZINE)

The system provided a way out for Rita Henley Jensen. She tells why it worked then—and doesn't now.

J am a woman. A white woman, once poor but no longer. I am not lazy, never was. I am a middle-aged woman, with two grown daughters. I was a welfare mother, one of those women society considers less than nothing.

I should have applied for Aid to Families with Dependent Children when I was 18 years old, pregnant with my first child, and living with a boyfriend who slapped me around. But I didn't.

On a particularly warm midsummer's day, I stood on High Street, directly across from the main entrance of the vast Columbus campus of Ohio State University, with an older, more sophisticated friend, wondering what to do with my life. With my swollen belly, all hope of my being able to cross the street and enroll in the university had evaporated. Now, I was seeking advice about how merely to survive, to escape the assaults and still be able to care for my child.

My friend knew of no place I could go, nowhere I could turn, no one else I could ask. I remember saying in a tone of resignation, "I can't apply for welfare." Instead of disagreeing with me, she nodded, acknowledging our mutual belief that taking beatings was better than taking handouts. Being "on the dole" meant you deserved only contempt.

In August 1965, I married my attacker.

Six years later, I left him and applied for assistance. My children were 18 months and five and a half years old. I had waited much too long. Within a year, I crossed High Street to go to Ohio State. I graduated in four years and moved to New York City to attend Columbia University's Graduate School of Journalism. I have worked as a journalist for 18 years now. My life on welfare was very hard—there were times when I didn't have enough food for the three of us. But I was able to get an education while on welfare. It is hardly likely that a woman on AFDC today would be allowed to do what I did, to go to school and develop the kind of skills that enabled me to make a better life for myself and my children.

This past summer, I attended a conference in Chicago on feminist legal theory. During the presentation of a paper related to gender and property rights, the speaker mentioned as an aside that when one says "welfare mother" the listener hears "black welfare mother." A discussion ensued about the underlying racism until someone declared that the solution was easy: all that had to be done was have the women in the room bring to the attention of the media the fact that white women make up the largest percentage of welfare recipients. At this point, I stood, took a deep breath, stepped out of my professional guise, and informed the crowd that I was a former welfare mother. Looking at my white hair, blue eyes, and freckled Irish skin, some laughed; others gasped—despite having just acknowledged that someone like me was, in fact, a "typical" welfare mother.

AFDC Recipients, 1992

An Ethnic Breakdown*

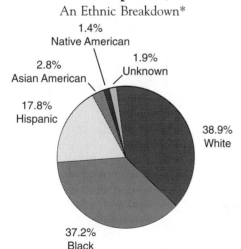

1.4%
Native American

1.9%
Unknown

2.8%
Asian American

17.8%
Hispanic

38.9%
White

37.2%
Black

*As recorded by the U.S. Department of Health and Human Services

Occasionally I do this. Speak up. Identify myself as one of "them." I do so reluctantly because welfare mothers are a lightning rod for race hatred, class prejudice, and misogyny. Yet I am aware that as long as welfare is viewed as an *African American* woman's issue, instead of a *woman's* issue—whether that woman be white, African American, Asian, Latina, or Native American—those in power can continue to exploit our country's racism to weaken and even eliminate public support for the programs that help low-income mothers and their children.

Today, my children and I still represent typical welfare recipients. The statistics I would cite to back up that statement have been refined since the 1970s and now include "Hispanic" as a category. In 1992, 38.9 percent of all welfare mothers were white, 37.2 percent were black, 17.8 percent were "Hispanic," 2.8 percent were Asian, and 1.4 percent were Native American.

However, the focus must be on the dramatic and unrelenting reduction in resources available to low-income mothers in the last two decades.

Fact: In 1970, the average monthly benefit for a family of three was $178. Not much, but consider that as a result of inflation, that $178 would be approximately $680 today. And then consider that the average monthly payment today is only about $414. Payments keep going down—in terms of real dollars.

Fact: The 1968 Work Incentive Program (the government called it WIN; we called it WIP) required that all unemployed adult recipients sign up for job training or employment once their children turned six. The age has now been lowered to three, and states may go as low as age one. What that means is you won't be able to attend and finish college while on welfare. (In most states a college education isn't considered job training, even though experts claim most of us will need college degrees to compete in the workplace of the twenty-first century.)

Fact: Forty-two percent of welfare recipients will be on welfare less than two years during their entire lifetime, and an additional 33 percent will spend between two and eight years on welfare. The statistics haven't changed much over the years: women still use welfare to support their families when their children are small.

By making war on welfare recipients, political leaders can turn the public's attention away from the government's redistribution of wealth to the wealthy. Recent studies show that the United States has become the most economically stratified of industrial nations. In fact, Federal Reserve figures reveal that the richest 1 percent of American households—each with a minimum net worth of $2.3 million—control

Recent studies show that the United States has become the most economically stratified of industrial nations. In fact, Federal Reserve figures reveal that the richest 1 percent of American households—each with a minimum net worth of $2.3 million—control nearly 40 percent of the wealth.

Monthly AFDC Payments vs. Cost of Living
For a Family of Three

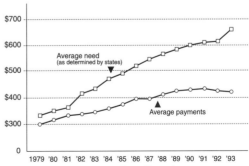

Source: U.S. Department of Health and Human Services

(i) See *Don't worry, He won't get far on foot: The Autobiography of a Dangerous Man*, by John Callahan and David Kelly, William Morrow, New York, 1989; or exerpts in "Welfare Hell" by Callahan and Kelly in *Mother Jones*, May 1989.

nearly 40 percent of the wealth, while in Britain, the richest 1 percent of the population controls about 18 percent of the wealth. In the mid-1970s, both countries were on a par: the richest 1 percent controlled 20 percent of the wealth.

The purpose of this anti-welfare oratory and the campaigns against sex education, abortion rights, and aid to teenage mothers is to ensure a constant supply of young women as desperate and ashamed as I was.

To accomplish their goals, political leaders continually call for reforms that include demands that welfare recipients work, that teenagers don't have sex, and that welfare mothers stop giving birth (but don't have abortions). Each "reform" addresses the nation's racial and sexual stereotypes: taking care of one's own children is not work; welfare mothers are unemployed, promiscuous, and poorly motivated; and unless the government holds their feet to the fire, these women will live on welfare for years, as will their children and their children's children.

This type of demagoguery has been common throughout our history. What sets the present era apart is the nearly across-the-board cooperation of the media. The national news magazines, the most prestigious daily newspapers, the highly regarded broadcast news outlets, as well as the supermarket tabloids and talk-radio hosts, have generally abandoned the notion that one of their missions is sometimes to comfort the afflicted and afflict the comfortable. Instead, they too often reprint politicians' statements unchallenged, provide charts comparing one party's recommendations to another's without really questioning those recommendations, and illustrate story after story, newscast after newscast, with a visual of an African American woman (because we all know they're the only ones on welfare) living in an urban housing project (because that's where all welfare recipients live) who has been on welfare for years.

14 • A Response to Jensen

DAWN MARIE COOK
(LETTER TO THE EDITOR, MS. MAGAZINE)

It would have been helpful to know why Rita Henley Jensen failed to take precautions and got pregnant at 18 when she had no support. Why was her mate selection process so faulty that she was drawn to a man who was abusive? Then she had a second child.

There is no mention of why the father was not contributing child support. Was there any legal action?

In other words, how did Jensen get into this mess? And could it have been prevented?

The bulk of Jensen's article aimed at indignation. She wanted to know why the state of Ohio gave her only $204 a month. It should really have given her more, is her attitude. She seems oblivious to the fact that someone had to come up with that $204 a month, something neither she nor her ex-husband nor her family was able to do. It isn't just some pie-in-the-sky agency. It's people like me. I am about the same age as Jensen. My father died when I was 16, leaving my mom with four kids; there was no money for college, so I worked my way through school; I was not able to afford a graduate degree. I have had good jobs since, but I have paid horrendous taxes. Although I still consider myself a liberal, I have to admit that the sob stories are wearing thin.

In my opinion we have to impress on young women the consequences of getting pregnant without a job, a marriage, an education. Young men today seem to have a hit-and-run approach to sex. They don't seem to realize they are condemning their children to a life of poverty. But we can't just let it keep happening. Stop sleeping with them, or at least take precautions. And we have to lobby for laws that pressure men to take responsibility for their offspring.

Young people can control what happens to them; we need to let them know that—to give more help on the front end rather than the back end.

Dawn Marie Cook
Yankeetown, FL

15 • Millions of Persons in Poverty

The majority of people in poverty are white. While people of color do have proportionally *higher* rates of poverty, the graph indicates just how pervasive poverty is. *The War on Poverty* of the late 60s appeared to diminish the number of people in poverty and keep that number stable until 1978. At that time, high unemployment and cuts in social spending seemed to result in a corresponding increase in people below the poverty line.

Millions of persons in poverty, 1967–94
by race

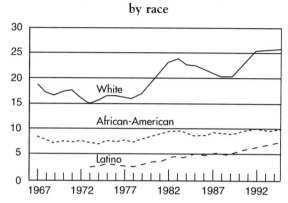

Source: U.S. Bureau of the Census: "Income, Poverty, and Valuation of Non-Cash Benefits." Also, Current Population Report, P-60, No. 185, "Poverty in the U.S., 1992." For further information refer to *The New Field Guide to the U.S. Economy* or contact the Center on Budget and Policy Priorities at 202-408-1080.

Note: Basis for calculating figures on this graph shift slightly between 1991 and 1992, 1981 and 1982, etc. based on differences in sampling procedures. In 1992 the figures were calculated based on the 1990 decennial census, whereas 1982–1991 were based on the 1980 decennial census. Poverty is defined as the minimum amount an individual or family needs to purchase the basic necessities of life (such as food, shelter, and clothing). In 1994, this was calculated as $11,821 for a family of three.

16 •   Welfare: Facts and Fiction

MS. MAGAZINE

*W*hen politicians and pundits talk about welfare reform, their rhetoric is often riddled with false assumptions and disinformation. It's time to set the record straight.

FALSE ASSUMPTIONS:

✗ **Myth:** The welfare system is bankrupting the country.

✔ **Reality:** The Aid to Families with Dependent Children (AFDC) program makes up 1 percent of the federal budget. With food stamps, the welfare system accounts for only 3 percent of the entire budget.

✗ **Myth:** Low-income women have many children in order to get fat AFDC checks.

✔ **Reality:** On average, the states provide only about $67 a month per additional child. The likelihood that a woman will have additional children decreases the longer she stays on AFDC.

✗ **Myth:** Cutting women off welfare will promote individual responsibility, ending illegitimate births.

✔ **Reality:** Recent studies have found no statistically significant links between AFDC benefits and nonmarital births.

✗ **Myth:** Those who work are not poor.

✔ **Reality:** In the1970s, a full-time, minimum-wage worker with two children lived above the poverty line. Today, the same family ends up with $8,840 a year—far below the 1995 poverty line of $12,188.

WHAT REAL REFORM WOULD LOOK LIKE:

• At current wage and benefit levels, neither work nor welfare alone can bring a family out of poverty. Genuine welfare reform would require widespread job creation with adequate pay and the prospect of stable, long-term employment.

• Most welfare recipients want to work but lack the education and skills to obtain jobs that pay a living wage. High-quality education and job training programs must be supported and expanded. Women who participate in such programs, including postsecondary education and training for nontraditional occupations, have higher earnings and are less likely to return to welfare.

• In order to work or to participate in training or educational programs, poor parents need access to high-quality, affordable child care and elder care. Poor families also need universal and comprehensive health care, including abortion and other reproductive health services.

To prevent poor people from having to resort to welfare, other benefits such as unemployment insurance, paid family leave, and temporary disability insurance must be expanded to cover all low-income people.

ⓘ See Linda Bridges, "Home Lessons from Abroad," *National Review*, June 26, 1995, pp. 41–42.

In *CENSORED! The News That Didn't Make the News—and Why* (Chapel Hill, N.C.: Melburne Press, 1993), pp. 28–29, Carl Jensen presents a cogent and articulate argument that challenges the notion that most serious crimes in the United States are committed by young black men. In the face of this common assumption, here articulated by Richard Cohen of the *Washington Post*, Jensen asserts that corporate crime and violence cost society much more than street crime. Because street crime is easier to report, often provides dramatic visuals for television, and requires a lesser degree of investigative effort, white-collar crime is not perceived as a major social problem. Most media organizations have a stronger affiliation with corporate America, and thus have an interest in not "rocking the boat." The fact that the government did not prosecute most of the Savings and Loan scandal criminals both excused and rewarded this hidden sort of criminality. Our contributors are telling us that the center once populated by a growing middle class is becoming a narrow and desolate border crossing.

17 • To Tell the Truth: The Proliferation of Really Big Lies—1990s Style

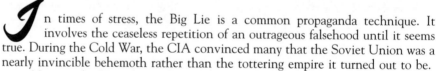

HERBERT JACOB *(THE CHICAGO TRIBUNE)*

*I*n times of stress, the Big Lie is a common propaganda technique. It involves the ceaseless repetition of an outrageous falsehood until it seems true. During the Cold War, the CIA convinced many that the Soviet Union was a nearly invincible behemoth rather than the tottering empire it turned out to be.

Now, as the United States faces the stress of international competition, the Big Lie once again dominates political analysis. Today's Big Lie has at least three components, which have been repeated incessantly. They include:

- Welfare has been a failure.
- The states can administer programs better than the feds.
- Government has grown by leaps and bounds and has become too big.

The failing that is laid to welfare policies is that they are unsuccessful in lifting the poor into the ranks of the working population. The major welfare programs, however, were never designed to lift people out of poverty. Aid to Families with Dependent Children and Unemployment Compensation were designed to keep needy Americans from starving, and they have done so.

An increasing number of Americans are poor—not because of the failure of welfare policies but because of the failure of the economic system. Now that our workers compete with those from Mexico, Guatemala, Indonesia, China and many other places where wages are tiny and living standards desperately low, it has become unprofitable to employ Americans.

In fact, the United States has done better than most in curbing unemployment. It enjoys a lower unemployment rate than Germany, France, England, and Italy. However, neither unemployment nor poverty are the consequence of welfare programs in these countries. They are the result of competition with poorer nations.

A second Big Lie is that state governments are more efficient than the federal government because the states are "closer to the people." Closer yes, but far less visible. The media pay much less attention to the goings-on in state capitals than in Washington, with state politicians and bureaucrats facing much less scrutiny. What federal agency matches the sorry record of the Illinois Department of Children and Family Services? Where are political contributions more necessary than in bidding for state public works contracts? Who has been more delinquent in paying its Medicaid bills or in funding public education? State politicians, of course, welcome block grants with no strings attached. If past experience is a guide to the future, block grants will create enormous opportunities for shady deals that will enrich state politicians and their cronies.

The third Big Lie is that government has grown too big.

For those who want no government, any government is, of course, too large. But compared to government elsewhere in the world, the federal government is not exceptionally large.

One common way to gauge the size of a government is to look at the amount of money it takes in taxes. In 1993, all but one of the 22 most industrialized countries taxed a higher percentage of its gross domestic product than the United States. For instance, West Germany taxed 9.4 percent more than the U.S., Britain took 6.2 percent more, and France levied 14.4 percent more.

Compared to the recent past, the federal budget remained almost constant, at about 22 percent, as a percentage of gross national product from 1975 to 1994. Meanwhile, expenditures for human services, rather than ballooning, have increased only 1.5 percentage points in real dollars.

The unfortunate consequence of the Big Lie is that with its constant repetition, much of the public comes to believe it—regardless of the facts. Policymakers devise solutions to problems that do not exist, while real problems continue to fester.

Ending welfare as we have known it will not decrease poverty; shifting programs to the states will not make them more efficient or effective; decreasing the size of the federal government will not empower people.

Instead, they lead to neglect of the country's real social problems, such as the growing income inequality, anxiety produced by fear of unemployment and

The unfortunate consequence of the Big Lie is that with its constant repetition, much of the public comes to believe it—regardless of the facts. Policymakers devise solutions to problems that do not exist, while real problems continue to fester.

uninsured illness, and inadequate education for our youth, to name only a few. All will return to haunt us before we reach the year 2000. As many of us learned from our parents, it does not pay to lie.

See the documentary film *Manufacturing Consent: Noam Chomsky and the Media* directed by Mark Achbar and Peter Wintonick (Necessary Illusions Films). This film distills the essence of Noam Chomsky's voluminous writing on propaganda and power: (1) that democracy is "a game for elites" whose central problem is managing opinion, not courting participation; (2) that the U.S. government, like any state, is fundamentally immoral and deceitful; (3) that private ownership of resources is the planet's most urgent problem as we exit the 20th century; and (4) that average people have an impressive capacity to recognize truth if they hear it. For thirty years Chomsky has been on a mission to restore memory, common sense, and a concern for human consequences to our denuded politics. (Available for $40 from Z *Magazine*, 18 Millfield St., Woods Hole, MA 02543, 508-548-9063, Fax 508-457-0626.)

A conservative perspective on class can be found in Carl F. Horowitz, "Searching for the White Underclass," *National Review*, September 11, 1995, p. 52.

Race in the USA— Exorcising Our Demons

2

I wonder why I must sit
and ponder the strange
and new? Sometimes I
think I'm all but
different but different
I'll always be.

From "The Oceanside," written
by Izzy Justice at age 14 in Zanzibar, Tanzania (Africa)

In some parts of North America, diversity is seen as being only about race, and limited to the treatment of African Americans in a society dominated by Euro Americans. But other sins of the past besides slavery haunt our social house as well. Consider the struggle for cultural and economic survival and against cultural and acutal genocide on the part of North America's native peoples. We tremble at the fragile Canadian truce between Western Provinces, Ontario, Quebec, and the Maritimes. In another geographic area, many people in the U.S. southwest and west view themselves as living in "Occupied Mexico."

As a result of California's population and immigration patterns, people of color are reaching numerical parity with those described as "white." Even now it is a normal daily experience—at work and at play—to be in groups of people in which there is no distinct majority. Yet race, color, or other visible characteristics still serve as common markers for deciding who is "in" and who is "out." It is at once culturally instinctual in people's reactions to others and maddeningly artificial to anyone who looks at the facts. Why do we need this distinction? What purposes does it serve? How long shall we need it? Do our present political, economic, legislative, and diversity efforts dispel or reinforce damaging distinctions of race? Are advocacy and interest groups, racial and ethnic solidarities, dividing our nations, or are they simply continuing an age-old process of "acting like Americans," openly competing in a marketplace of ideas, resources, and opportunities?

Some groups in North America have gaping wounds whose bleeding begs to be stanched, while others seem to pick at the scabs of old hurts that might otherwise be healed and forgotten. How assimilated are we really? How much do we want to be? Can we have the advantages of both commonness and difference? If so, how? These are some of the questions our contributors attempt to shed light on in this section. Their answers are distinctly not "black and white."

18 •   Black Pride for White People

ADRIAN PIPER (TRANSITION)

Are you sure you don't have an African ancestor?

She's heard the arguments, most astonishingly that, statistically . . . the average white American is 6 percent black. Or, put another way, 95 percent of white Americans are 5 to 80 percent black. Her Aunt Tyler has told her stories about these whites researching their roots in the National Archives and finding they've got an African-American or two in the family, some becoming so hysterical they have to be carried out by paramedics.

—Elaine Perry, *Another Present Era*

Estimates ranging up to 5 percent, and suggestions that up to one-fifth of the white population have some genes from black ancestors, are probably far too high. If these last figures were correct, the majority of Americans with some black ancestry would be known and counted as whites!

—F. James Davis, *Who Is Black?*

The fact is that the longer a person's family has lived in this country, the higher the probable percentage of African ancestry that person's family is likely to have—bad news for the Daughters of the American Revolution, I'm afraid. And the proximity to the continent of Africa of the country of origin from which one's forebears emigrated, as well as the colonization of a part of Africa by that country, are two further variables that increase the probability of African ancestry within that family. It would appear that only the Lapps of Norway are safe.

A number of years ago I was doing research on a video installation on the subject of racial identity and miscegenation, and came across the Phipps case of Louisiana in the early 1980s. Susie Guillory Phipps had identified herself as white and, according to her own testimony (but not that of some of her black relatives), had believed that she was white, until she applied for a passport, when she discovered that she was identified on her birth records as black by virtue of having one thirty-second African ancestry. She brought suit against the state of Louisiana to have her racial classification changed. She lost the suit but effected the overthrow of the law identifying individuals as black if they had one thirty-second African ancestry, leaving on the books a prior law identifying as black an individual who had any African ancestry—the "one-drop" rule that uniquely characterizes the classification of blacks in the United States in fact though no longer in law. So according to this long-standing convention of racial classification, a white who acknowledges any African ancestry implicitly acknowledges being black—a social condition, more than an identity, that no white person would voluntarily assume, even in imagination. This is one reason that whites, educated and uneducated alike, are so resistant to considering the probable extent of racial miscegenation.

No reflective and well-intentioned white person who is consciously concerned to end racism wants to admit to instinctively recoiling at the thought of being identified as black herself. But if you want to see such a white person do this, just peer at the person's facial features and tell her, in a complimentary tone of voice, that she looks as though she might have some black ancestry, and watch her reaction. It's not a test I find or any black person finds particularly pleasant to

ⓘ See *Race: How Blacks & Whites Think & Feel About the American Obsession*, by Studs Terkel (New York: Anchor Books, $12.95, ISBN 0-385-46889-X).

See *Two Nations: Black, White, Separate, Hostile, Unequal*, by Andrew Hacker. (New York: Scribner's Sons, 1992, $24.95, ISBN 0-684-19148-2). Using the techniques of both philosophy and statistical social science, Hacker examines the racial divide between whites and blacks in America. He examines the effects of existing racial inequalities on such issues as families, crime, work, and education and contends that racial segregation as a social and human division "surpasses all others—even gender—in intensity and subordination."

"But I am not tragically colored. There is no great sorrow dammed up in my soul, nor lurking behind my eyes. I do not mind at all. I do not belong to the sobbing school of Negrohood who hold that nature somehow has given them a lowdown dirty deal and whose feelings are hurt about it."

—Zora Neale Hurston, *I Love Myself When I Am Laughing . . .* , *A Zora Neale Hurston Reader*, Alice Walker, editor (Old Westbury, N.Y.: The Feminist Press, 1979), p. 17.

apply (that is, unless one dislikes the person and wants to inflict pain deliberately), and having once done so inadvertently, I will never do it again. The ultimate test of a person's repudiation of racism is not what she can contemplate *doing* for or on behalf of black people, but whether she herself can contemplate calmly the likelihood of *being* black. If racial hatred has not manifested itself in any other context, it will do so here if it exists, in hatred of the self as identified with the other—that is, as self-hatred projected onto the other.

When I was an undergraduate minoring in medieval and Renaissance musicology, I worked with a fellow music student—white—in the music library. I remember his reaction when I relayed to him an article I'd recently read arguing that Beethoven had African ancestry. Beethoven was one of his heroes, and his vehement derision was completely out of proportion to the scholarly worth of the hypothesis. But when I suggested that he wouldn't be so skeptical if the claim were that Beethoven had some Danish ancestry, he fell silent. In those days we were very conscious of covert racism, as our campus was exploding all around us because of it. More recently I premiered at a gallery a video installation exploring the issue of African ancestry among white Americans. A white male viewer commenced to kick the furniture, mutter audibly that he was white and was going to stay that way, and start a fistfight with my dealer. Either we are less conscious of covert racism twenty years later, or we care less to contain it.

Among politically committed and enlightened whites, the inability to acknowledge their probable African ancestry is the last outpost of racism. It is the litmus test that separates those who have the courage of their convictions from those who merely subscribe to them and that measures the depth of our dependence on a presumed superiority (of any kind, anything will do) to other human beings—anyone, anywhere—to bolster our fragile self-worth.

When I turned 40 a few years ago, I gave myself the present of rereading the personal journals I have been keeping since age 11. I was astounded at the chasm between my present conception of my own past, which is being continually revised and updated to suit present circumstances, and the actual past events, behavior, and emotions I recorded as faithfully as I could as they happened. My derelictions, mistakes, and failures of responsibility are much more evident in those journals than they are in my present, sanitized, and virtually blameless image of my past behavior. It was quite a shock to encounter in those pages the person I actually have been rather than the person I now conceive myself to have been. My memory is always under the control of the person I now want and strive to be, and so rarely under the control of the facts. If the personal facts of one's past are this difficult for other people to face too, then perhaps it is no wonder that we must cast about outside ourselves for someone to feel superior to, even though there are so many blunders and misdeeds in our own personal histories that might serve that function.

For whites to acknowledge their blackness is, then, much the same as for men to acknowledge their femininity and for Christians to acknowledge their Judaic heritage. It is to reinternalize the external scapegoat through which they have sought to escape their own sense of inferiority.

19 · Treason to Whiteness Is Loyalty to Humanity

AN INTERVIEW WITH NOEL IGNATIEV

*N*oel Ignatiev is coeditor of *Race Traitor*, a journal of the new abolitionism, the motto of which is "Treason to whiteness is loyalty to humanity." He is a long-time activist in radical movements and has written numerous articles and pamphlets, including "The White Blindspot" (1967, co-authored with Ted Allen) and *How the Irish Became White*.

What is a race traitor anyway?
IGNATIEV: A traitor to the white race is someone who is nominally classified as white, but who defies the rules of whiteness so flagrantly as to jeopardize his or her ability to draw upon the privileges of the white skin.

Why did you decide to launch a journal?
IGNATIEV: C. L. R. James says somewhere that in this world if you have an idea and you get together with a few other people and you publish your idea, you never can tell what will happen. The other coeditor, John Garvey, and I are both admirers of James, and so we decided to follow his advice.

Who are your readers?
IGNATIEV: They range from university professors to skinheads who resent Nazi attempts to appropriate their culture. We are hoping to reach those so-called white

Subscriptions to *Race Traitor* are $20 for four issues for individuals, $40 for institutions. Sample copies are $6. Write to PO Box 603, Cambridge, MA 02140-0005.

(i) *How the Irish Became White,* by Noel Ignatiev, 233 pp., (Routledge, $25, ISBN 0-415-91384-5). 1-800-634-7064.

(i) *Uprooting Racism: How White People can Work for Racial Justice,* by Paul Kivel. (Philadelphia, Penn.: New Society Publishers, 1996, $14.95, ISBN 0-865671-338-3). 1-800-333-9093.

people who are uneasy with the definition of themselves as "white" and who are aware on some level that whiteness is a problem for themselves and others.

Have there been any reactions to the name?
IGNATIEV: Everyone who sees it is curious, which of course was part of the idea. We are looking for those readers who will see it and experience the shock of recognition—"hey, that's me." We did include a slogan, "Treason to whiteness is loyalty to humanity," to make it clear that we were not asking black people to become traitors to their race.

What is the history of the concept of "race"?
IGNATIEV: "Race" has meant various things in history. We use the term to mean a group that includes all social classes in a situation where the most degraded member of a dominant group is exalted over any member of a subordinate group. That formation was first successfully established in the seventeenth century. By then, there already existed a trade across the Atlantic in laborers. Traders from Europe and Africa both sold their countrymen and were not held back because they were of the same color as those they sold. Slavery was a matter of economics. At the time, it was the most efficient way of guaranteeing a labor force—provided it could be enforced.

To enslave Europeans in the New World would have cut off the emigration of laborers from Europe. To make slaves of the Native American groups as a whole would have created problems on the frontier and would have encouraged the natives to give sanctuary to runaway laborers. After some experimenting, hereditary, lifetime servitude was fastened exclusively on Africans. Even limiting slavery to people from one continent did not by itself mean that races existed as social formations.

To see the contrast, look at Brazil and the islands of the Caribbean. There, the slaveholders were from Europe, the middle classes were of mixed descent, and the slaves were African. People who on the North American mainland would have been called "black" were part of a free middle class and helped to police the slaves. In those places, what appeared to be a color distinction was essentially a distinction of class.

As Theodore Allen points out in *The Invention of the White Race,* the white race meant not only that no European Americans were slaves. It meant also that all European Americans, even laborers, were by definition enforcers of slavery. In the Chesapeake Bay Colony (Virginia and Maryland), people from Africa and people from Europe worked together in the tobacco fields. They mated with each other and ran away and rebelled together at first. At the end of the 1600s, people of African descent, even those who were free, lost certain rights they had had before and that even the poorest and most downtrodden person of European descent continued to enjoy. In return for these privileges, European Americans of all classes came to be part of the apparatus that maintained Afro-Americans in chattel slavery (and themselves in unfreedom). That was the birth of "race," as we use the term.

Is there such a thing as a "white culture"?
IGNATIEV: No. There is Italian culture and Polish, Irish, Yiddish, German, and Appalachian culture; there is youth culture and drug culture and queer culture; but there is no "white" culture—unless you mean Wonder bread and television game shows. Whiteness is nothing but an expression of race privilege. It has been said that the typical "white" American male spends his childhood as an Indian, his adolescence as an African American, and only becomes white when he reaches the age of legal responsibility.

What do you mean by the "new abolitionism"?
IGNATIEV: We believe that so long as the white race exists, all movements against what is called "racism" will fail. Therefore, our aim is to abolish the white race. Most anti-racists, even while they oppose discrimination, believe that racial status is fixed and eternal. We hold that without social distinctions, "race" is a fiction. The only race is the human.

20 · Patterns of Behavior

BOB ABRAMMS INTERVIEWS TOM KOCHMAN

*T*om Kochman is one of the foremost researchers on cultural differences in patterns of communication among U.S. ethnic groups. His classic work *Black and White: Styles in Conflict* has long served as a practical guide for people willing to cross racial barriers in business, education, or social life.

BOB ABRAMMS: Your work has come under fire in the past few years. Critics claim that your black and white "patterns of behavior" are stereotypes that don't speak to workforce interactions. Training audiences resist some of your research findings because they don't seem to fit across class or regional differences. For example, in the South there was an older generation of African Americans who worked in white homes. They deliberately taught white linguistic patterns to their kids as a way of assimilating. Could it be that patterns are different outside Chicago, where you did most of your research?

TOM KOCHMAN: A lot depends on the class level. My research is a work of science. And often science and politics do not make happy bedfellows. I was describing patterns of difference that exist for those for whom they are true. If it's not true for others, then it may be that they do not participate in the culture being

ⓘ *Black & White: Styles in Conflict,* by Thomas Kochman (Chicago: University of Chicago Press, 1981, $10.00, ISBN 0-226-44955-6). Distributed by ODT (1-800-736-1293).

(i) **The "dozens"** is a form of verbal banter usually involving mutual insults and considerable creative humor. There are forms of direct insults to the other person, usually referred to as "woofing," "sounding," or "ranking." "The dozens" refers to indirect insults (e.g., "Your mama's so low, she plays handball against the curb") usually applied to relatives rather than the other person directly. It follows a ritual form of escalating exaggeration and serves as a testing ground to "toughen" the players to withstand verbal insults without resorting to violence. Superiority is achieved by matching wits and "topping" your adversary's putdowns.

(i) **"Signifying"** is a form of hinting or insinuation. It involves meaning more than you are willing to say. The receiver needs to discern the missing part by interpreting the motive of the sender, going above and beyond what's being said. There is also another version of signifying which means to instigate and stir up trouble (as in the song "Signifying Monkey," where the monkey goads the lion into fighting the elephant).

described. At the same time, many, especially middle-class, blacks would rather not have sections of the work speak about the black population. They feel implicated by what other blacks do or say.

ABRAMMS: It causes problems for people who don't want to feel identified with it.

KOCHMAN: Right. Material dealing with profanity, playing "the dozens," signifying, and male/female relations generally gets targeted because blacks are stereotyped every day for many of the patterns we describe. To avoid the stereotype, many people would like to disassociate themselves from those patterns.

ABRAMMS: Your research shows patterns that were true up through 1980. Are they just as prevalent in the inner city today?

KOCHMAN: No question. The patterns have become even more visible in the past twenty years. One can see Scotty Pippin and Alonzo Mourning of the NBA almost getting into playing "the dozens" on TV. The patterns are still strong and relevant to the population of which they are true. Culture doesn't change much. And black culture is quite traditional. The public is always confused when we talk about "black" and "white," so now I use the term "African American" and "Anglo" because I want them to stand for ethnic labels rather than race labels.

ABRAMMS: Yes.

KOCHMAN: If you say "black" and people understand it as a race label, they will object, as you pointed out. And there are Southern blacks highly influenced by white middle-class values. Not feeling themselves described by the patterns I have been defining, they wonder how can I call them "black" patterns. But, this shows a fundamental misunderstanding. It is culture that defines behavior, not race. If I grew up in China, I might be "white," but I'd speak Chinese and my whole values system would be much more Chinese.

We are talking about patterns of difference. The force of our work is how it illuminates why communication fails. Taken at that level, it is most powerful. But people are asking us how representative these patterns are of the population as a whole and in terms of regional and class differences. The two issues are separate. I know that the patterns are highly representative because of how frequently breakdowns occur—that hasn't changed in the 30 years that we've been in this business.

ABRAMMS: What key points of leverage would improve interracial relations?

KOCHMAN: It's more than simple exposure. We've worked with interracial couples and with a biracial family network who used the book as their bible for years. I have some students examining how much a vested interest in the relationship might encourage people to explore remedies for problems they generate.

ABRAMMS: What do you find?

KOCHMAN: It doesn't really happen—a conflict is a conflict is a conflict. And when people hit the wall on a problem, they tend to avoid it and run away from it or they handle it the way anybody else would handle a conflict.

ABRAMMS: So just knowing the dynamics doesn't create a key point of entry?

KOCHMAN: It helps. But, like in therapy—you can understand the Oedipus Complex but you still need psychoanalysis to know how it affects you. So the best way to do this work is to incorporate it in a "therapeutic" kind of environment. Our workshops do this.

ABRAMMS: So, not just intellectual theorizing . . .

KOCHMAN: People need to see firsthand how patterns have infiltrated how they think and view the world and how they behave and so on. Then it begins to become transforming.

ABRAMMS: Can you give us one thing that would work for, let's say, the white population?

KOCHMAN: Here's an example. When a situation gets emotionally charged, white men tend to shut down. So, when a white man is being confronted by a black in a passionate way, as long as the situation is issue-focused rather than a personal attack, there's no reason for concern. He should just stay with it, stay engaged, and not shut down.

ABRAMMS: Match the feeling level?

KOCHMAN: Yeah, develop a capacity to handle it. In workshops we ask, "When does your heart start to palpitate?"

ABRAMMS: And it's different for WASPS than it is for Jews or Italians or people with Mediterranean backgrounds because they're more comfortable with that.

KOCHMAN: Up to a point. I'm not sure it's exactly the same . . . Japanese, Chinese, and some other East Asians will tell you their heart starts to palpitate *if you force them to confront you.* White women, white men—Anglos say their heart starts to palpitate *when you confront them,* while blacks say, "My heart starts to palpitate *when you don't let me confront you.*"

ABRAMMS: [Laughs]

KOCHMAN: We have to make people comfortable with these different styles, not just understand them. That calls for things like role playing.

ABRAMMS: How about one tip for the African-American?

KOCHMAN: He or she needs to understand that when Anglos withdraw, it's not because they don't care; it's because they fear the intensity. Blacks tend to think that whites have all the power, so they shouldn't be afraid of confrontation. But, in fact, whites do fear that the relationship is at risk when a hot, passionate confrontation occurs. So whites, on the one hand, need to develop their capacity to hear the energy, passion, and emotion, while blacks may have to learn to ratchet down their intensity to get their message across. Both sides are dealing so much with *how* things are said that they can't get to *what* is being said.

21 • The Busy Citizen's Discussion Guide to Racism and Race Relations

STUDY CIRCLES RESOURCE CENTER

*T*he purpose of this activity is to examine some common viewpoints about the current state of race relations in this country and to think about some of the beliefs that underlie those views.

VIEWPOINT 1—Racism is a powerful force that we must eliminate.

Racism is pervasive and powerful in America, harming African-Americans, Hispanics, Asian Americans, Native Americans, Arab-Americans, and, less directly, whites. Discrimination on the basis of race deprives many Americans of a good education, good jobs, promotions, decent housing, and access to credit. For example, even when blacks have the same level of education, they earn less than whites. This kind of discrimination means that minorities often lack economic opportunity, status, and other important sources of self-esteem.

VIEWPOINT 2—Blacks and other minorities still suffer from past forms of racism.

Even though discrimination has declined significantly over the past 25 years and there are more opportunities for racial and ethnic minorities, most minorities continue to receive a strong (though sometimes subtle) message from our society that they are not as capable as others. African-Americans, in particular, have a horrible legacy—that of slavery and 100 years of deprivation after the Civil War. It is unrealistic to expect any culture to overcome hundreds of years of oppression in a generation or two; we as a society must recognize that we are dealing with a legacy of past injustices. Though African-Americans have a unique history of oppression, other racial and ethnic groups have suffered oppression as well.

(i) A free information packet about Study Circle programs is available from SCRC; 860-928-2618, Fax 860-928-3713, e-mail: scrc@neca.com

VIEWPOINT 3—The biggest problem people of color face is a declining economy.

African-Americans and Hispanics do have a harder time making it than whites, but this is not due primarily to racism and discrimination. It is largely because economic opportunities have declined at a time when many minorities are still at the bottom of the economic ladder. Over the past 20 years, our economy has lost the low-skill jobs that once sustained the working poor and the manufacturing jobs that once lifted poor people into the middle class. As a result, blacks and Hispanics are stuck at the bottom of the economic ladder and are not able to move up the way Italians, Irish, Jews, Polish, and other ethnic groups once did.

VIEWPOINT 4—Some minority cultures don't value hard work or schooling. This is the main problem.

Racism no longer holds back minorities as it once did. The evidence is a thriving black middle class, the success of Asian Americans and some Hispanic groups, and the success of foreign-born blacks in comparison with native-born African-Americans. Racism has become a crippling fixation for minorities; the image of victimization has isolated and weakened the black community in particular. Many of the problems of poor minorities are due to a dysfunctional culture that fails to emphasize education and hard work. In addition, the welfare system discourages initiative and leads to an ever-expanding number of families headed by single mothers. The climate of crime and violence in many poor minority communities further discourages work on anything other than mere survival.

VIEWPOINT 5—Racism will never be eliminated. People of color will do better if they focus on building from the strengths of their own cultures.

Too much time has been lost trying to fit in with the values of white culture. Even those people of color who have "done everything right" and who have attained success according to the standards of the majority culture continue to face racism on a daily basis. It is time for people of color to realize that many white people will never give up or share power. Rather than trying to change white people's attitudes, people of color should focus on themselves. They should strive to build cultural, political, social, and economic institutions that build on the strengths of their own cultures.

QUESTIONS ON THE VIEWPOINTS

1. How powerful and widespread is racism in America?
2. Does one of the viewpoints come close to your own?
3. What experiences, beliefs, and values might lead a reasonable person to support the views that are different from your own?

"The black community has strong undercurrents of conservatism. Nearly 90 percent support voluntary prayer in schools. Over 90 percent approve of requiring able-bodied welfare recipients to work for benefits. Over 50 percent consider themselves pro-life. About 60 percent approve of denying parole for repeat violent offenders."

—Jack Kemp (Co-director of Empower America) in *National Review*, May 16, 1994, p. 40)

4. Are there viewpoints not represented here, or perhaps a combination of the views, that you think best describe how widespread racism is in our country?
5. How widespread is racism in our community?
6. How does this discussion of racism in America and in our community affect our ideas about dealing with it?

22 • Barney's in Bankruptcy

JOHNNIE L. ROBERTS (NEWSWEEK)

Johnnie L. Roberts, staff writer for *Newsweek*, describing an incident that occurred in 1990, when he was preparing to receive a newswriters award. *Newsweek*, January 22, 1996. His reflections indicate an increasing realization of the intricacies of class and race in our current social complex.

"*I* had a queasy feeling about Barney's from the start. The store felt off-limits. . . . I quickly picked a Hugo Boss suit (on sale for $600) . . . I returned for my suit two weeks later. With the bag in hand, I shopped for a shirt and tie. There in a locked case, like a piece of jewelry, was the Armani tie for me. The sales clerk handed it to me. I quickly handed it back, after seeing the $85 price tag, and headed for the exit. But a security guard met me as I approached the door. "Come with me," he said. I didn't realize he was addressing me, so I kept walking. "Come with me," he said again. "You stole a tie." Of course, I hadn't, and told him to ask the tie clerk. He refused. Suddenly it dawned on me: Just as many African-American men have long suspected about ritzy retailers, Barney's had targeted me as a shoplifter because I'm black.

"I've since concluded that race was only part of the story. Barney's is really about elitism. Skin color was only one of its ways of sorting out the regular Joes and Janes from the hip crowd that passes through its doors."

See *Faces at the Bottom of the Well: The Permanence of Racism*, by Derrick Bell (New York: Basic Books, 1992, ISBN 0-465-06814-6). P.O. Box 588, Dunmore, PA 18512-0588 1-800-331-3761. In this collection of reflective pieces, dialogic narratives, and historical fables, Bell explores the persistence of racism in determining the social and economic condition of African Americans. He argues that racism is so ingrained in American culture and its historical heritage that no matter what blacks might do to better themselves, racism will not abate in America until whites begin to see their own well-being linked to the elimination of racism from the culture.

It is often helpful to go back to original sources, and revisit great leaders in the struggle for racial equality. Some of Malcolm X's works are easily available today and can make a profound impact on our understanding of the issues. Take, for instance Malcolm's famous speech "The Ballot or the Bullet," which sounded so militant when it was broadcast in the 1960s. Now, it sounds fair-minded and reasonable. Was Malcolm's perceived "militancy" simply the shock to the '60s white audience never having heard a powerful African American man? Listen to the tape yourself! It is available for $5 (plus $3 postage) from Pathfinder Bookstore, 780 Tremont St., Boston, MA 02118, 617-247-6772, Fax 617-247-6834. The text of the speech is found in *By Any Means Necessary* (Boston: Patherfinder Press, $15.95, ISBN 087348-759-1). A catalog that includes many Malcolm X resources is available from Pathfinder Press, 410 West St., New York, NY 10014, 212-741-0690, Fax 212-727-0151.

Malcom X

History provides some insight and irony into the legacy we imagine we have as Americans. While we preach freedom and lofty ideals, these are often contradicted by a closer look at our past.

Our nation's military action after annexing the Mexican territory of Texas (the Texas War, 1845–46) was primarily because Anglos demanded the right to own slaves, a condition abhorrent to the government and people of Mexico. The Mexicans were willing to make nearly any concession to the demands of the Anglos, but allowing slavery within their borders was totally unacceptable. Thus, the war that ensued, in which Davy Crockett, James Bowie, and the rest fought at the Alamo, was a war for the right to own slaves—not generally how we learned it in school.

Sometimes dialogue occurs informally and richly as in the case of the following story, with all the advantages and pitfalls of spontaneity. Powerful dialogue processes can assist understanding and conflict resolution. Many of the pieces that follow invite us to see other aspects of dialogue, examine the obstacles, and offer tips and insights to overcome them.

23 · The Museum of Slavery?

LANCE MORROW (TIME MAGAZINE)

I say, "blacks should focus on whatever increases black self-respect and pride. That is the answer." He—old friend, old comrade—leans across the table, voice angry, eyes flame throwing. I should not have said "should."

"Listen," he starts, meaning, *Listen, Whitey.* "After everything that has happened, no white man has the right to tell blacks what they should be doing—about anything!"

I have a temper too. I stifle an impulse to fire back what W. C. Fields called "an evasive answer." Instead I pause and let the adrenaline subside; I roll my eyes to the ceiling and raise my open palms, priestlike: Peace.

But I am right—presumptuous and prim but on the money: self-respect. The answer is in the black mind. Forget about the white mind. The Muslims have been saying it for years.

But when a white man says such things, the truth, arriving from the wrong direction, becomes an enemy truth to blacks—less welcome than a lie. (*Enslave them, and then lecture them about self-respect—cutely done, Mr. Charles.*) Still, my Inner Ranter is awake and would push my friend even further. He wants to say, "Forget about racism, about racists. They are always there, and irrelevant. What matters is the content of the black mind, not the white. Building the black mind, its morale." I do not say it. I have no right. My friend ascribes the ills of the universe to racism.

My friend is handsome, brainy, son of a distinguished family, successfully married, light-skinned in a city (Washington) where—a source of ideological discomfort—light skin proclaims the black elite. He was educated in the Ivy League, has climbed high in his profession. But precisely the reasons for which he should feel self-respect, airtight reasons for a white man, raise confusing interior questions about his identity as a black man. Or so I surmise. Hence the anger. Ellis Cose wrote a book called *The Rage of a Privileged Class* about black executives and law partners who earn half a million dollars or more a year and feel sorry for themselves. My friend is a flashing electrical display of privileged rage.

And thus upon our lunchtime dialogue at Washington's Jefferson Hotel (named for that numinous slave-owning paradox) there descends the ancestral "twoness," something of the familiar racial veil W. E. B. DuBois wrote about in 1903.

But my friend and I retreat from the battlefield. We part as friends. For days I continue our conversation in my mind.

See *The Rage of a Privileged Class*, by Ellis Cose (New York: HarperCollins, 1993). 1-800-237-5534.

I look up DuBois's great book *The Souls of Black Folk* and admire again its rolling thunder: "After the Egyptian and Indian, the Greek and Roman, the Teuton and Mongolian, the Negro is a sort of seventh son, born with a veil, and gifted with second-sight in this American world—a world which yields him no true self-consciousness, but only lets him see himself through the revelation of the other world. . . . One ever feels his twoness—an American, a Negro; two souls, two thoughts, two unreconciled strivings." Will DuBois's famous refrain—"the problem of the Twentieth Century is the problem of the color line"—be just as valid in the twenty-first? I like to doubt it.

What will cure the twoness? So many of the problems remain the same. But everything is changed too, mainly because of the emergence of a black middle class. I take up Glenn Loury's *One by One from the Inside Out: Essays and Reviews on Race and Responsibility in America*. Loury, a professor of economics at Boston University, is black and writes, among many other things, "No people can be genuinely free so long as they look to others for their deliverance."

In my imaginary conversation, I echo Loury: affirmative action merely confuses the racial issue, ridiculously placing all blacks in the same category and obscuring the immense differences between the black middle class and the black poor. The need is not affirmative action for the black middle class (for whom it may turn into a moral scam and irrelevance). The imperative is massive intelligent help for the poor, whose condition is an American apocalypse—a disgrace to the nation and, although many may not accept it, a disgrace to the black middle class. That middle class preaches conservative values to its children but excuses the destructive world of the poor as a somehow "authentic" snoop-doggie gangsta-rap culture whose misery results from white racism. That continuing misery, you see, is also a form of moral capital for the black middle class.

Yet at our lunch it occurred to me that the essential problem also revolves, at a deeper level, around myths. We have the founders' story (Washington et al.), the frontier story (endless folklore there) and the Ellis Island story (sepia-tinted immigrant myth). What is the great void in the national tale?

"What would you think," I ask my friend, "about a museum and memorial on the Mall in Washington, something called the American Museum of Slavery and Freedom—a national acknowledgment of the history? There is still this terrible suppression of what happened—or half-suppression. There's denial and ignorance—or else a lot of fatuous political correctness. And yet American culture has been more powerfully formed by black energies than almost anyone knows. Wouldn't it accomplish something to lift the history into full sunshine? The Vietnam Memorial, after all, worked in a healing way."

"Oh, it's a good idea," my friend says. "It wouldn't solve anything, though."

I think: It might be a modest start.

(i) *Brothermen: The Odyssey of Black Men in America*, by Herb Boyd and Robert Allen. (New York: Ballantine Books, 1995).

Divided by Color: Racial Politics and Democratic Ideals, by Donald R. Kinder and Lynn M. Sanders (Chicago: University of Chicago Press, 1996, $27.50, ISBN 0-226-43573-3), 420 pp.

Two excellent resources for books by and about women of color are: *Kitchen Table Press*, P. O. Box 908, Latham, NY 12110, and South End Press, 116 St. Botolph Street, Boston, MA 02115, 1-800-533-8478.

(i) See "One Drop of Blood" by Lawrence Wright, *The New Yorker* (July 25, 1994) and "Who's What?: The Crazy World of Racial Identification" by Wright, in the *Cultural Diversity Sourcebook* (call 1-800-736-1293).

24 • Color Blind

MARGARET L. ANDERSEN AND PATRICIA HILL COLLINS

*R*acism does not exist in a vacuum . . . Race, gender, and class are intersecting systems–experienced simultaneously, not separately. Do not think of any one category in the absence of the others. People's experiences with race and racism are framed by their location in this overarching system of race, class, and gender privileges and penalties. Race possesses not only objective dimensions resulting from institutionalized racism; it simultaneously has subjective dimensions of how people experience it. For example, some people of color grow up with relative class privilege; yet, this does not eliminate racism. . . . All people of color encounter institutional racism, but their actual experiences with racism vary, depending on social class, gender, age, sexuality, and other markers of social position.

25 • African-Americans and Automation

JEREMY RIFKIN (UTNE READER)

*T*he story of automation's impact on African-Americans may be prophetic of what lies ahead for the rest of the workforce. In the early years of the 20th century more than 90 percent of the black population in the United States still lived below the Mason-Dixon Line, and the vast majority was tied to agriculture.

Then, in 1944, an event took place in the rural Mississippi delta that was to change the circumstances of African Americans forever. On October 2 an estimated 3,000 people crowded onto a cotton field just outside of Clarksdale, Mississippi, to watch the first successful demonstration of a mechanical cotton picker. The onlookers were awed by the sight. Each machine could do the work of 50 people. For the first time since blacks had been brought over as slaves to work the agricultural fields in the South, their hands and backs were no longer needed.

The push of mechanization in Southern agriculture combined with the pull of jobs and less overt discrimination in the industrial cities of the North to create what Nicholas Lemann called "one of the largest and most rapid mass internal movements of people in history." More than 5 million black men, women, and children migrated north in search of work between 1940 and 1970.

Although most African Americans were unaware of it at the time of their trek north, a second technological revolution had already begun in the manufacturing industries of Chicago, Detroit, Cleveland, and New York that once again would lock many of them out of gainful employment. In the mid-1950s, automation began to take a toll in the nation's factories. Hardest hit were unskilled jobs in the very industries where black workers were concentrated. Between 1953 and 1962, 1.6 million blue-collar manufacturing jobs were lost. In *The Problem of the Negro Movement*, published in 1964, civil rights activist Tom Kahn quipped, "It is as if racism, having put the Negro in his economic place, stepped aside to watch technology destroy that place."

Companies started to build more automated manufacturing plants in the newly emerging suburban industrial parks. Automation and suburban relocation created a crisis of tragic dimensions for unskilled black workers in the inner cities. The newly laid interstate highway system and the ring of metropolitan expressways being built around cities favored truck over train transport of goods, providing a further incentive to relocate plants to the suburbs. Finally, employers anxious to reduce labor costs and weaken unions saw relocation as a way to create distance between plants and militant union concentrations in urban neighborhoods.

Eventually these same anti-union feelings pushed companies to locate plants in the South, in Mexico, and overseas. The corporate drive to automate and relocate manufacturing jobs split the black community into two distinct economic groups. While many blacks were able to take advantage of the loosening grip of outright discrimination and join the middle-class mainstream of American life, millions of unskilled African-American workers and their families became part of what social historians now call an underclass—a permanently unemployed part of the population whose unskilled labor is no longer required and who live a marginal existence, often as welfare recipients or in the underground economy of drugs and crime.

Jeremy Rifkin

(i) This material is drawn from *The End of Work* by Jeremy Rifkin (New York: Putnam Publishing, 1995, $24.95, ISBN 0-87427-779-8), 350 pp. 1-800-847-5515.

26 • Money Involved

DON L. DISE (LETTER TO THE *SUN*)

In 1946 the country was shifting to a peacetime economy, and my wife and I were trying to restart the house-building business World War II had interrupted.

We needed to hire some carpenters, and I placed an ad in the Chicago Tribune. The phone rang a few nights later.

"You have an ad in the paper for carpenters."

"Yes."

"My brother and me are both carpenters."

"How much experience do you have?"

"Lots. Our dad was a carpenter."

"So was mine. When can you start work"

"I better tell you something first. We're colored."

"Do you have a union card?"

"Yes, sir."

"I'm color blind."

"We can start Monday."

Nay and Pete were waiting at the job site Monday morning. I introduced them to our superintendent, Roy, who gave them the worst possible assignment, but it was soon apparent that Nay and Pete were the best carpenters on the crew.

After I found Roy in the corner tavern for the second afternoon in a week, I fired him and asked Nay if he wanted to be superintendent.

He said, "There's going to be repercussions."

I said, "I'm willing if you are."

The next morning I called all the men together and said, "Roy doesn't work for us anymore. Nay is the superintendent. You're working for him."

Someone said, "I'm not workin' for no nigger."

I said, "You're fired. Anyone else have anything to say?"

Silence.

"OK. Let's go to work."

The men grew to respect Nay because they had confidence in his ability. Our company prospered, and Nay prospered. He and his

(i) *The Sun* is a magazine of essays, interviews, fiction, and poetry. In it writers share their lives with remarkable candor. Six issues for $15. Order from: 107 North Robertson St., Chapel Hill, NC 27516. 919-942-5282; Fax 919-932-3101.

wife lived in a flat on Chicago's West Side. Soon they bought the building. After that they bought an eight-unit apartment building across the street.

Nay and I had many meetings over the next several years about our company and its future and about his aspirations. He was concerned about race relations as blacks moved into white neighborhoods. He said he and his wife were trying to be better landlords to their white tenants than white owners had been, but most whites were mad, scared, and running.

One day, a doctor we knew offered to sell Nay a sixteen-unit building. Nay said he knew the building from the outside and wanted to see more, so I got the keys and we went to inspect it.

In the foyer was a bank of locked mailboxes with the names of the tenants on each one. Nay looked. The name on every mailbox was Latino.

Nay said, "Hell, they ruined this building. They let all these damned Puerto Ricans move in here."

I said, "Nay, you s.o.b. You've been preaching race relations to me for years and now you talk like that."

"Yeah," he said, "but there's money involved here."

Don L. Dise
Grand Cayman Island
British West Indies

Just exactly who is black and how *much* black makes one black is starting to be reassessed. The issue is a Pandora's Box crammed with subjects—such as color discrimination and interethnic prejudice—that are usually verboten in public discussion. . . .

There is potential for great strength—and great strife—in diversity. Many African-Americans who are sympathetic to multiracial Americans' wish for enhanced self-definition worry that in its weakening grasp on the levers of power, white American society is embracing the multiracial movement as a convenient divide-and-conquer mechanism—another way of buying time before their time is fully up.—Karen Grigsby Bates, excerpted from *Emerge: Black America's Newsmagazine*, June 1993. All rights reserved.

27 • Shades of Black

KAREN GRIGSBY BATES (*LOS ANGELES TIMES*)

Contrary to so many stereotypes, the African-American community is the true melting pot of American society, the real version of the mythical one we all were taught about in elementary school. Because of the vagaries of slavery and this country's ancient insistence that even one drop of black blood defines a person as black, African-Americans have for decades looked like one of Jesse Jackson's favorite analogies: We are this country's "Coat of Many Colors." Or, in my own fond but less reverent metaphor, we are a crazy quilt of ethnicities, features, and colors.

"Why do we only call ourselves black?" I asked my mother, semiseriously, during a recent family reunion. "If you look at it logically, we're not just black; not only are there white folks and Native Americans in our family, we know who they are."

Mother, who has little patience with my "what-if" devil's advocacies, gave me an exasperated look. "We were raised black, we see ourselves as black and society sees us as black," she said, with the slow enunciation one uses when explaining fundamental things to small children.

What we call ourselves, and how larger society defines us, is at the center of an escalating debate within the black community. A new generation of mixed-race children, born of the mid '60s Summer of Love, when interracial dating and marriage began to increase sharply, is coming of age. In addition, more black people who had considered themselves monoracial are taking a long look at the varied fruit of their family trees and are deciding that multiracial is a more accurate description of them, as well. These trends, coupled with the growing interest in genealogical exploration spurred on by Alex Haley's "Roots," have prompted a new push for an official census category for biracial and multiracial people.

Much of the traditional black community looks upon this movement with little patience. Like my mother, many feel that if you look black, you are, for practical purposes, black. (It has been estimated that as many as 80% of African-Americans are mixed with something else, usually American Indian.) Your phenotype, a set of physical characteristics based on race or ethnicity, makes you part of the club. And if you have black blood but don't *look* black, your black ancestors and identification with the black community also make you black.

It sounds complicated, but it's consistent, according to New York writer Itabari Njeri, who has written and lectured on multiracial issues for nearly a decade. "Black is not a color; it's a culture," Njeri says sharply. "The reality of the

I suspect that when—if—we ever reach a point where race is a neutral factor in how we are seen as individuals, when one's color is no more potent than one's choice of perfume, then the need for a multiracial category will probably be met with less suspicion.

New World black experience is this: We are a Creolized culture." So, Njeri argues, black Americans need to do what Caribbean blacks have done for centuries: acknowledge all the ethnic strains we possess, not merely the ones that are visible to the naked eye.

Me? I'm torn. Not about being black—Mother is right: It is indeed how we were raised and how we identify ourselves culturally. But I also see the multiracial proponents' point: Why should society have the right to define one, simply because of one's looks? I'm beginning to accept part of their argument. It makes sense to me, for example, that the children of interracial marriages define themselves as multiracial. For them, such a category is a psychological comfort that allows them to officially embrace both parents, both sides of a well-defined family tree. But I'm still grappling with extending the concept to those adults who, like me and many others, may have some blood other than African running through our veins.

G. Reginald Daniel, who lectures in African-American and Latin American studies at UCLA and in sociology at UC Santa Barbara, notes that "every country has its way of dealing with diversity, but we are the only country that uses that 'one-drop' rule." The mandate's original definition was oppressive: White slaveholders decided that even one drop of black blood made a person black, and that children of the unions with black women usually went unacknowledged by mainstream society, which preferred to lose them in a convenient social oblivion.

The very concept of multiracialism with an African strain makes many people jumpy, for if there are individuals who are *black*-looking and multiracial, then, obviously, they have to be mixed with black and something else. Frequently, that something else is white, which means that there are a lot of multiracial *white*-looking Americans, too, who aren't aware of it—or who choose not to acknowledge it.

Some things are hard to face—like the probability that Thomas Jefferson had several children with his black slave, Sally Hemings—children who, by laws he helped draft, were considered black. And chattel. . . .

"We hear a lot about black fathers who shirk their responsibilities to their families," says author Bebe Moore Campbell, "but the first deadbeat dads in this country were white slave owners, most of whom didn't honor or care for their children."

Times are changing. Some African-Americans are cautiously starting to explore the other components of their ancestry while remaining politically tied to the black community. One is Linda Villarosa, an executive at *Essence* magazine. Villarosa—whose father is Latino, African-American and American Indian and whose mother is African-American—says she and her sister for many years did not use the Spanish pronunciation of their last name. "For a long time when people asked what I was, I would say, 'Black, *period*.' But eventually I realized that not acknowledging the other things in me would almost be a backlash against those parts, and I'm not ashamed of them either. Now when people ask, I tell them I'm

> "We hear a lot about black fathers who shirk their responsibilities to their families," says author Bebe Moore Campbell. "but the first deadbeat dads in this country were white slave owners, most of whom didn't honor or care for their children."

black *and* Hispanic *and* Native American. The deepest part of me identifies as black, but by pronouncing our surname the Spanish way, my sister and I can pay homage to those ancestors, too."

I suspect that when—if—we ever reach a point where race is a neutral factor in how we are seen as individuals, when one's color is no more potent than one's choice of perfume, then the need for a multiracial category will probably be met with less suspicion. Until then, given this country's history, I will have a hard time using the label *multiracial* to describe people with two black parents but varied ancestry. Race is still too salient a part of our national being, and it doesn't exist in a vacuum.

 Jon Katz shows how technology can help in overcoming racism by providing a vehicle for conversations that people have become unable to have face-to-face. Perhaps the interracial home visits that were organized to do this in the 1960s will occur again in cyberspace in coming years.

28 ·   Guilty

JON KATZ (WIRED)

*W*hile we still come together under the aegis of public institutions to thrash out our shared values, laws, and understandings, the notion of an America united by common views of attainable equality, justice, and individual freedom is a myth. And the one institution most responsible for spotting and disclosing this big story, as well as providing a forum in which we can come to terms with it, has abdicated its duties. The role of modern journalism as a mechanism for meaningful cultural debate is a great hoax, exposed by Orenthal James Simpson and the spectacle he's provoked in Los Angeles.

Technology lets newspapers, radio, and television bring us the words and pictures more quickly, clearly, and overwhelmingly than ever, but the press has lost the will to tell us what those images mean.

The nature of modern politics has altered the meaning of detachment. To the gay person seeking a governmental response to AIDS or to the underclass mother whose family is engulfed by drugs and guns, a journalist's attitude of distance about such life-and-death issues constitutes a hostile act. Such audiences will soon find other media. So too the young, who have abandoned newspapers, TV, and radio in staggering numbers for media that offer strong points of view, frank exchanges of ideas, graphic visual presentations, and lost of irony and self-deprecation.

Decades back, when newspapers were homogeneous—published by white men for white men—objectivity worked in both the marketing and the journalistic sense.

But as the nation became more diverse, and as new technology provided fierce competition, objectivity paralyzed more than professionalized. Cable, VCRs, computers, and modems have created a vast new cultural outlet, not only for new kinds of advertising such as music videos but for the outspoken opinion, vivid writing, visual imagery, and informality the young prefer. Ascending media—Web pages, Oliver Stone films, Comedy Central programs, online discussions, MTV news—make no pretense of being "objective," comprehensive, or even substantial.

What would subjective mainstream news media look like?

In the case of the Simpson story, journalists would report not only on the trial, but on the racial climate in Los Angeles, the economics of justice, the overwhelming impact of media, and the glaring inadequacies of the jury system. They would present the trial's daily developments, but would be free—encouraged, in fact—to state opinion as long as they were supported by facts and strong reasoning, and free to change their minds *with* explanation.

But as things stand, our society has no mechanism to try O. J. Simpson rationally. We can't deal with the debilitating social tensions of the case. And our legal process virtually guarantees that informed, fair-minded people be barred from juries.

It seems clear that the justice system can be overwhelmed by large infusions of money, influenced by mass concentrations of media, and paralyzed by racial divisions.

As the drama of the Simpson trial already demonstrates, a jury no longer does what it was meant to do (function as the true conscience of the community) but represents those parts of the community, those tribes, to which individual jurors belong.

Jurors are identified by race, and it is virtually assumed that just as the loss of an African-American juror is a setback for the defense, the dismissal of a white or Hispanic juror is a defeat for the prosecution.

In modern America, we might consider empaneling jurors willing to acknowledge and discuss racial perceptions and biases, instead of forcing them to pretend they have none.

ⓘ Malcolm CasSelle and E. David Ellington are the founders of NetNoir, the purpose of which is to "digitize, archive, and distribute Afrocentric culture in cyberspace." Visit NetNoir via America Online (keyword NetNoir) or at its Web site (http: /www.NetNoir.com). Also see Web magazine *Meanderings* edited by Cuda Brown. It focuses on African-American issues and concerns. *Meanderings* is available at http://www.webcom.com/ sppg~/meanderings/me.html or write to Brown at editor@meanderings.com.

Sometime in the spring of 1995, according to numerous polls and surveys, it became clear to most white Americans—roughly 70 percent—that O. J. Simpson was probably guilty, that the DNA and other evidence was substantial, that the idea of a massive police conspiracy to frame him was ludicrous, and at best a desperate play by high-powered lawyers. Almost at the same time, it became equally clear to most African-Americans—also about three-quarters—that Simpson was innocent and that a police conspiracy was not only possible but likely.

It also became clear to both groups and everyone else that the Simpson jury was probably not going to convict him and would stalemate primarily as a result of racial differences. Journalists passed along the poll results but seemed unable to react to the fact that these findings had become the big story, not an interesting sidelight.

Mobility, diversity, and media exposure alter groups' expectations, generate instability, cement differences, exacerbate conflict. Instead of assimilating, tribes retain their own values and reject many of those imposed by the cultures they find themselves in.

Journalists are one tribe in Los Angeles, whites another, African-Americans another, along with the police, defense attorneys, prosecutors, and jurors.

This is a new politics of entrenchment, where sides dig in and fight for every bloody inch of ground, where the function of media is to transmit pictures and quotes of people shouting at one another.

Our journalists should be shaping and commenting upon the debate, not simply mirroring and exacerbating it. This is where new media's potential should be realized. But so far, new media have also failed.

Although big online systems such as *Prodigy* are as corporate and tepid as other mainstream media, they have too many live chat rooms and public topics to be as safe and noncontroversial as they'd undoubtedly like to be. Smaller BBSes, computer conferencing systems, and Web sites have no history of objectivity; public policy and politics are fiercely debated, and almost nothing is off-limits.

The biggest journalistic breakthrough made by online news has been reconnecting individuals to stories like this [the Simpson trial], giving them a chance to bypass journalists and ask questions, express themselves, share concerns. But with so many voices speaking at once, it's difficult for most people to find what they most want or need to hear. This is fertile ground for good, subjective journalism if there ever was one.

The possibilities are enormous. America Online could easily set up black-white forums on which individuals could speak frankly about race and begin a dialogue in a medium that permits users to encounter people they would otherwise never meet. Black people could message about their perceptions of racism and justice, white males could talk about their fear of displacement, scholars could come online to answer questions and share their research findings.

ⓘ See *News Values* by Jack Fuller (Chicago: University of Chicago Press, 1996, $22.95, ISBN 0-226-26879-9), 256 pp.

Every online user knows that this kind of communication often breaks down barriers, forcing sender and receiver to deal with each other as individuals rather than as group members.

There is already a precedent for opposing political forces to communicate directly via this technology. During the debate over gays in the military, gay soldiers spoke directly to wary veterans on CompuServe.

The Northridge, California, earthquake, reported first on Prodigy via wireless modem, made online communications a news medium in the traditional sense of the term. Four hours after the bombing in Oklahoma City, Internet Oklahoma (ionet) had created a World Wide Web site offering news, lists of survivors, and hospital telephone numbers. Inevitably, as the number of online users grows, online news will converge with a massive story, and digital news will become part of the media mainstream.

If one tenet of our age is that information wants to be free, its companion is that media wants to tell the truth. Neither information nor media get what they want much of the time; this is one of the great ironies of the information revolution and the sad legacy of the O. J. Simpson trial.

GENDER AND SEXUAL ORIENTATION— UNDERSTANDING AND RELEARNING OUR ROLES

3

Perhaps at no time in history have the roles of women and men been so in flux as they are today in the workplace, the home, and in society at large. Reading the literature and listening to the gender role debate one can sense an overwhelming need on the part of so many voices to be right and prove the other wrong. Perhaps this indicates how important the issues have become to the participants. Some men (and women) blame women for abandoning their familial and civilizing roles, while many women (and some men) see men as incorrigible oppressors—violent, abusive, barbarian. Strident voices accuse gays, lesbians, and bisexuals of perverting family values, while other voices denounce straight people for creating an unreal, exclusivist culture that marginalizes many of their own kind as well as those whose sexual orientation is different.

This section examines the frustrations and progress of women and gay people in both the workplace and society. It begins, however heretically or daringly inclusive you may see this, with the pain of men, in particular Euro American men, on the job and in other social settings. Identified with "the system," demonized and accused of the oppression of the rest of the world, men are only beginning to look for an equal but different voice in the chorus of diversity. It is perhaps incongruous that some of the foremost champions of diversity are Euro American men who use their value system and the power and leadership they find that they possess to empower others. The majority of Euro American men are bewildered by accusations of power and privilege heaped upon them at a time when they perceive their own circumstances quite differently.

The focus then turns to sexual orientation. Generally speaking, our contributors have tried to see this as a normal part of the diversity dialogue, about normal people living normal lives in normal circumstances, while many fellow citizens see them as anything but normal. Gay people face enormous challenges, but their experiences can contribute valuable insights and perspectives to others of us whose gender roles are being redefined.

Finally, our contributors revisit women's issues, some seemingly intractable, others showing signs of progress. There is also some important breaking of taboos as lesbians and black women address sex-biased assumptions and behaviors in their own ranks. In the past, men and women brought benefits to each other, albeit within the context of more highly defined gender roles. The question remains today: How can we or should we create partnerships that enable us to work together while expanding our notions of who we are? Or are we consigned to a future in which we are more isolated and supposedly independent from our partners (gay or straight)? When Leonard Cohen (in his album "Future") sings optimistically about relationships, few of us believe it. Nonetheless, our contributors in this section offer a few ideas and tools for bridging the widening gap between how things are and how we hope they become.

Among the most comprehensive treatments of sexual harassment is the 1994 book by Susan L. Webb, *Shock Waves: The Global Impact of Sexual Harassment.* The book provides a clear overview of the nature of sexual harassment issues and legislation in the United States, then goes on to give a status report on sexual harassment in countries throughout the world and additional attention to developing issues in the United States. The final pages look ahead at the next steps in each area of the world and offer perspectives and tips for the task of ending sexual harassment. There is a generous resource directory in the Appendix. The book ($11.95 paper, $19.95 hardbound, plus $2 postage and handling) is available from MasterMedia Limited, 17 E. 89 St., New York, NY 10128, 1-800-334-8232 or 212-260-5600, Fax: 212-348-2020.

29 • The Code of Honor: A Key to Including European-American Men

GEORGE F. SIMONS

*M*en of many backgrounds grow up with what is sometimes called "a code of honor." Explicit or implicit, it is a set of standards by which men judge each other and the norms of behavior toward which they strive. When these standards are made explicit it is not because all men in a specific group behave in accordance with them, but because when at their best, they believe they should. When cultural shifts occur men may be tempted to rebel against or even repudiate these values or, on the contrary, try to regain or reaffirm them as an anchor in the sea of change.

We have listed such a "code of honor" in the margins on the following pages. It contains elements often, but not exclusively, found in the traditional values system of European-American men. This particular articulation of the "code" has emerged from years of discussions in men's workshops and support groups.

Items in such a code of honor can be at the root of both these men's strengths and their weaknesses. Like any cultural norms, they are meant to support the survival and success of a group in dealing with its environment. "Defending one's territory" (both internal and external), to use an example from this code, can be an important prerequisite for public peace and personal tranquillity; it can also give rise to paranoia and aggressiveness if its execution is inappropriate.

As with all such values today, applying them requires ongoing dialog *among men* in particular, while taking into account the changing environment and the needs and rights of others. Having men "do their own work" is critical at a time when men's culture, and in particular "white" men's culture, is criticized and

THE CODE

Defend your territory.
Don't be pushed around.
Stay free.
Guard your home.
Be prepared.
Serve your country,
your people.
Love nature.
Protect the outdoors.
Keep the faith.
Defend your honor.

Care for women and children.
Be a provider.
Be faithful.
Be strong.
Be a coach and a model for
younger men.

Play fair.
Level the playing field.
Give the other guy a chance.
Take turns. Everybody gets a hearing.
Don't play favorites.

Be a team player.
Be loyal.
Compete for your team or organization.
Make and keep commitments.
Give your best effort.

Be an adventurer.
Be brave. Take risks.
Explore new territory.
Be self-reliant.
Don't be a "whiner."

Tell the truth.
Own up to mistakes and failures.
Call others on their failures.
Decry injustice.
Speak up for what is right.

Do right.
Obey legitimate authority.
Observe the chain of command.
Work hard for a living. Don't take handouts.
Free the oppressed. Fight for the underdog.

Do good.
Be a leader.
Put others' needs first.
Rescue the victim.
Give community service.

disparaged in much diversity discourse and in the public media. Men need to review these values with other men who both understand the values and bring their experiences to bear on how to apply them to everyday life. Here the wisdom of other men or a men's peer group is a great help in digesting input from women and others outside the group.

When men's values are discussed in today's politically charged diversity debate, they are more than likely to be dismissed as outdated if not actively disparaged as "dysfunctional, patriarchal and patronizing." Rarely do we hear the necessary distinction being made between *masculinity* (the socialization of men into satisfying and useful roles) and *patriarchy* (a label for what's not working in the inherited social system). When men's values are taken seriously and honored, they can serve to enable the men who hold them to adapt their roles to an increasingly diverse culture. Often a traditional value simply needs to be applied to include people different from themselves in carrying it out, e.g., seeing how "fairness" applies to previously excluded groups. Sometimes it needs to be reinterpreted to achieve its objectives in new circumstances. For example, men committed to "caring for women" can change the traditional ways they have carried this out (now seen as "patronizing") into attitudes and actions that make them effective allies to women. This, of course, cannot be a one-way street. Men need allies, too, and women will have to learn to do this in new ways as well.

Today, though we hear more and more about "inclusion," in practice "white" men often continue to be "trashed" as the enemies of diversity, the oppressors, and the source of "backlash." True inclusion will involve understanding them as having a culture and a values system that can be addressed and used successfully as an integral part of the diversity effort.

Those who are reluctant to do this have to take off their blinders about how the traditional values of European-American men have made the struggle for personal and civil rights conceivable and possible and its efforts successful in the United States. True, among the "Founding Fathers" of the nation were slave holders. Most, judged by today's standards, held very narrow views about the roles of women and the rights of the propertyless. However, the logical consequences of their philosophy motivated subsequent generations of men and women to extend the values and ideals of freedom and equality first enjoyed by upper-class men to all comers of whatever gender, race, or ethnicity. The system they actually created, despite its blocks and hindrances, enables non-traditional participants to pursue democracy on an ongoing basis as well as enjoy a great deal of it. This original philosophy still inspires millions of immigrants and refugees to prefer the United States, despite its dangers, as their first destination.

Some of the standards of European men can pose obstacles and challenges to cultures with other value systems. Their jingoistic interpretation can make U.S.

Americans self-righteous and imperialistic toward peoples of other nations and backgrounds. Fundamentalist interpretation of the "code" fuels the angers and swells the ranks of the ultra right.

Still, men's standards (not just the codes of European-American men but those of men of other groups as well) belong in the diversity debate. Accepting and discussing them consciously and with respect, as we would the values of any other culture, provides an entry point for making all men an integral part of the dialog about the future of the nation's culture, workplace, and social structure. Multiculturalism that does not hear, or dismisses the male voice out of hand, sabotages itself by excluding an important part of the reality with which it wants to come to terms.

The "code" does not pretend to be fully correct or complete. It is only one attempt to articulate elements of one kind of male acculturation, though we believe it rather accurate for many men. Having groups of men articulate their own code and discuss it with each other and others is a more useful way for them to enter the diversity discussion. For European-American men, in particular, doing this helps them disentangle their own male culture (the way things are for them) from the dominant role their values have played in shaping the larger culture (the way things are done around here). With a culture or cultures of their own, European-American men acquire a voice of their own in the diversity dialog. They no longer appear twice their natural size to others. On the other hand, as long as they are simply identified with dominance, they are by definition excluded from making any contribution of their own to the identification and solution of systemic problems.

"White Privilege and Male Privilege: A Personal Account of Coming to See Correspondences Through Work in Women's Studies," by Peggy McIntosh, in *Race, Class and Gender: An Anthology*, Patricia Hill Collins and Margaret L. Andersen, editors (Belmont, Calif.: Wadsworth, 1992). McIntosh examines concrete, specific privileges—earned and unearned—and how they are expressed in daily life. Among these she is primarily concerned with the inherent privileges one enjoys in American society by being white and male as well as less immediately recognized advantages. She uses methods of comparative analysis gained through her work in women's studies and constructs useful comparisons between those privileges conferred by gender and those that are conferred by race.

30 •   Men Changing Men

ROBERT L. ALLEN AND PAUL KIVEL (MS. MAGAZINE)

*W*hy do men batter women? We have to discard the easy answers. Portraying batterers as ogres only serves to separate "them" from "us."

ⓘ For more information, write to the Oakland Men's Project, 440 Grand Avenue, Suite 320, Oakland, CA 94610, or call 510-835-2433; Fax: 510-835-2466.

ⓘ *Men's Work: How to Stop the Violence That Tears Our Lives Apart*, by Paul Kivel (New York: Ballantine, 1992, ISBN 0-345-37939-X).

But men who batter and men who don't are not all that different. Male violence is normal in our society and vast numbers of men participate. Men batter because we have been trained to; because there are few social sanctions against it; because we live in a society where the exploitation of people with less social and personal power is acceptable. In a patriarchal society, boys are taught to accept violence as a manly response to real or imagined threats, but they get little training in negotiating intimate relationships. And all too many men believe that they have the right to control or expect certain behavior from "their" women and children; many view difficulties in family relationships as a threat to their manhood, and they respond with violence.

"ACT LIKE A MAN" BOX

When we do this exercise, it gets undivided attention because most have experienced being humiliated by an older male. Indeed, the power of this exercise is that it is so familiar. When asked what they learned from such encounters, boys often say things like: A man is tough. A man is in control. A man doesn't cry. A man doesn't take crap.

We write the boys' comments on a blackboard, draw a box around them, and label it the "Act Like a Man" box. Men in this culture are socialized to stay in the box. We ask: What happens if you step out of it, if you stop acting tough enough or man enough? Invariably we hear that you get called names like "fag," "queer," "mama's boy," "punk," "girl." Asked why, boys say it's a challenge, that they're expected to fight to prove themselves. Homophobia and fear of being identified with women are powerful messages boys get from an early age, and they are expected to fight to prove that they're tough and not gay—that they're in the box.

How safe is it to stay in the "Act Like a Man" box? Usually, most admit that it isn't safe, because boys and men continually challenge each other to prove that they're in the box. When a boy or man is challenged, he can prove he's a man either by fighting the challenger or by finding someone "weaker"—a female or a more vulnerable male—to dominate.

"STAND UPS"

To get men to reflect on their experiences and behaviors, we ask everyone to be silent, and then slowly pose a series of questions or statements, and ask men to stand every time one applies to them. For example, we may ask,

Have you ever:

- worried you were not tough enough?
- been called a wimp, queer, or fag?
- been told to "act like a man"?
- been hit by an older man?
- been forced to fight?

- been physically injured and hid the pain?
- been sexually abused, or touched in a way you didn't like?
- used alcohol or drugs to hide your pain?
- felt like blowing yourself away?

Later in the workshop we ask,
Have you ever:

- interrupted a woman by talking louder?
- made a comment in public about a woman's body?
- discussed a woman's body with another man?
- been told by a woman that she wanted more affection and less sex from you?
- used your voice or body to intimidate a woman?
- hit, slapped, shoved, or pushed a woman?
- had sex with a woman when you knew she didn't want to?

Each participant is asked to look around and see other men standing, which helps break down their sense of isolation and feelings of shame. Since we are not a therapy group, no one is questioned or confronted about his own experiences. All of our work involves challenging the notion that males are naturally abusive and that females are natural targets of male abuse. We give boys and men a way of analyzing social roles by drawing insights from their own experiences, and help them to recognize that social interactions involve making choices, that we can break free of old roles by supporting each other in choosing alternatives to violence.

31 • The "Born That Way" Trap

LINDSY VAN GELDER (MS. MAGAZINE)

*W*hen the Episcopal Diocese of Newark recently established a ministry to welcome gay people into the church, the bishop told *The New York Times*: "We are not ready to accept the prejudice and ignorance that homosexuality is a matter of choice or reflects moral depravity." And when *Child* magazine published a sympathetic article on how straight parents can learn to be

See *Helping Teens Stop Violence*, by Allen Creighton with Paul Kivel (Alameda, Calif: Hunter House, 1992, $11.95, ISBN 0-89793-116-5), 1-800-266-5592.

*M*y father asked
me if I am gay
I said, "Does it matter?"
He said, "No, not really."
I told him, "Yes."
He said, "Get out of my life."
I guess it mattered.
My Boss asked me if I am gay.
I said, "Does it matter?"
He said, "No, not really."
I told him, "Yes."
He said, "You're fired, faggot."
I guess it mattered.
My friend asked me if I am gay.
I said, "Does it matter?"
He said, "No, not really."
I told him, "Yes."
He said, "Don't call me
your friend."
I guess it mattered.
My lover asked, "Do you
love me?"
I said, "Does it matter?"
He said, "Yes."
I told him, "I love you."
He said, "Let me hold
you in my arms."
For the first time in my life
something matters.
My God asked, "Do you
love yourself?"
I said, "Does it matter?"
He said, "Yes."
I asked, "How can I
love myself?
I am gay."
He said, "That is the way
I made you."
Nothing again will matter.

—Anonymous
(from the Internet)

supportive of their gay children, the lead quoted a gay man who recognized his sexual orientation when he was barely out of kindergarten. "Many people believe that a person chooses to be a homosexual, which is ludicrous," he explained to anxious parents.

I hear the same sentiment in liberal circles everywhere. Even *Dear Ann* and *Dear Abby* agree: Being gay is something a person has no more control over than race or gender. Therefore, it's unfair to deprive us of our rights.

The people who say these things are all on my side. But they make me very, very nervous.

For starters, I personally don't think I was "born this way." (In fact, when I'm feeling hostile, I've been known to tell right-wingers that I'm a successfully "cured" hetero.) Until I was in my early thirties, I fell in love with men, took pleasure in sleeping with them, and even married one. But like most women, I experienced most of my closest emotional relationships with female friends. The only thing that made me different was that at some point I got curious about lesbian feminist claims that it was possible to combine that intense female intimacy with good sex. The good sex part turned out to be vastly easier than I anticipated. Even so, there was no immediate *biological* reason to stop having sex with men or to start living as a lesbian. Coming out was, for me, a conscious decision—every step of the way.

Nor am I an aberration, at least among women. Virtually every self-identified gay man I've ever met has been convinced that his sexuality is a biological given, but lesbians are a mixed bag. My own wildly unscientific estimate is that it's a pretty even split between the born lesbians and the born agains. We talk about these differences within the lesbian community (and we bitch about the other side of the born-again syndrome—women who choose to stop being lesbians and go off with men). But out in the Big World, it's invisibility as usual. The gay party line reflects the universal male experience in this culture, not the complexities of the lesbian world.

Sexism? Probably. But the truth is that the "Born That Way" line has the public relations edge. At the root of a lot of homophobia is a fear that gayness is somehow contagious. If people really did fit into neat little either/or sexual pigeonholes from birth, no one would be able to say that gay teachers could possibly "recruit" their students. Parents of gays would be off the blame hook. Straights wouldn't have to feel threatened by passing queer attractions.

It seems like a quick-win strategy. But I suspect that it's shortsighted—and I'd say so even if it didn't ignore the experience of so many lesbians.

Remember when we got sucked into arguing not just about a woman's right to control her own body, but about whether the fetus was in fact a human being? We're making the same mistake here: letting the other side set the terms of this debate. The fundamentalists believe that being gay is definitely a matter of choice—specifically a matter of choosing to sin. Instead of turning about and saying, "Get your church out from between my legs, pal," we've essentially thrown up our hands and said, "But we can't *help* being this way."

Inherent in that response is the implication that if we could help it, we would. Even when that isn't what we mean, it's what a fair number of straight people hear, including some of our allies. It's easier for some of them to pity us as bearers of a genetic flaw than to respect us as sexual equals. Not challenging them might gain us some votes, but in the long run it means that we're subtly putting the word out that it's O.K. to regard us as sexually handicapped.

We're also staking our lives on scientific research that at the moment is a crapshoot. I recently saw a debate on a computer bulletin board about whether gay men should be allowed to serve as Boy Scout leaders. The homophobes trotted out the usual drivel about child abuse; the liberals argued back that gay people are born, not made; the homophobes countered with testimonials from various ministries claiming to "cure homosexuality"; the liberals answered that most of these supposed rehabilitations don't last. But what if scientists do find a

The truth is that the "Born That Way" line has the public relations edge. At the root of a lot of homophobia is a fear that gayness is somehow contagious.

Created Equal: Why Gay Rights Matter to America, by Michael Nava and Robert Davidoff. (New York: St. Martin's Press, 1995, $8.95, ISBN 0-312-11764-7).

The authors assert the purpose of the Constitution is to protect individual rights. The denial of equal rights to gays and lesbians, therefore, makes a direct challenge to the rights of all Americans.

biological "cure" someday? How many of us would really want to swallow that vaccine? What if they could identify a gay fetus through amniocentesis? Amusing as it is to contemplate our side waving giant photos of tiny (limp?) fetal wrists outside fundamentalist clinics, it really isn't that funny—or that farfetched.

Or what if they discover that there's no biological basis to sexual orientation? Are we willing to promise that on that day, we'll give back any gay rights we've managed to win and march off to the psychic showers?

I'd rather see us acquire some new political underpinnings. As inspiring as the civil rights and feminist struggles have been to most of us, I think we have to stop trying to fit gay rights onto the same grid. Every time we talk about race, gender, and sexual orientation in the same breath, we merely invite more tedious debate on whether gays are a "real" minority group or just people with an elective "lifestyle."

Instead, I'd like us to start referring en masse to another bedrock American liberty: the right to worship in the faith of one's choice. Through much of history, people have been forced to change their religions or to practice them underground. The United States was founded upon a rejection of such "solutions," and they're recognized as oppressive worldwide. The principle here is *freedom of expression*. It doesn't matter if you're a Jew or Quaker because your parents were, or if you converted as an adult. You're still protected.

Most of all, I want us to get off the defensive with all these tight-assed bigots. The we-can't-help-it argument is a cop-out. It pretends that sex is something that white rats in a maze do because their hormones tell them to—not something humans do for fun. If there's anything we as feminists ought to be supporting, it's a frank, unapologetic celebration of sexual choice.

I'm personally for the right of happy heterosexuals to "experiment" with same-sex love and perhaps find that they like it. I'm for the right of bisexuals to opt for gay relationships, even though they don't have the excuse that they have no other choice. And I'm for the right of gay people to choose to act on their sexuality, whether society approves of it or not.

An excellent and thorough history of gay life in America is found in *About Time: Exploring the Gay Past,* by Martin B. Duberman (A Seahorse Book, ISBN 0-914017-13-6 P.O. Box 294, Village Station, NY 10014). Prior to 1969 (the year of the Stonewall riots) there was virtually no public record of homosexuality in America. Duberman's research and scholarship has unearthed oral records and private documents to chronicle this history from the 1820s through the mid-1980s.

An up-to-date investigation into gay and lesbian social life can be found in *American Gay* by Stephen O. Murray (Chicago: University of Chicago Press, 1996, $16.95, ISBN 0-226-55193-8).

32 •   Homophobia—Counting the Costs

AMY J. ZUCKERMAN AND GEORGE F. SIMONS

*H*omophobia, the fear of gay people, causes both heterosexual and gay people to react in strange ways. Sometimes it forces gay people into "the corporate closet," i.e., they go to great lengths to hide their sexual orientation at work. Homophobia separates people who could enjoy each other's company and work together productively. It may cause them to avoid each other or sabotage each other's efforts. In some cases, homophobia results in harassment, violence, or expensive litigation that can destroy the lives of the individuals involved and drain the organization's resources.

Here are examples of situations where the costs are adding up. In the space beneath each example, list what you believe would be one personal cost to the people involved and one cost to the organization to which the individuals belong. When you have finished, compare your answers to those of the authors. Here is an example:

Sarah never talks about herself when the others are discussing their husbands and wives. She knows that they think she is cold and reserved, but she is afraid to tell them about her life with her woman partner for fear of being rejected or even fired.

Personal cost: Damaged relationships among the coworkers; the job becomes uncomfortable for Sarah and those around her.

Organizational cost: Sarah always feels on guard. She may quit for a more comfortable job. Time and money spent to replace her.

Now you try it. What do you think the costs are in each of the following situations?

1. When the other managers—all men—go to lunch, they have gradually stopped inviting Wilson, who is rumored to be gay.
2. Mae Linn gives preferential treatment to gay men when hiring applicants. She believes that they are more creative and sensitive and will treat women better than straight men will.
3. Since telling others that she is a lesbian, Jayne has noticed that David, a coworker, has begun to make passes at her. She has heard via the grapevine that he has told his buddies that she will be "a real challenge."
4. Stephen has felt depressed for a few weeks and has given people around the office different explanations. When his coworkers discover that he and a long-term male lover just broke up, they wonder what else Stephen is hiding.

ⓘ This activity can be adapted to focus on other social identities as well, e.g., race, class, geographic origin, religion.

PLAYER   diversiPLAY™

Role play this scenario with a colleague or friend. Read this role for yourself, give the book to your partner to read the section printed on the facing page. Then role play the situation for a few moments and discuss the experience together.

You try to be a good ally to the lesbian and gay people where you work. One of your normally quiet co-workers says to you, "How gay people live their lives is their own business. I'm for being fair, but I really get angry when they flaunt it in everybody's face?" Your role play partner will play the role of this co-worker as try to find out what triggered this outburst and respond in a helpful way.

5. Rosita has heard that several of the caregivers at the day-care center where she leaves her children are gay. She is embarrassed to discuss the issue with her supervisor Carmen. She simply tells Carmen that she can no longer work mornings.

6. Angelo is afraid to tell his subordinates to get back to work and stop playing tricks on their gay coworker. He is afraid that his subordinates will think of him as soft, or even suspect that he is gay, even though he is not.

7. When some people where Thomas works find out he is gay, his coworkers and even his manager make AIDS jokes in front of him.

8. Judy, a lawyer and a lesbian, is the first to be laid off from her $55,000-a-year position when her firm faces downsizing. She feels she was first to be fired because of the senior partners' homophobia.

Here are some of the authors' responses to these situations. Read them to see if they add to your understanding of the issues. Do you agree or disagree? If so, why?

Personal Cost

1. Wilson becomes an outcast. His colleagues fail to confront their prejudice. Lack of trust on both sides grows. Loss of profitable networking.

2. Individuals devalued, stereotyped.

3. Humiliation for both parties. Hostile work environment for Jayne.

4. Gossip. Mistrust.

5. Living in fear for her family and children. Loss of income or job.

6. Loss of personal respect for all involved. Damage to Angelo's career as manager.

Organizational Cost

1. Loss of valuable perspectives, consensus, and team spirit among the group.

2. Wrong people may be hired. Mae Linn's bias will reveal itself, causing hurt, perhaps a claim.

3. Possibly an expensive harassment lawsuit. Dysfunction due to homophobia.

4. Strained working relationships.

5. Work loss. Her beliefs are seen as disruptive to work schedules. The company's tolerance of employee diversity decreases.

6. Breakdown of work discipline. Potential hostile environment lawsuit.

7. Thomas is upset and considers quitting. He is upset because his coworkers joke about the tragedy of AIDS. They are uncomfortable with his sexuality.

8. Loss of professional standing, money, and time job-searching.

7. Company could get reputation as hostile toward gays and lesbians. Cost of replacing Thomas. If the firm tracks or fires people it suspects are HIV-positive, it could be sued.

8. Judy may sue if her firing was discriminatory.

Sexual Orientation in the Workplace: Gays, Lesbians, Bisexuals and Heterosexuals Working Together, by Amy J. Zuckerman and George Simons. A workbook ideal for all levels of the organization and all sexual orientations. Presents a nonthreatening way to look at how sexual orientation affects the workplace. George Simons International, P.O. Box 7360, Santa Cruz, CA 95061-7360; 408-426-9608, Fax 408-457-8590, e-mail: gsintaz@aol.com.

The cards on pages 70 and 71 are two of more than 5,000 in the database of *DIVERSOPHY™: Understanding the Human Race*, a board game for up to 6 persons. You'll find several examples of them throughout the *Fieldbook*. Players are tested on facts and appropriate behavioral choices, share their culture and diversity experiences, and undergo the risks of working in a multicultural environment. $199. Additional card sets ($99) include: The Gender Deck (concerning men and woman; gays, lesbians, and bisexuals; and sexual harassment in the workplace); Doing Business with the USA; Doing Business with U.S. Latinos; Doing Business with Mexico; Doing Business with Canada; Doing Business in Europe; Doing Business with Japan; Diversity Role Plays; Sexual Orientation Deck. Conference DIVERSOPHY™ is for one-time use in large groups. Each package ($139) can be used for up to 72 people in groups of 6 for up to 1 1/4 hours of play. Contains program planner and facilitator guide. Available from George Simons International, P.O. Box 7360, Santa Cruz, CA 95061-7360; 408-426-9608, Fax 408-457-8590, e-mail gsintaz@aol.com (GSI also produces custom decks upon request).

PARTNER diversiPLAY™

Read these instructions SILENTLY before starting the role play. Play the role to represent the following point of view, whether or not you agree with it.

You feel that you are fair-minded. You grudgingly accepted gay co-workers at work, against your strict religious principles. But what you saw in the Gay Pride Parade on TV seemed for you not only outrageous but obscene. You wonder if the gay people you work with are actually all like this.

33 · Management Women and the New Facts of Life

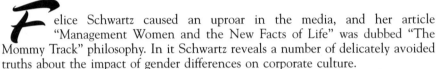

FELICE N. SCHWARTZ (*HARVARD BUSINESS REVIEW*)

*F*elice Schwartz caused an uproar in the media, and her article "Management Women and the New Facts of Life" was dubbed "The Mommy Track" philosophy. In it Schwartz reveals a number of delicately avoided truths about the impact of gender differences on corporate culture.

"The cost of employing women in management is greater than the cost of employing men. This is a jarring statement, partly because it is true, but mostly because it is something people are reluctant to talk about. A [1988] study by one multinational corporation shows that the rate of turnover in management positions is 2½ times higher among top-performing women than it is among men. A large producer of consumer goods reports that one half of the women who take maternity leave return to their jobs late or not at all. And we know that women also have a greater tendency to plateau or to interrupt their careers in ways that limit their growth and development. But we have become so sensitive to charges of sexism and so afraid of confrontation, even litigation, that we rarely say what we know to be true. Unfortunately, our bottled-up awareness leaks out in misleading metaphors ("glass ceiling" is one notable example), veiled hostility, lowered expectations, distrust, and reluctant adherence to Equal Employment Opportunity requirements."

Schwartz proposed a two-track system for advancing women and enabling them to achieve their full potential: (1) "career-primary" for those wishing to compete with men [and] who will not be devoting significant time to a family life, and (2) "career-and-family" for those who will be taking time for childbirth and child-rearing and who "are willing to trade some career growth and compensation for freedom from the constant pressure to work long hours and weekends."

She outlines practical strategies for increasing the utilization of both types of women, as well as for eliminating the somewhat different kinds of barriers that each group faces. She discusses how the corporation can benefit from employing both groups. If all of her suggestions were embraced, they'd probably leave only one unasked question: "When will men get the opportunity to choose whether to participate on one track or the other?"

ⓘ "Management Women and the New Facts of Life" by Felice N. Schwartz (*Harvard Business Review*, January/February 1989). Reprint # 89110. Reprints available from HBS Press, Reprint Service, Soldiers Field, Boston MA 02163; 617-495-6192, Fax 617-495-6985. Reprints are $5.50 each plus shipping & handling.

34 • Confronting Sexism in Black Life: The Struggle Continues

BELL HOOKS (Z MAGAZINE)

*I*f our black ancestors hadn't believed wholeheartedly in sexist assumptions about gender roles, they would not have insisted that a primary horror of slavery was the "emasculation" of black men. During and after slavery, black male leaders like Frederick Douglass and Martin Delaney urged black men to assume the role of patriarch, to be providers and protectors. They recognized that slavery had undermined black male authority. Most of the Africans enslaved in this country had been brought from societies where gender hierarchies already existed, where female status was most often subordinate to that of males. For many black people the reinstitutionalizing of black patriarchy was seen as a means to recover collective dignity and self-respect. There was little concern about the reality that the call to strengthen black patriarchy would condone and perpetuate coercive black male domination of black females. [Manning] Marable emphasizes that violence is key to maintaining a sexist order: "Rape, spouse abuse, sexual harassment on the job are all essential to the perpetuation of a sexist society. For the sexist, violence is the necessary and logical part of an unequal, exploitative relationship. To dominate and control, sexism requires violence. Rape and sexual harassment are therefore not accidental to the structure of gender relations within a sexist order." The call for black patriarchy was an affirmation of black men's right as men to control and dominate black women.

It is precisely this gendered way of interpreting the holocaust of slavery that makes it difficult for black people to take sexism seriously. The rhetoric of the 1960s black power movement consistently used metaphors about restoring a crippled and castrated black manhood to describe not only the pain of white supremacy but the way in which that pain could be eliminated. Freedom for black folks became synonymous with the affirmation of patriarchy. Black females who questioned black male sexism were easily targeted as betrayers of the race.

bell hooks

35 •   Teenage Pregnancy

ROSEMARIE WHITE-STARR
(LETTER TO GEORGE SIMONS)

Dear Dr. Simons,

In answer to a question you asked about teen pregnancy, I am
able to share the following from research and from the
Jamestown, New York YWCA program's 21-year experiences:

- Teen pregnancy occurs most frequently when young
  women do not have any goals or see hope for the future.
- Young women feel unloved. It translates, "If I have a baby,
  the baby will love me. I will have someone who loves me."
- Over 60 percent of the teen mothers have been sexually
  abused or molested and therefore have learned that saying
  no had no power or meaning. The message is, "I am
  powerless to make a decision about my sexual activities
  and my body."
- The message that most teenagers who get pregnant receive
  is that they are only valued as sexual objects. ("I have no
  value as a person. I am just an object of pleasure.")
- A positive adult who over a period of time consistently
  communicates real caring helps in reducing the likelihood
  of pregnancy.
- Most of the boyfriends are significantly older than the teen
  mothers. If all high school males who were sexually active
  used condoms, 80 percent of the young women would be
  pregnant anyway. The fathers are not in high school.
- While self-esteem plummets for all adolescents, male and
  female, it is the female whose self-esteem and goals suffer
  the most. This is why Take A Daughter To Work Day was
  started by the Ms. Foundation. At 8 years of age many
  girls will have dreams and ambitions for the future which
  evaporate or become compromised with the onset of
  adolescence.

The American Association of University Women conducted
excellent research on this topic. A group of 5th graders were

See *Teen Mothers—Citizens or Dependents*, by Ruth
Horowitz (Chicago: University of
Chicago Press, 1996, $14.95,
ISBN 0-226-35379-6).

asked the following questions: The boys were asked to pretend that they were girls and tell what career goals they had. The girls were asked to pretend they were boys and give their career goals. The girls responded with many goals and professional occupations. The boys did not mention professional careers as often and several said they would commit suicide rather than be a girl.

Some very powerful messages are being sent by the culture to the pre-adolescent which predisposes some girls to pregnancy and lessens career goals for most. Of course success in career goals is tempered by race, ethnicity, and class views of education.

Rosemarie White-Starr
Jamestown, NY

The problems: "Take Our Daughters to Work," the public-education program sponsored by the Ms. Foundation for Women, was launched in 1993 in response to disturbing research findings on the adolescent development of girls. Studies by Harvard University researchers, the American Association of University Women (AAUW), and the Minnesota Women's Fund indicate that during adolescence girls often receive less attention than boys in school and in youth-serving programs, suffer from lower expectations than do their male counterparts, and tend to like or dislike themselves based on aspects of their physical appearance. It is during these formative years that countless girls also grapple with eating disorders, negative body image, teen pregnancy, poverty, discrimination, substance and sexual abuse, and distrust in the promises of education.

The solution: Those are the problems. Fortunately, the Ms. Foundation for Women has the solution—to prevent these problems from taking root by helping girls to strengthen their resiliency.

Research has shown that when caring adults intervene in girls' lives, girls are more likely to grow up with confidence, in good health, and ready to fulfill their dreams. In planning a day to celebrate girls—by taking them seriously and listening to their ideas—girls began to believe in themselves, their abilities, and by extension, their futures. Held on the fourth Thursday in April around the country (and in fourteen countries around the world) millions of girls between the ages of 9 and 15 will go to work with adult mentors—parents, grandparents, cousins, aunts, and friends—to learn first-hand the exciting range of life options open to them, while also getting the attention they deserve. (Ms. Foundation for Women, 120 Wall St., 33rd floor, New York, NY 10005, 1-800-676-7780, 212-742-2300, Fax 212-742-1653, e-mail: msfdn@interport.net.)

36 · Managing by Gender

JUDITH C. TINGLEY (SKY)

Because women now compose about 40 percent of middle management ranks, are pressing toward senior management, and work in many industries that were previously considered male territory, the gender difference is hard to ignore.

Neither gender is quite sure how to deal with the other—as managers, superiors, or subordinates. Trying to look and act like men usually doesn't work well for women, and treating women as "one of the boys" is no longer an effective approach for men. Men and women are knocking heads and shaking their heads, putting up with each other while putting each other down. Because men and women communicate in different ways, their style of management often looks and sounds different. Judith Rosener, a professor at the University of California at Irvine, distinguishes between the *transformational* style of women and the *transactional* style of men. *Transformational* style is process-oriented, involving subordinates, sharing information, and empowering employees. The male *transactional* style is task-oriented and exchanges incentives and pressures for performance. An individual's power comes with his title and position in the organization is often used to influence others.

Many men and women in management recognize the stereotypes about the "right" management style for their gender. They try to avoid being branded as too soft or too tough to do the job well, while risking broader management skills to adapt to different situations. It is clear that "one size does not fit all."

Should a male manager deal with a female subordinate differently than he would a man? Are women so sensitive that male bosses need to walk on eggshells? Do men's egos keep them from dealing effectively with female bosses? Is the issue power or gender? Does treating someone as an equal mean treating him or her the same or differently?

George Simons, co-author of *Transcultural Leadership*, says, "The male-female difference represents the biggest cultural difference that exists. If you can learn the skills and attitudes to bridge the gender differences in communication, you will have mastered what it takes to communicate and negotiate with almost anyone about almost anything."

Believing in the magnitude of gender disparity, I coined the word "genderflexing"™ to describe the adaptive process that men and women can use to communicate more effectively with one another in the workplace.

Genderflexing means "temporarily using communication behaviors typical of the other gender to increase your influence." Just as you'd learn to speak some

Is the issue power or gender? Does treating someone as an equal mean treating him or her the same or differently?

Spanish if you were working with a Spanish speaker, you learn to speak some "male" if you're working with men, or some "female" if working with women.

Here are some genderflexing ideas for male managers working with female subordinates:

1. Listen and ask rather than tell. Generally speaking, when women bring up a problem or concern, they want you to know what's going on and to understand their thoughts and feelings about the problem. Male managers often assume they should solve the problem, so they quickly jump in to advise. Unlike many men, women often have no problem asking for advice if they think they need it, but they don't necessarily want advice unless they ask for it.
2. Treat your female subordinate equally in the sense that she has the same opportunities as men to deal with tough tasks, interesting projects, hard or physical work if that's in her job description.
3. Be flexible in how you communicate. You needn't be excessively polite, but you may need to avoid or use fewer male expressions, jokes, or military and sports analogies. If in doubt, ask. Norms have changed. Even the woman you've worked with for a long time may no longer accept conversation that once was okay.
4. Give more positive feedback about performance than you might to men. Both sexes appreciate frequent, positive comments that fit the situation, but some psychologists contend that women probably have a higher need for approval than men. Stick to genuine compliments about performance rather than appearance.

If you're a female manager dealing with a male subordinate, here are some genderflexing ideas for you:

1. Recognize that some men may not particularly like working for a female boss. Try not to take it personally. Recognize ego issues, based on traditional views of gender and power. Without patronizing or challenging, accept his discomfort—unless it interferes with his performance.
2. Be direct, concise, and to the point in conversation. If you are concerned about his understanding all the details, put your words in writing. Recognize that men are less likely than women to say they don't understand, don't get it, or need help.
3. Requiring help makes many men feel weak, so if you think he does need help, find another way to say so. Offer suggestions you'd like him to consider in solving the problem. If you have strong feelings and thoughts, then tell him clearly and directly what you want. "I

ⓘ See *Genderflex: Men & Women Speaking Each Other's Language at Work*, by Judith C. Tingley (New York: AMACOM, $19.95, ISBN 0-8144-0266-6), 135 W. 50th St., New York, NY 10020-1201; 212-586-8100.

PLAYER **diversiPLAY™**

Role play this scenario with a colleague or friend. Read this role for yourself, give the book to your partner to read the section printed on the following page. Then role play the situation for a few moments and discuss the experience together.

As one of the few women in an, until recently, all-male sales force, you are getting a lot of teasing from the men. You feel that this is not malicious and even enjoy some of it. Your co-workers are in their own way initiating you into the team. Your role play partner however has just teased you in front of a client and this is not okay. Tell him exactly why not and what you expect of him.

PARTNER   diversiPLAY™

....
*Read these instructions SILENTLY before starting the role play.
Play the role to represent the following point of view, whether or
not you agree with it.*

Play the role of the man. You find it hard to understand why the
player is upset. You were "just being friendly," and besides, that's
how the guys behave with each other. You will grudgingly accept
her point, however, if she makes it well.

want you to call Jim, Mary, and Joe and meet with
them before moving into phase two." He can't read
your mind, and softening the message can muddy the
waters.

4. Lighten up. Because women often feel they are not
taken seriously, they sometimes take themselves too
seriously. A good sense of humor, generously used, is a
great way to become more credible and comfortable
with co-workers and subordinates. Humor says that its
user is confident and in control.

Men and women can adapt to working with one
another as colleagues, subordinates, or superiors:
keeping communication collaborative instead of competitive; learning the vocabulary and stories of the
other gender; respecting the other's strengths; and
learning from each other.

A homeless woman making her bed in a shelter in New York.
While diversity initiatives in many organizations are discussing
lifestyle options, a growing number of people in their workforces
are homeless. One of their options is often the either-or choice
between food or shelter.

Women Make Movies is a national nonprofit multicultural media organization dedicated to the production, distribution, and exhibition of films and videotapes by and about women. In addition to its International Distribution Service and Membership Program, for those wishing to support the feminist media, Women Make Movies has several other programs:

- Production Assistance—Fiscal Sponsorship, Resource Center, Screening Room, Skills Bank, Media Workshops and Seminars.
- Women of Color Database—An ongoing, comprehensive detailed listing of women of color video and filmmakers.
- Production Division—Produces a limited number of films and videotapes to enhance their distribution collection.

Sample titles include: *Visions of Spirit: A Portrait of Alice Walker; Positive Images: Portraits of Women with Disabilities; Trade Secrets: Blue Collar Women Speak Out.*

For more information or to receive a catalog contact: Women Make Movies, Inc. 462 Broadway, Suite 500 C, New York, NY 10013; 212-925-0606, Fax 212-925-2052.

Gender Resources

With its dual mission of enabling women in business and the professions to achieve their maximum potential and to help employers capitalize on the talents of female employees, Catalyst is the leading nonprofit organization focusing the attention of business leaders and public policy makers on women's workplace issues. For over thirty years Catalyst has conducted research and provided updates on trends affecting women in the workforce. Its solutions-oriented reports combine an in-depth look at the barriers and opportunities for women with concrete how-to advice to achieve a workplace where women advance. Its annual Awards Dinner and Conference honors up to three outstanding corporate initiatives and explores their accomplishments in depth. For a listing of publications or more information, write Catalyst, 250 Park Ave. S., New York, NY 10003-1459; 212-777-8900, Fax 212-477-4252.

The National Film Board of Canada publishes *Beyond the Image*, a catalog fully describing films and videos about women's culture, politics, and values. Beginning with the Canadian government's decision in 1974 to support International Women's year, Studio D has won many awards and international acclaim. For information or to receive a copy of the catalog, write to Women's Marketing D-5, National Film Board of Canada, P.O. Box 6100, Station A, Montreal, Quebec H3C 3H5 or call Atlantic Canada 1-800-561-7104; Quebec 1-800-363-0328; Ontario 800-267-7710; Western and Northern Canada 1-800-661-9867. In the United States, write the National Film Board of Canada Library, 22-D Hollywood Ave., Hohokus, NJ 07423, or call 201-652-0426, Fax 201-652-1973.

Significant works over the last thirty years on feminist thought include:

1963—*The Feminine Mystique*, by Betty Friedan (New York: Dell Publishing)
1971—*The Female Eunuch*, by Germaine Greer (New York: McGraw-Hill)
1975—*Against Our Will*, by Susan Brownmiller (New York: Fawcett)
1981—*Common Differences: Conflicts in Black and White Feminist Perspectives*, by Gloria I. Joseph and Jill Lewis (New York: Doubleday)

1982—*In a Different Voice*, by Carol Gilligan (Cambridge, Mass.: Harvard University Press)

1982—*All the Women Are White, All the Blacks Are Men, but Some of Us Are Brave: Black Women's Studies*, edited by Gloria T. Hull, Patricia Bell, Barbara Smith (Old Westbury, N.Y.: Feminist Press)

1984—*This Bridge Called My Back: Writings by Radical Women of Color*, edited by Gloria Anzaldua and Cherrie Moraga (Watertown, N.Y.: Persephone Press)

1984—*Sister Outsider*, by Audre Lorde (The Crossing Press)

1990—*The Second Shift*, by Arlene Hochschild (New York: Avon)

1990—*Feminism/Postmodernism*, edited by Linda J. Nicholson (New York: Routledge)

1990—*Sexual Personae: Art and Decadence from Nefertiti to Emily Dickinson*, by Camille Paglia (New York: Random House)

1991—*Backlash: The Undeclared War Against Amerian Women*, by Susan Faludi (New York: Anchor)

1992—*Race-ing Justice, En-Gendering Power*, edited by Toni Morison (New York: Pantheon)

1994—*Unequal Sisters*, edited by Vicki L. Ruiz & Ellen Carol DuBois (New York: Routledge)

1994—*Fire with Fire: The New Female Power and How to Use It*, by Naomi Wolf (New York: Fawcett)

1995—*Listen Up*, edited by Barbara Findlen (Seattle, WA: Seal Press)

1995—*To Be Real*, by Rebecca Walker (New York: Anchor Books)

1996—In *These Girls, Hope Is a Muscle*, by Madeline Blais (New York: Warner Books)

DIVERSE AMERICA— ITS RICHES AND CHALLENGES

As Roosevelt Thomas (interviewed in Section 10) insists, the primary issue of diversity in North America is not our differences but the *mix* of our differences. Though territorial boundaries often separate us into neighborhoods and ghettos, it seems natural for Americans to spill over into and sometimes even deliberately walk over each other's space. Precisely because the "mix" Thomas refers to brings with it both conflict and new possibilities—challenges and riches, we choose to define diversity as "the sum total of the potential that exists in a group of people because of their differences,"

In the first three sections of this book we explored differences of class, race, and gender and sexual orientation. Here our contributors discuss other differences that are part of the diversity equation. Through their eyes we see a diverse people, vibrant, interacting, doing business, sometimes exuberant and sometimes in pain. They examine ways these differences affect how we work and do business with each other and how we explore each other's feelings about our pluralism.

Interacting with each other in diverse America brings to the foreground our own cultural preferences, our stereotypes, and our prejudices. All of these must be dealt with successfully if we are to harvest the added value that so many contributors say diversity promises us. The activities included will help measure our exposure to each other and reduce the biases that erode our mutual respect and prevent us from collaborating.

See *A Different Mirror: A History of Multicultural America*, by Ronald Takaki (Boston: Little, Brown and Company, 1993, $27.95, ISBN 0-316-83112-3). Takaki's pathbreaking survey of American history seeks to correct past scholarship in which America has been defined too narrowly. Takaki synthesizes ideas from recent literature on the histories of groups previously ignored in American history such as Chicanos, Asian Americans, African Americans, Native Americans, and Irish Americans, thereby creating a more complex portrait of the United States. The product of this synthesis is a history of the United States where race, class, and gender are shown to have been central in shaping people's access to and attitudes toward American citizenship and inclusion. See also Howard Zinn's classic, *A People's History of the United States* (New York: HarperCollins, 1995, $12, ISBN 0-06-092643-0; 1-800-736-1293).

Days of Obligation: An Argument with My Mexican Father, by Richard Rodriguez (New York: Viking, 1992, $11, ISBN 0-14-009622-1). In this collection of autobiographical essays, Rodriguez explores his own place in the world as well as the complex relationship of the United States to the larger world, and especially to Mexico. He argues that these two countries inherited different cultures from Western Europe: one Protestant, the other Catholic; one comedic, the other tragic. The clashing and blending of these two cultures, according to Rodriguez, continues to have profound consequences for North America and the world. See also "The Fear of Losing a Culture" in *Time* (7/11/88).

Ethnic Options: Choosing Identities in America, by Mary Walters (Berkeley: University of California Press, 1990). Waters conducted interviews with white suburban Americans to determine "why people choose a particular ethnic identity from a range of possible choices;

how often and in what ways that ethnic identity is used in everyday life; and how ethnic identity is intergenerationally transferred within families." She finds that ethnic identity does have meaning for individuals; it is, however, most often constructed in relation to family habit rather than to models existing in larger ethnic communities.

37 • Let's Make a Deal!

DEENA LEVINE

You work in the Customer Care department of a Home Development Corporation in Southern California. An Iranian client moved into his new home, having gone through the pre-move-in inspection where, apparently, everything was fine. Two weeks later, he calls you. The conversation goes like this:

CLIENT: Hello, this is Hossein Barkour and I'd like to tell you about a little problem in my new home.

CUST. CARE REP: Sure. We'll try to be of help. Go right ahead.

CLIENT: One of the outlets in my living room is not in the same place as it was in the model home. This isn't right. It has to be changed.

CUST. CARE REP: I understand the problem, but I have to tell you that changing it would involve extensive electric work. How important is moving it?

CLIENT: Very important. You promised me a home just like the model. It has to be changed.

CUST. CARE REP: This is very difficult.

CLIENT: Look, I'll call it even if you pour concrete in my atrium and lay the tiles.

CUST. CARE REP: (Surprised and, for a moment, speechless)

Culture tip: For Iranians, personal cleverness or what is called "zerenghi" is a highly prized attribute in business situations such as bargaining. The concept involves knowing how to manipulate certain structures and situations to one's own advantage.

What is happening here? How should you interpret it? How should you react?

Living and working in a multicultural world challenges our everyday assumptions about how we do business and especially how we judge the values and behaviors of other people. This story is a good example of how different values give rise to confusion and unwarranted negative judgments of others.

This is excerpted from *The Dynamics of Cross-Cultural Selling: What You Don't Know May Be Costing You Sales,* a 2-hour training audiocassette by Deena Levine. Available from 510-947-5627.

Action tip: Do not take it personally when a negotiating strategy seems out of line. Try not to let any of your own negativity surface or to overreact to such transparent bargaining attempts. Remain calm and simply explain where you do and do not have flexibility.

38 • Inventory of Exposure to Various Cultures

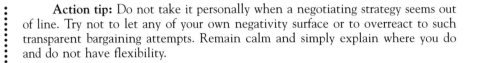

DIANNE LAMOUNTAIN

*M*ost people would agree that exposure to a culture leads to increased understanding and comfort with that culture. Scientific research supports this idea. Use the following list to review your exposure to various groups and assess your level of comfort. Ask yourself the following questions:

- What is my level of exposure to this group (limited, some exposure to, worked closely with, live in my neighborhood, good friends, lived with)?
- How do those I know from this group view the world differently than I do (relationship to time and to authority, self vs. group, etc.)?
- What are the differences in the way they communicate (personal space, level of emotion, who looks at whom, difference in other non-verbal signals, etc.)?
- Do they, as a group, have any beliefs or ways of doing things with which I feel uncomfortable or that I feel are wrong?
- Do they, as a group, have different beliefs or ways of doing things that I feel contribute added value to our work group?
- Do I feel differently now than I did when I first was exposed to someone from this group? If so, what caused the change and how long did it take?

The list is meant to be representative, not all-inclusive. As you go through the list, add other groups that come to mind.

Africans (specify countries)

_____

African-Americans

_____

Amish

_____

Arab Nationals (specify countries)

_____

Buddhists

_____

Caribbeans (specify countries/islands)

_____

Central Americans (specify countries)

_____

Chinese

_____

Europeans (specify countries)

_____

Gays, Lesbians, and Bisexuals

_____

Hindus

_____

Japanese

_____

Jews

_____

This list is from *The Questions of Diversity*, a spiral-bound collection of diversity diagnostic questionnaires, checklists, inventories, and assessment instruments for organizations to use in an internal audit of diversity awareness and multicultural competence. The book is sold copyright-free, enabling users to administer the quizzes within their organization. A disk-based version is also available.

(Contact: ODT, Inc., P.O. Box 134, Amherst, MA 01004, 1-800-736-1293; Fax 413-549-3503.)

Mexicans

_____

Mormons

_____

Muslims

_____

Native Americans (specify nations)

_____

People with disabilities

_____

Southeast Asians (specify countries)

_____

South Americans (specify countries)

_____

Countries of the former Soviet Union (specify republics/ethnic groups)

_____

Others?

_____
_____
_____
_____

Another useful diversity awareness tool is *Barnga: A Simulation Game on Culture Clashes*, by Sivasailam Thiagarajan and Barbar Steinwachs. *Barnga* demonstrates how cultural differences affect human interactions. Players divide into small groups, each of which receives a standard deck of playing cards and a slightly different set of rules. Participants then move from group to group, initially believing they all know the same rules but gradually coming to understanding that others have different information. This simulates the culture shock people experience when entering another culture, where they must learn new rules in order to function effectively in cross-cultural interactions. Order *Barnga* from Intercultural Press (see Contributors section).

Although this case study might seem extreme, it illustrates the critical importance of cultural competency within a multicultural workplace. It is crucial that employees understand the necessity of having awareness of, and sensitivity to, cultural norms outside of their own.

39 · The Manager in a Multicultural Organization

JOY BODZIOCH

*L*uis has been a manager at a large Southwestern telecommunications company for two years. He is proud of his ability to get along well with every worker on his very diverse team. One of Luis's team members is Anh, a young Vietnamese man who immigrated to the United States six months ago. Anh is an excellent worker: His technical skills are superior and he works many extra hours to get the job done. Since Anh speaks little English, he stays pretty much to himself. Luis may not speak with him for several days at a time.

One day last week, Anh happened to glance up as Luis walked past his work station. Luis smiled and greeted Anh with a cocked thumb and extended forefinger gesture, the typical cowboy "pistol" salute. But Anh was unfamiliar with the friendly gesture; he interpreted Luis's cocked thumb signal as a threat, for the next day he brought a gun to work! Fortunately, a co-worker saw Anh put the gun in his locker and reported it to Luis who, in shock and dismay, passed the information on to Bill, the director of human resources.

When Bill confronted Anh, Anh explained that he had brought the gun for self-protection, because his manager Luis, was planning to kill him! After discussions with both Anh and Luis, Bill concluded that in Anh's culture, hand gestures were often interpreted literally, and Anh had not been in America long enough to understand the cultural differences. Although Luis had taken the company's standard management training course, cultural differences had never been discussed, so he had no idea that Anh might react as he did. The fact that Anh's co-worker accidentally saw the gun was the only thing that averted a potential tragedy.

Myrna Araneta, Manager of Organization Effectiveness at Procter and Gamble, has developed a "Management Diversity Feedback Survey," which helps managers obtain candid feedback in their actions in leading and supporting diversity in the workforce. The survey includes an interpretative tool and worksheet for the recipient's personal reflection and action plan. Reach her for further information at 2 P&G Plaza, Tower North 5, Cincinnati, OH 45202; 513-983-8417, Fax 513-983-1814 or 0603.

See *Experiential Activities for Intercultural Learning*, edited by H. Ned Seelye. This book contains an essay on the theory and practice of intercultural learning and 33 activities intended to foster understanding of the various aspects and levels of intercultural contact. These exercises are practical and purposeful and they are designed to help adolescent and adult learners acquire the special skills needed to communicate across cultural boundaries. The activities can be used with a variety of audiences. Order *Experiential Activities* from Intercultural Press (see Contributors section).

AARP WORKS teaches job-search skills to midlife and older workers through a series of workshops offered at more than 70 sites nationwide. AARP WORKS is also carried on Mind Extension University, the educational cable T.V. network. To find a site near you, write AARP Work Force Programs, 601-E. St., NW, Washington, D.C. 20049. To register for the cable series, call 1-800-777-MIND (6463), 9 a.m. to 5 p.m.

40 • What Is Your Aging I.Q.?

NATIONAL INSTITUTE ON AGING

TRUE OR FALSE?

_____ 1. Everyone becomes "senile" sooner or later, if he or she lives long enough.

_____ 2. American families have by and large abandoned their older members.

_____ 3. Depression is a serious problem for older people.

_____ 4. The numbers of older people are growing.

_____ 5. The vast majority of older people are self-sufficient.

_____ 6. Mental confusion is an inevitable, incurable consequence of old age.

_____ 7. Intelligence declines with age.

_____ 8. Sexual urges and activity normally cease around age 55–60.

_____ 9. If a person has been smoking for 30 or 40 years, it does no good to quit.

_____ 10. Older people should stop exercising and rest.

ANSWERS:

1. **False.** Even among those who live to be 80 or older, only 20–25 percent develop Alzheimer's disease or some other incurable form of brain disease. "Senility" is a meaningless term that should be discarded.

2. **False.** The American family is still the number-one caretaker of older Americans. Most older people live close to their children and see them often; many live with their spouses. In all, 8 out of 10 men and 6 out of 10 women live in family settings.

3. **True.** Depression, loss of self-esteem, loneliness, and anxiety can become more common as older people face retirement, the deaths of relatives and friends, and other such crises—often at the same time. Fortunately, depression is treatable.

4. **True.** Today, 12 percent of the U.S. population are 65 or older. By the year 2030, one in five people will be over 65 years of age.

5. **True.** Only 5 percent of the older population live in nursing homes; the rest are basically healthy and self-sufficient.

6. **False.** Mental confusion and serious forgetfulness in old age can be caused by Alzheimer's disease or other conditions that cause incurable damage to the brain, but some 100 other problems can cause the same symptoms. A minor head injury, a high fever, poor nutrition, adverse drug reactions, and depression can all be treated and the confusion will be cured.

7. **False.** Intelligence per se does not decline without reason. Most people maintain their intellect or improve as they grow older.

8. **False.** Most older people can lead an active, satisfying sex life.

9. **False.** Stopping smoking at any age not only reduces the risk of cancer and heart disease, it also leads to healthier lungs.

10. **False.** Many older people enjoy—and benefit from—exercises such as walking, swimming, and bicycle riding. Exercise at any age can help strengthen the heart and lungs, and lower blood pressure. See your physician before beginning a new exercise program.

Public domain material published by the U.S. Department of Health & Human Services (Public Health Service/National Institutes of Health).

See *Coming of Age: The Story of Our Century by Those Who've Lived It*, by Studs Terkel (New York: The New Press). Studs Terkel's book assembles reflections from 70 Americans over the age of 70. The participants are sharp observers of the changes that have transformed American society in their lifetimes, including labor organizers, environmentalists, reform politicians, radical priests and ministers, pioneering proponents of gay and lesbian rights, as well as corporate lawyers, investment bankers, public pitchmen, and homicide detectives. Almost all lament the collapse of workplace solidarity, institutional loyalty, and civil society, and some note the limited basic skills of today's youth.

American Business and Older Workers: A Road Map to the 21st Century is a study of employers' attitudes toward workers age 50 and older and provides tips about what older workers can do to stay employable. To order one free copy send a request with the title and stock number (D13827) to AARP Fulfillment, 601 E St., NW, Washington, D.C. 20049.

The Gray Panthers, also known as Gray Panthers Project and Fund, is a national advocacy group for older Americans. Reach them at 2025 Pennsylvania Ave., NW, Ste. 821, Washington, D.C. 20006, 202-466-3132, Fax 202-466-3133. Membership information: 1-800-280-5362.

"Think of me as an 18 year-old with 30 years' experience."

—a downsized executive in a job-hunting interview.

41 •   Diversity in Canada

LYDIA PHILLIPS AND DANIELLE CÉCILE

*T*he cultural make-up of Canadian society has become very diverse in recent years. A new pattern of immigration has changed cities such as Vancouver, Toronto and Montreal. Looking ahead to future trends, we see that this diversity will continue to increase.

Recent statistics show that among Canadians today:

- 42 percent have origins other than British or French
- 4 percent have Aboriginal origins
- 15 percent have a disability
- 38 percent of adults have some level of difficulty with every day reading material
- 16 percent of Canadians live below the poverty line

By the year 2006 the proportion of Canadians who are visible minorities will probably be between 13 and 18 percent. In Toronto and Vancouver, this could be up to 50 percent. By the year 2021, there will be twice as many seniors as there are today.

Canada's population growth depends on immigrants arriving every year.

Canadian Aboriginals fought for Canada in the two World Wars, but were not allowed to vote until 1960.

Canadians of Chinese, Japanese, and Indian heritage also fought for Canada in the two World Wars, but were not allowed to vote until after the second World War. They were also forbidden to work in certain professions and occupations.

Canada had the lowest rate of acceptance for immigration of Jews fleeing the Holocaust.

Aboriginal rates of unemployment, poverty, literacy and disability are far higher than in the general Canadian population.

The majority of New Canadians have higher educational levels. They are also less likely than their fellow Canadians to be on social assistance.

More than one in five Canadians over 65 years lives below the poverty line.

More than one in five of Canada's children live in poverty.

People with disabilities have incomes lower than those of the general population. In 1990, 43 percent of people with disabilities had an income below $10,000.

(i) "Diversity in Canada" is from the Diversity Action Kit of the Cooperative Housing Federation of Canada, which can be contacted at 311-225, rue Metcalfe Street, Otawa, Canada, K2P 1P9; 613-230-2201; 1-800-465-2752; Fax 613-230-2231.

(i) See *Multiculturalism in Canada: The Challenge of Diversity*, by Augie Fleras and Jean Leonard Elliott (Scarborough, Ont.: Nelson Canada, 1992), a solid synthesis of the political, cultural, and historical context of the Canadian experiment in multiculturalism.

42 • Asian Americans: Common Stereotypes & Corresponding Cultural Explanations

TOY-PING TAIRA

Observed Behavior of Asian Americans	Common Stereotypical Misinterpretations	Possible Cultural Explanation
Non-confrontational	Passive; does not care one way or another	Values harmony; sees disagreements as being in disharmony
Quiet; reserved	Has no opinions	Values opinions of others and fitting in with group
Agreeable; dependable follower	Unassertive; no leadership qualities	Values what is good for group; can be assertive and a leader if needed for the group
Industrious	Make good "worker bees"	Values carrying their share of work; believes hard work will be recognized and rewarded
Technically and scientifically competent	No management competence or leader-type charisma	Values science as universal language crossing cultural barriers; believes leadership comes in many forms
Deferential to others	Not committed to own opinions, judgments, or preferences	Values being respectful of others; believes in "saving face" for self and others; values age and wisdom
Very American behavior	Looks Asian; must be of different culture	Born in United States; values American heritage

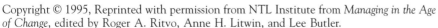

Copyright © 1995, Reprinted with permission from NTL Institute from *Managing in the Age of Change*, edited by Roger A. Ritvo, Anne H. Litwin, and Lee Butler.

Valuing Their Differences—Asian Americans & Pacific Islanders focuses on Asian American stereotyping, and promotes valuing of human differences. The package includes Training Facilitator Guides, 15 Participant Workbooks and 6 videos: *All Orientals Look the Same* views stereotypes and prejudices about Asians and Pacific Islanders. *My Brown Eyes* tells of a young immigrant on his first day of school in the United States. *Me, Mom, and Mona* explores intercultural and intergenerational differences in a Chinese Canadian family. *East of Occidental* highlights the history of Asian communities in Seattle. *Animal Appetites* explores the legal issues surrounding the killing of one dog by an Asian American. *Meeting at Tule Lake* reflects upon the incarceration of Japanese Americans during World War II.

Nonprofit: $650, for-profit $1,195. Call 415-552-9550, Fax 415-863-0814, or write NAATA/CrossCurrent Media, 346 Ninth St., 2nd floor, San Francisco, CA 94103.

43 • Asian Americans' Awkward Status: Some Feel Whites Use Them as "Racial Wedge" with Others

BENJAMIN PIMENTAL (SAN FRANCISCO CHRONICLE)

*L*arry Alcantara is a middle manager in a West Coast city government agency, and when his boss asked him recently to discipline an employee accused of incompetence, he found himself in a troubling position.

The boss is white. The employee is black. And Alcantara, a Filipino American, could not help but wonder whether he had been chosen to discipline the employee because he, too, is a minority.

Department executives had been unhappy with the employee's performance for years, but, according to Alcantara, they never did anything for fear of a discrimination complaint. They decided to take action, he said, only when Alcantara was in place to do the job.

"Having a minority supervisor over a minority employee, they no longer had that fear," said Alcantara, who asked that his firm not be identified. "I ended up saying (to the employee), 'The rules of the game have now changed.'"

It is a concern shared with increasing frequency among Asian Americans in offices and schools nationwide—especially in West Coast cities like San Francisco, Los Angeles, and Seattle where thousands have risen into middle management in the past generation.

Though they have fared relatively well in the work force compared to African Americans, Latinos and other minority groups, many Asian Americans feel they are becoming a "racial bourgeoisie"—a buffer class between the white majority, which has most of the power, and the minorities, who have less.

The belief is not universally held by Asian Americans or by white executives. But in dozens of interviews, Asian Americans expressed concerns—and uneasiness—much like Alcantara's. They are a "shock absorber" between whites and blacks, said one; they are a "racial wedge" used to divide minorities, said others.

Many Asian American executives, managers, and professionals are taking a closer look at their status as the minority of choice and at their relations with other people of color.

"It started with this bizarre model minority thing . . . this image of the white man holding an Asian American up . . . and telling other minorities . . . 'If you minorities just work as hard as the Asians, then you too will be able to succeed.' *"*—Kathy Imahara, a Japanese American attorney in Los Angeles

The notion that Asian Americans have become a racial wedge is not based on some grand conspiracy but is the result of the complex social dynamics of an emerging multiethnic society, analysts say.

Since the civil rights era of the 1950s and '60s, the door to opportunity has been opened slowly—and sometimes grudgingly—to minorities. And in the past two decades, the number of Asian immigrants and Asian Americans in the work force has risen exponentially, sometimes provoking tension from other minority groups.

While whites hold most top management posts in the state bureaucracy, Asian Americans, who make up 10 percent of California's population, hold a disproportionate number of civil service professional jobs, far more than blacks or Latinos. And in some settings, such as California hospitals, Asians occupy more mid-level positions than any other minority.

But success, analysts say, sometimes cuts both ways: Asian Americans are stereotyped as more competent and reliable than other minorities.

At the same time, they may be dismissed as unassertive nerds and poor communicators. They can get stuck in the mezzanine of the workplace hierarchy and often are locked out of the upper echelons.

For that reason, white managers might not recognize the unique dilemmas that an Asian American manager might face.

Last year, the Federal Glass Ceiling Commission interviewed 14 Asian American male executives—and not one identified himself as a "minority."

Many Asian Americans feel they are becoming a "racial bourgeoisie"—a buffer class between the white majority, which has most of the power, and the minorities, who have less.

"Immigrant communities generally tend not to know the history and to buy into the biases and prejudices of the dominant group. Unfortunately, becoming American often means buying into the prejudices. They want to identify upward. They don't want to identify with those at the bottom."—Bill Lee, regional counsel with the NAACP Legal Defense Fund, Los Angeles.

44 · Marketing to Generation X

KAREN RITCHIE
(AMERICAN DEMOGRAPHICS)

Divorce, diversity, and declining incomes shape the consumer behavior of Generation X. With a broader definition of family, young adults may give consumer advice to many friends and relatives. As cautious romantics, they may create stable marriages and make smarter buying decisions. They accept racial and sexual diversity as facts of life. And they hate advertisements that use hype or insincerity.

Today's young adults are perhaps closer to their parents than any recent generation has been. Rather than breaking ties with parents during the turbulence of adolescence and moving on to new adult families, the members of Generation X tend to rebound after college and other brief experiences of independent living. Then, as adults, they must redefine their relationships with the same parents, siblings, and stepparents they grew up with.

In fact, Generation X is helping to form a new extended American family, one that includes close friends, stepparents, adopted and half-siblings, live-in lovers, and a host of diverse relations. An important aspect of this new extended family often involves a renewed bond between Generation X and older family members. In a 1993 survey conducted for *Details* magazine, 51 percent of Generation X said they "admire their parent(s) more than anyone else," and 29 percent described their mother or father as "my best friend." Clearly, even after Xers move out on their own, many continue to depend on an emotional and social connection with parents, as well as varying degrees of financial support.

See William Strauss and Neil Howe's *Generations: The History of America's Future* or Howe and Strauss' article "The New Generation Gap" in the December 1992 issue of the *Atlantic Monthly.*

Organizations recruiting for a diverse work force will find important national data in *Diversity Recruitment Sourcebook.* Supplements of demographics on the schools in four regions—the Northeast, South, Midwest, and West—are also available from the National Association of Colleges and Employers (NACE) by calling 1-800-544-5272 or 610-868-1421.

diversiSMARTS™

The more schooling a person gets today the more likely he or she is to be tolerant.

True or false.

Because young adults now remain at home longer, many marketers underestimate their importance as consumers. If marketers have not considered the degree to which the parent-child relationship changes over time, they may not have noticed that many Xers have become "designated decision-makers" for their parents or other relatives. This may be especially true in those areas where young adults have particular expertise, such as electronic equipment, computers, or in some cases, automobiles. Since so many Xers were children of working parents, they were given shopping chores early on. An Xer may have begun by picking up milk at the store and progressed to specifying a new computer. Now she is hiring a contractor to remodel the house for her parents or advising on the purchase of a new car.

Many Xers maintain contact with a large network of relatives and friends, including several different family branches. In this manner, a single Xer with a high degree of expertise about computers, for example, may consult in several households and be a significant influence on purchasing decisions in all of them.

Today's young adults will eventually get married. But they will do so later in life than boomers did, and their marriages may represent a return to a more stable lifestyle than we have seen in recent decades. First of all, Xers are playing the statistics in favor of lasting marriages: they are marrying at a later age, which may increase the maturity and stability of each partner and the economic stability of the marriage.

Marriage for Generation X will probably not mean the formation of a totally separate nuclear family. Boomers who married earlier often saw getting married as another aspect of adolescent separation, a badge of independence and adulthood, and many boomers were therefore anxious to put space between their old family and their new spouse. Generation X will be more settled and more accustomed to the extended family that evolved during their single years.

In the workplace, Generation X will continue the balancing act between career and home but will keep in mind the lessons of the baby boom. Today's young adults do not question the achievements of boomer women in the workplace, but they often question the price of those achievements. Boomer women, some of whom have spent a lifetime opening new opportunities for

Generation Xers don't dislike advertising. They dislike hype. They dislike overstatement, self-importance, hypocrisy, and the assumption that anyone would want to be disturbed at home by a salesperson on the telephone.

(i) *Voices: AT&T People Speak Out On Diversity* is a videotape (18 minutes) that has been used as a discussion starter with AT&T employees, as well as AT&T clients and vendors. It is provocative and insightful, and is available as a public service for $9.80 (including shipping and handling) from 1-800-600-5855 (WRS, Box 44290, Pittsburgh, PA 15205).

(i) See *Marketing to Generation X*, Karen Ritchie, Lexington Books, New York, 1995.

Diversity in Corporate America is a directory of corporations, associations, and consultants involved in managing diversity initiatives. Available from the Institute for Corporate Diversity, P.O. Box 2106, Minneapolis, MN 55402. 1-800-650-4747, 612-338-1231, Fax 612-337-9694.

(i) For more information about the 1993 *Details* magazine survey on the attitudes of young adults, telephone 212-598-3797. *Marketing To Generation X* is available for $25 from the American Demographics Marketing Power Catalog; 1-800-8281 133.

women, are understandably puzzled when Generation X women preface a statement with, "I'm not a feminist, but. . . ." Boomers are concerned when Generation X women are quick to claim the benefits of feminism and equally as quick to disavow any association with it.

Boomer men and women who have worked hard to gain the success they enjoy do not understand when an Xer expresses a reluctance to make personal sacrifices for the sake of career. Boomer women were willing to sacrifice some of their family life in return for a chance at a career. Generation X women have a clear shot at the executive suite, but often have been working since high school and long for a change of pace. They place a greater importance on the home and family life they missed as children and are unwilling to compromise that ideal for a job. While Xer women will continue to work, they will not sacrifice their personal lives or families to the degree that boomer women did.

Marketers would be wise to note this temperature change, but should not read it as a return to the 1950s. Boomer women made the market for power suits, Rolex watches, Saabs, and BMWs. For Generation X, balance and perspective will be a primary goal. Look for a continued emphasis on leisure activities and family entertainment, economical and functional clothing, quality day care, and home offices.

Apartment furnishings and appliances in smaller or more portable configurations will be useful to young singles and young married couples alike. Small, economical automobiles like the Geo Metro and the Chrysler Neon are already popular with this market.

Any product or service that feeds the need of young, single Xers to stay in touch and in control at the same time will do well. The future is bright for carphones, beepers and pagers, answering machines, computer mail, and fax machines. These are necessities—not luxuries—to Generation X.

Banks, insurance companies, and credit cards would do well to overcome their long-standing mistrust of applicants without credit ratings and to look for ways to provide services to Generation X. Their good work history, high aspirations, and consumer savvy will ultimately make them good customers.

Copyright © 1995, *American Demographics*, Ithaca, New York. Reprinted with permission.

 diversiSMARTS™

Answer to the DIVERSOPHY®

False. Once considered true, this trend has been reversed in the present under-30 generation. Researchers suggest that this is due to the lack of historical focus and the fact that many of this generation see themselves as victims of reverse discrimination.

45 · Psychological Disability, the Workplace and the American Character

GEORGE SIMONS INTERVIEWS ELIZABETH HENRY POWER

GEORGE SIMONS: What is a psychological disability? Could you give some examples?

ELIZABETH HENRY POWER: A psychological disability is a mental-emotional condition that causes a person to meet the criteria for a disability as set forth by the Americans with Disabilities Act (ADA), which means that one or more major life activity is impaired. Such people are legally protected from discrimination in the workplace. However, as with any law, some conditions are exempt.

There are lots of factors involved in discussing disability. Under the law, one must look at whether the person is only perceived as having a disability or has actually been diagnosed, and whether the disability occurred in the past or is still going on. And, of course, how severe it is — all the while following rules about under what circumstances it can be brought up and discussed.

Disabilities can include those such as genius and retardation as well as phobias, Post Traumatic Stress Disorder (PTSD)—a lot of Vietnam vets experience this—bipolar depression, and other labels that indicate inappropriate abnormality. Included are learned conditions such as PTSD and dissociation as well as biological ones such as bipolar disorder and schizophrenia.

SIMONS: You experience one of these disabilities. Could you describe it and tell me how this affects your work? For example, do you need workplace accommodations for this? How does having such a disability actually contribute to your workplace performance?

POWER: In 1990 I was diagnosed with Dissociative Identity Disorder, then labeled "Multiple Personalities Disorder" or simply MPD. I was working as a technical writer and instructional designer in an automotive factory at the time. I also had my own consulting firm. Then, the major effects were the challenges of acquainting myself with the internal process, identifying and learning to manage triggers for shifting and switching, and staying productive (which I was doing before diagnosis).

The diagnosis exaggerated the issues as they were becoming known, so it seemed that I got worse before I got better! I had never known how much of my day was missing, even though it all got handled. At first, constant droning noise or sudden noise could result in my "spacing out." The accommodations I created were

> When people value my differences instead of demeaning or belittling me, I perform much better at work. In situations where people value the assets that are related to my disability, such as multiplistic thinking, internal group process, and a more systems-oriented view, I can contribute significantly.

to build in timers to help me stay alert to the passing of time (like egg timers). I educated a core group of people for support and created reminders and positive triggers that allowed me to adjust as I got to know myself better. It was a challenge.

Now, five years later, what I experience has very little similarity to back then. Droning noise doesn't bother me as much as random noise. I become startled just like everyone else when I hear a sudden noise.

Of the many "me's" who became known, most have come together, so I no longer have the sense that there is a crowd inside trying to get their own space and time. We generally share and collaborate. I find I am still more affected by emotional events than others may be, and I work to protect myself more effectively. Sometimes different versions of me may be more prominent, but this is now much more subtle than it was. I don't lose information or time, and there is very little internal conflict.

I own my own business, so I build in my own accommodations. For example, I use a laptop computer to help me keep track of time and events—ACT (Symantec's time management software) has become my walk-around personal secretary. It helps me stay focused: I really can't attend very well to spoken information, so I type things on the laptop as I hear them. This helps me remember them better. I spend a lot of time in reading, thinking, and writing, and less around large crowds, which I find a little difficult—too many inputs. I do really well with groups and in stand-up presentations (I am an international consultant and trainer), as long as I can get time to recharge.

When people value my differences instead of demeaning or belittling me, I perform much better at work. In situations where people value the assets that are related to my disability, such as multiplistic thinking, internal group process, and a more systems-oriented view, I can contribute significantly. This is especially true when people ask questions and accept the process I use as valid.

On the other hand, when I am greeted with fear and unasked questions, when I am lumped in with the media-driven image of "people like that," or harassed about "making things up," my performance is lowered—and short-term—I won't stick around long.

SIMONS: It has been said that Attention Deficit Disorder (ADD) is somewhat specific to U.S. culture. Is that true, and, if so, could you tell us why you think that is so?

POWER: I suspect that ADD is a disease of a multimedia culture, one that affects the ways in which brain function develops. Some research indicates that ADD is often another type of childhood dissociative disorder, not nearly as far down the line as MPD. If that's so, since about 30 percent of the kids diagnosed ADD can also be diagnosed with a dissociative disorder, then it takes on a whole different meaning.

Why? Because dissociation is a consequence of exposure to trauma, including injury, illness, relocation, and seeing violence—as well as all the types of abuse that can be named. If the connections are there, we may be seeing the outcome of our culture in kids with learning disabilities caused by the steady diet of life that adults, especially our media, feed them.

Descriptive Video Service (DVS®) is a national service that makes movies on video, public television programs, and some cable programming accessible to people who have difficulty appreciating movies and television due to limited vision. DVS provides narrated descriptions of key visual elements without interfering with the audio or dialogue of a program or movie. Information about DVS on video and television can be obtained by calling the DVS Information Line. Call 1-800-333-1203 for a schedule of TV programs, for locations of public television stations offering DVS, for a listing of video titles, to place a video order, or to ask for other information.

Managing Our Selves; Building a Community of Caring is a workbook for persons with MPD/DD concentrates on self-management through active decision making and the development of internal collaboration among others. It is appealingly written in a straightforward and slightly folksy style. Available from E. Power & Associates, P.O. Box 2346, Brentwood, TN 37024-2346, 615-371-1320, Fax 615-383-8870.

46 • Blond Hair, Black Hair

ROBERTO RODRIGUEZ AND PATRISIA GONZALEZ (SAN FRANCISCO CHRONICLE)

*C*ristina Saralegui, a syndicated television talk show host recently wrote a column, distributed by *The New York Times* Syndicate, titled "Bashing Hispanics Who Are Too White."

Saralegui, who has blond hair, green eyes and white skin, raises a topic that is commonly whispered among Latinos—resentment against Latinos who look white.

In her column, she points out that in 1989, her first year on the air, she was subjected to hate mail by Latinos who objected to her white persona. As a result, she went on a "What is a Real Hispanic?" crusade throughout the country.

Her conclusions were that Latinos come in all colors and that all Latinos are basically the same, united by language and culture. Her statements, however, reveal she doesn't seem to comprehend the nature of the resentment heaped upon her.

To this day, outside of the "help," brown and black populations are conspicuously absent from Spanish-language media. Blondes predominate in soap operas and commercials, as movie stars, game show hosts, models, entertainers, and newscasters.

ⓘ See also "Teaching Guide to the Eye of the Storm" found in *The Cultural Diversity Fieldbook Supplement* by Hopkins, et. al. (ODT, 1996); 1-800-736-1293.

If we were to answer her question on the basis of watching Spanish-language television—both in the United States and in Latin America—the response would be that real Latinos are blond, have blue or green eyes, and are light skinned.

The reality is that the vast majority of Latinos have brown skin or black skin, black or brown hair, and black or brown eyes.

She states that having spent her entire life in Miami, she was discriminated against by Latinos but never has been subjected to "prejudice of any kind from English-speaking Americans." It's a statement commonly made by Latinos who look white.

By her own admission, she reveals that her experience is radically different from that of the majority of Latinos—who historically were subjected to legal discrimination and who continue to face prejudice of many kinds.

Those who object to this media distortion should direct their anger not at her but at the Spanish-language media, which consciously and unconsciously continue the centuries-old tradition of denigrating the indigenous, mestizo, and African elements of Latino culture. . . .

Many observers see this as an indicator of a deep inferiority complex. Others view it as a blatant racism by the owners of Spanish-language media.

The truth is that it is a little bit of both.

The inferiority complex is not new. The idea that white is good and dark is bad was brought over by Europeans and beat into the Indian, African, and mestizo populations. To this day, people compliment newborn babies by saying, "Que guerito" ("How light-skinned"), which is synonymous with saying, "How beautiful."

Its destructive nature on the psyche of non-whites is called "stigmatic injury" and was the basis of the victory in Brown v. Topeka Board of Education. Kenneth Clark, a psychologist from the City University of New York, who helped Thurgood Marshall in the historic desegregation case, proved through his experiment with white and brown dolls that black children are psychologically damaged by discrimination and segregation. His studies showed that black children preferred the white dolls because they viewed them as "the good dolls."

A test back then on Latino children would have produced the same results. The same test might produce the same results on Latino children today.

Other studies show that even whites are affected by this type of discrimination. One such experiment, "Blue Eyes, Brown Eyes," was conducted by Jane Elliot, in an Iowa third-grade classroom, shortly after the death of Martin Luther King Jr. One day, students with blue eyes were told they were superior and the students with brown eyes were inferior. Then the roles were reversed. Elliot found that the students who were told they were inferior began to drop off in their school work and were isolated in the play ground. That experiment, which has been replicated often and has been the subject of a number of award-winning documentaries, buttressed Clark's work.

For Latinos, that stigmatic injury is so severe that many adopt European standards of beauty and denigrate all things Indian, African, or mestizo. In its most severe form, many change their names, dye their hair, use blue or green contact lenses and attempt to "pass" for white.

To her credit, Saralegui did conclude that just as "black is beautiful," so too are brown and all the other colors of the human rainbow, including white. Unfortunately, children will never know that if all they ever see is blondes on TV.

47 • Bias Reduction Exercise

DONNA GOLDSTEIN

THE WHOOPI GOLDBERG VIDEO

In one powerful, poignant, and often very funny videotape, Whoopi Goldberg has created a cast of characters who cause us to examine our stereotypes and preconceived notions about a variety of individuals and groups. Among the characters portrayed are an African-American girl who desperately wants to be white; a disabled woman whose mere presence oftens disturbs those around her, as she copes with her disability; a junkie-thief with a Ph.D. who visits the hideaway of Anne Frank; and a thirteen-year-old Valley Girl coping with pregnancy.

Vignettes from this video have been used in prejudice reduction training in varied settings, where it has been found that people of all backgrounds relate to her characters and their stories. Empathy is built and participants find themselves re-examining their most cherished beliefs.

Following are guides for processing the vignette.

Time Frame: 45–60 minutes.

Audio-visual Materials: "Whoopi Goldberg" videotaped concert, Copyright © 1985 by Vestron Video (available at video stores for rental, or can be purchased for $29.95)

EMPATHIZING WITH DISABLED INDIVIDUALS

1. Participants view a ten minute segment of the concert tape. In this humorous and poignant vignette Whoopi portrays a woman who has an unnamed physically degenerative condition. She has recently become engaged to a wonderful guy, a reporter. At first she fears he was motivated by pity, but he encourages her to reconsider her own fears, to swim and dance, and to reject

OBJECTIVE:

To promote empathy, respect, appropriate interaction, and awareness of the challenges faced by disabled people.

previously self-imposed limitations. She discovers that she enjoys these activities, though others have difficulty including her in their world. In her final interaction with the audience she invites them to her wedding and the "disco-pool party" that will follow.

2. In small or large groups, brainstorm the key points. Some of these are:

• Disabilities are not contagious, though some people act as though they are.
• Pity and condescension are not helpful or appreciated.
• Disabled individuals can be invited to participate in almost any sport or activity and allowed to accept or decline the invitation as they choose.
• All people have emotional and physical needs.

3. To the group as a whole, pose the question "What is the primary message of this exercise?"

One key message stated by the character in the video is "Normal is in the eye of the beholder."

4. In pairs or small groups, participants are instructed to share their own "disabilities," such as poor eyesight, poor memory, lack of athletic skills, obesity, or inability to swim. Questions could include:

How have they dealt with the "disability"?
How have they been treated by others?
How does their "disability" make them feel?

If the facilitator has personal anecdotes to share, doing so can help start the discussion. For instance, I had a temporary disability that required me to walk with a cane for several months. Though some individuals were concerned and kind, a number of others were intrusive, rude or unhelpful. Some people made the assumption that I might also be unable to hear or to make decisions for myself.

5. In the large group, participants are invited to share the "disabilities" discussed in the previous session and the insights gained from the activity.

6. Depending on the goals of the program and the length of time available, try these complementary activities:

a. Organize a "Blindwalk", where participants take turns being blindfolded and exploring their environment under the supervision of a "sighted" partner.
b. Let participants attempt to navigate your facility in a wheelchair. For example, one group videotaped a group member trying to open a door and another struggling to get into a bathroom stall, as well as the dozens of people who walked by without offering to help.
c. Attend a wheelchair basketball game or a Special Olympics event.

See *On Prejudice, A Global Perspective*, Daniela Gioseffi, editor. (New York: Anchor Books, 1993, $16.95, ISBN 0-385-46938-1).

Films for the Humanities & Sciences® maintains a catalogue of video and videodisk programs for Multicultural Studies which includes African American, Hispanic American, Native American, and Asian American features, as well as multicultural issues and world cultures. For further information or to obtain a copy, write Films for the Humanities & Sciences, P.O. Box 2053, Princeton, NJ, 08543, 1-800-257-5126, Fax 609-275-3767.

Intercultural Sourcebook: Cross-Culture Training Methods, edited by Sandra M. Fowler and Monica G. Mumford, is an essential resource for anyone concerned with intercultural learning or the development of cross-cultural skills. Six methods of cross-cultural training are examined: role plays, contrast-culture training, simulation games, critical incidents, the culture assimilator, and case studies. Each is introduced by an article outlining the history and use of the method. This is followed by several articles applying the method. Order *Inter-Cultural Sourcebook* from Intercultural Press (see Contributors section).

The Awareness Collection Inc., 5568 Marita Lane, Columbus, OH 43235; 1-800-313-5606, Fax 614-451-1923 is a purveyor of gift items to be used as reminders and mementos of diversity initiatives and training programs. Created by the consulting and training firm of Pope and Associates, Inc., the collection has such useful items as diversity calendars, tote bags, clothing, and note cards.

An additional resource of excellent graphic materials (posters, banners, pins, mugs, etc.) is Rod Enterprises, 123 W. Bellevue Dr., #4, Pasadena, CA 91105, 818-577-8297, Fax 818-577-0199.

Toward Multiculturalism: A Reader in Multicultural Education, edited by Jaime Wurzel. This book illustrates both the dynamics of multiculturalism worldwide and the nature and challenges of multiculturalism in the United States. A range of subjects are discussed, including ethnocentrism, stereotyping, resistance to cultural norms, prejudice and conformity, socialization, verbal and nonverbal communication, and value orientations. Research studies and lively tales of personal experience are presented, from writers such as Peter Farb, Robert Kaplan, Sudhir Kakar, Hitoshi Fukue, and Studs Terkel. Order from Intercultural Press (see contributor section).

Crossing Cultures Through Film, by Ellen Summerfield. She makes a special case for the special nature of film in cross-cultural studies. Because films speak to the emotions as well as the intellect and provide an entry point into controversial topics which otherwise might be too uncomfortable to handle, they are a valuable teaching resource. It includes clear direction to educators on how to use films most effectively and how to capture and channel the reactions of the students. Over seventy films are discussed, and the book includes a section on film and video sourcing and availability. Order from Intercultural Press (see contributor section).

Tribes: How Race, Religion, and Identity Determine Success in the New Global Economy, by Joel Kotkin (New York: Random House, $12, ISBN 0-679-75299-4).

Three leading sources of information, training, and support materials for classroom-based diversity programs are listed below:

ADL: A WORLD OF DIFFERENCE Institute, is an education and diversity training program of the Anti-Defamation League. Operating in 29 U.S. cities, A WORLD OF DIFFERENCE workshops provide anti-bias training with a multicultural education perspective for all members of the school community: teachers, administrators, students, and parents. Since its inception over 230,435 elementary and secondary school educators have been trained to deliver their "A CLASSROOM OF DIFFERENCE" program. ADL provides extensive curriculum and support materials. Contact the Anti-Defamation League, A WORLD OF DIFFERENCE Institute, 823 United Nations Plaza, New York, NY 10017, 212-885-7800, Fax 212-490-0187.

The Teaching Tolerance Education Project has as its mission to make sure that every classroom in America is equipped with tools to help young people learn to live together in harmony. A new module designed for junior high school through college audiences is entitled "The Shadow of Hate: A History of Intolerance in America." The video, book, and teacher's guide is available at no charge to schools. Their first video and text kit, "America's Civil Rights Movement" is available for $25 (prepaid). *Teaching Tolerance* is about tolerance and diversity. All are available from the Southern Poverty Law Center, 400 Washington Ave., Montgomery, AL 36104, Fax 334-264-3121.

The National Conference is a human relations organization dedicated to fighting bias, bigotry, and racism in America. It promotes understanding and respect through advocacy, conflict resolution, and education. Over 100,000 elementary school students have benefitted from their role-playing program, "How to Get Along with Others." They provide free training programs (school systems pay direct expenses only) and have extensive support materials. Contact The National Conference, 71 Fifth Ave., Suite 1150, New York, NY 10003, 212-807-8440, Fax 212-727-0166.

Diversity Under Fire—Right, Left, and Center

North Americans have valued continuous improvement long before it was fashionable, both in society and in the workplace. Diversity efforts themselves have emerged from a belief that what is not working in our culture can be corrected, healed, fixed, renewed, made better. Now from this same cultural source, from this relentless discontent, comes the critique of efforts to make things better. Diversity, like every other effort or institution, comes "under fire" for what it has left undone and for what, at least in the critic's eyes, is done poorly.

Sometimes our dissatisfaction with diversity efforts is simply a matter of impatience with slow progress. At other times, it signals that certain efforts have served their purpose and should be renewed or replaced. The debate over one such effort, Affirmative Action, has taken on such massive proportions that we devote much of Section 9 to it.

In this section, we focus more on the philosophy and practice of diversity itself than on its legal scaffolding. Integration and inclusion are the buzzwords of late 1990s diversity management practitioners. Integration means that diversity needs to be an ongoing, indispensable part of everything we do in organizations, planning, teamwork, communication, quality efforts, personnel management, training, marketing, etc., rather than a special program. Inclusion means a shift in focus from paying exclusive attention to so-called legally "protected" groups, to helping everyone actively participate in and benefit from diversity efforts.

This shift is not easy, since it challenges a number of positions that have become "politically correct" dogma. Primary among these is the negative assessment that Euro American men both individually and as a group are "the problem" or the primary obstacle to successful diversity. If I belong to a class of people that has been historically discriminated against, and therefore am not at fault for where I am socially or economically, does it necessarily follow that someone must be blamed in order to change things? If, as is lately the case, the "white" man must become the scapegoat, how can he be an asset rather than an adversary in creating a more just society?

Downplaying the Anglo focus of Euro American culture in universities and schools to make room for the cultural treasures of the countless citizens of other backgrounds makes good sense, but this does not imply eliminating it altogether. It is important that we are all exposed to the richness of our own background and relevant perspectives of our neighbors' cultures. Eliminating Euro American culture or teaching it only to attack its deficiencies does not serve people of that background or prepare those of different backgrounds to function effectively in contexts where Euro American culture predominates.

Hardest to assess is the effect that emphasizing differences has on the bonds between diverse citizens and our search for the common good of all. As Arthur Schlesinger raises the question: How much emphasis on differences leads to disunity? Does today's disunity mean that we are walking close to the edge of anarchy? Are fundamental freedoms, such as our freedom of speech and assembly, being curtailed by political correctness? Does the stridency of "special interests" threaten the integrity of our North American nations? Does Canada's lingering constitutional crisis, for example, forebode similar polarization in the United States?

Perhaps, though, the conflict itself provides the raw material from which new and better relationships develop. Perhaps our divisions benefit us in the long run, by highlighting the work we have cut out for ourselves to create more equitable, inclusive societies. Much depends on our willingness and skills to hear the voices of our fellow citizens, left, right, and center.

These are some of the main issues on which our contributors seek to shed light in the following readings.

48 • Our Common Citizenship

DAVID S. BERNSTEIN

Eighty-one years ago, W. E. B. Du Bois introduced the magazine of the newly-founded National Association for the Advancement of Colored People, *The Crisis*, with these words:

"[*The Crisis*] will stand for the rights of men, irrespective of color or race, for the highest ideals of American democracy, and for reasonable but earnest and persistent attempts to gain these rights and realize these ideals. The magazine will be the organ of no clique or party and will avoid personal rancor of all sorts. In the absence of proof to the contrary it will assume honesty of purpose on the part of all men, North and South, white and black."

Du Bois understood the importance of appealing to the core values of this country in order to end discrimination against black Americans. He was not alone. Other giants of the civil rights movement, from Frederick Douglass to Booker T. Washington to Martin Luther King, Jr., despite differences on many points, recognized the power inherent in the manifesto of the Declaration of Independence: "We hold these truths to be self-evident, that all men are created equal, that they are endowed by their creator with certain inalienable rights. . . ." These men believed in the promise of America, and they believed that one day the American dream could be fulfilled by all men, regardless of color.

This editorial kicked off the first issue of *Diversity & Division: A Critical Journal of Race & Culture* in the fall of 1991. Eleven issues were published over a four-year period. Currently inactive, but its owner and editors hope to renew publication in the Summer of 1996. Subscriptions and back issues available for $4 each from: 45472 Holiday Dr., Suite 10, Sterling VA 20166; 703-709-6620; Fax 703-709-6615.

However, in the last twenty-five years, the issue of race has clouded many Americans' view of our nation. Certain black leaders, in particular, express cynicism about whether the American experiment is meant for anyone other than white people. Supreme Court Justice Thurgood Marshall, once a staunch defender of our core values, refers to the Constitution as fundamentally flawed. Other prominent black Americans demand that whites pay "reparations" to atone for slavery and Jim Crow.

This sort of thinking has penetrated beyond just a few black critics. In today's environment, where every "recognized minority group"—meaning Hispanics, Asians, Native Americans, blacks, et al.—has its own self-appointed leadership, the rhetoric of victimization has become standard fare. Aside from the obvious absurdity of lumping together people from dozens of different cultures under the term "Asian," "Hispanic," or the catch-all "minority," this way of thinking is inimical to American democracy. In America, millions of individuals from diverse racial and ethnic backgrounds have been molded into citizens by their adherence to common values. But a contrary concept—that America is not a society of citizens but a collection of races struggling for power—threatens the foundations of American democracy, and has poisoned our public discourse about race, making it the most talked about but least understood subject in the nation.

For many today, race is the defining characteristic of every individual. It is necessary, we are told, for people to feel good about their "racial identity" before they can feel good about themselves. But when character becomes equated with color, racial minorities will inevitably suffer the most. For if white Americans begin to believe, again, that the problems within poor black and Hispanic neighborhoods are the result of inferior genetics, then we can expect bigots to use this as a justification for a return to a Jim Crow society—or worse.

As a young black man, I and many of my peers are profoundly disturbed by these trends. We believe in the idea of an America of individuals, and in the concept of common citizenship. We recognize the danger of group categorization, the concept that allowed the horrors of slavery, the Holocaust, and apartheid, and now threatens to divide America into warring races and tribal factions.

W. E. B. Du Bois, *The Soul of Black Folk* (New York: New American Library, 1969). ISBN 5181423. Also on audiotape from Blackstone Audio Books, Ashland, OR, 1993. For further information on the life and writings of W. E. B. Du Bois, see the Pulitzer Prize-winning biography by David Lewering Lewis, *W. E. B. Du Bois: Biography of a Race*, (New York: Henry Holt, 1993).

Upheaval in the University—A six part program of audiocassettes (each 30-minutes long) that explore the increasingly contentious debate over the future of American higher education. Taped on location at campuses throughout the United States and hosted by Jonathan Karl. The program includes over 50 thought-provoking interviews with commentators like: William F. Buckley (*National Review*), Arthur Schlesinger Jr. (*The Disuniting of America*), Nadine Strossen (ACLU), Lynne Cheney (NEH), Robert Lukefahr (Madison Center), and Reginald Wilson (ACE). Three cassettes for $19.95 (price includes postage and handling, prepay by check or money order. Contact Leslie Brown, Radio America, 1030 15th St., NW, Suite 700, Washington, D.C. 20005; 202-408-0944, Fax 202-408-1087).

49 · White Men and Diversity

WARREN FARRELL

*I*ncorporating the feelings of white men gives white men a stake in the diversity process so they become supporters rather than resisters. But incorporating their feelings is more easily said than done. Why? Most presentations about white men get caught in one of two traps: either the compassion for white men discounts the perspectives of women and minorities; or, we set out to sensitize the white man to minorities without sensitizing the minorities to the white man.

But wait . . . haven't white men been expressing their feelings for centuries? No. The way a white man became successful was to *repress* his feelings, not express his feelings. Understanding that begins our sensitivity training—what would the white man say if he had learned to express his feelings?

A NEW FRAMEWORK FOR HOW BOTH SEXES AND ALL RACES CAN UNDO THE MISUNDERSTANDINGS OF THE PAST QUARTER CENTURY.

Feminism did a wonderful job of freeing women from stereotyped sex roles. Yet no one freed men from their stereotyped roles. Specifically, the women's movement helped women become free to be whoever they wanted to be—mother, executive, secretary, plumber or some combination thereof. But as the women's movement helped women who were denied the option to work outside the home achieve that option, we made the false assumption that men had always had the option to work. In fact, men never had the *option* to work; they had always had the *obligation* to work.

By missing the fact that earning income was the male obligation, we falsely concluded that men producing income meant men had the power. But *power is not about being obligated to earn money that someone else spends while the earner dies*

Question for dads

Ask your dad (or an older male in your social circle): "(Dad), if you didn't have (me and) the family to support, what would you most loved to have done with your life?"

SHOE JEFF MacNELLY

SEAGULL-AMERICANS. PEACOCK-AMERICANS. MALLARD-AMERICANS...

WE ALL HAVE SOMETHING IN COMMON.   YEAH.

HYPHENS.

Reprinted by permission: Tribune Media Services.

sooner. Power is not about obligation; it is about control over one's life. Does this mean women had the power? No. *Historically, neither sex had power; both sexes had roles:* the women's role, to raise children; the men's role, to raise money.

Our blindness to men's obligation created a double standard in the way we viewed the sexes' roles: we labeled women's role of raising children "sacrifice," "contribution," and "slavery." But when it came to men's role, we ignored the sacrifice the men made to earn money (often to make his children's life better while he died earlier), and instead called his obligation "privilege." And "patriarchy," "power" and "dominance."

This left a generation of men feeling misunderstood. It prevented them from hearing that diversity programs might include them.

What experiences does the successful heterosexual white man have in common with other men, such as the African-American man, poor man, homeless man, the Native American man and the gay man? Each lives in a world in which men are ridiculed, ignored or ostracized if they are either not successful, or do not use that success to support a woman. African-American men are ridiculed by African-American women when they aren't successful; poor men and homeless men are ignored; Native American men were worshipped until their defeat by white men prevented them from being successful providers. Gay men were ostracized by everyone because they refused to even play the game: the game of using their success to support a woman.

Why have heterosexual white men gone from hero to villains? Until recently, almost all heterosexual white men supported women for life. But in the 1960's, divorces left millions of women, who had grown up with

---

PLAYER diversiPLAY™

Role play this scenario with a colleague or friend. Read this role for yourself, give the book to your partner to read the section printed on the facing page. Then role play the situation for a few moments and discuss the experience together.

One of your European-American co-workers has an excellent performance record in his or her past 14 years with the company and relates well to others. Recently, this person seems upset. When you ask, she or he complains of being "run over by affirmative action" and says, "my career is at a standstill." Respond sensibly and sensitively to your role play partner who will play the role of this co-worker.

the dream of Prince Charming supporting her for life, instead faced with the reality of that dream falling apart all around her. Disappointed dreams breed anger.

At the same time, the white man feels caught between a rock and a hard place: still feeling he will not receive a woman's love if he consistently earns less money than a woman, but now feeling that if he earns more money he will be *accused* of it ("You have the power") rather than loved for it.

In my corporate workshops, I ask each participant to understand how we have blinded ourselves to men's deepest desires—their real power—by asking themselves, "Have you ever asked your dad, **'Dad, if you didn't have me and the family to support, what would *you* most loved to have done with your life?'**"

PARTNER diversiPLAY™

Read these instructions SILENTLY before starting the role play. Play the role to represent the following point of view, whether or not you agree with it.

You are impatient for a promotion and a raise. Your daughter is entering college this year and you have a son who will start next year. You are upset because your child does not qualify for financial aid although you are having a hard time making ends meet. Nothing, you feel, will make up for damage to your career that the preferential treatment of women and minorities caused.

This exercise helps each participant see how, as many of our dads followed income rather than fulfillment, they may have forfeited doing things that were more creative—like art and music—because, well, art history pays less than engineering or construction. Our dad, then, may have taken a job he liked less but earned more so his children could take jobs that they liked more that earned less, and so his wife could have a decent home over her head.

This experience, then, transfers a core understanding about men from the intellectual level to the emotional level: That *men never had the option to work*, they had the obligation to work; that fulfilling that obligation was not "male privilege" or "male dominance," but the fulfillment of responsibility.

This allows us to look at earning money as the traditional male form of nurturing—his financial womb; his contribution to love. Men who performed the obligation well received approval, just as women who performed their obligation of "good mother" well received approval. Obviously both sexes performed these obligations because they loved their family and received satisfaction from their happiness. But this is love, not "patriarchy," "privilege" and "male dominance."

Just as Betty Friedan defined for women "the problem that has no name," I am defining for men "the problem that has a deceptive name"—men's socialization to call "power" what any other group would call powerlessness. For example, if *only* women, Jews, or Blacks had to register for the draft, they would call it genocide. In contrast, men learned to call it "power" and to even accept medals as bribes "to die." Similarly, if we told only women that being female meant being expected to earn money someone else spent while she died sooner, no woman would call that expectation "power." Men do. This paradigm shift in our view of power is harder to grasp than it would have been before the women's movement, because as we have empathized with women's experience of powerlessness, we made the false assumption that men's expectations to assume responsibility in government and business was male privilege rather than the male role.

50 · The Disuniting of America

ARTHUR M. SCHLESINGER JR.

(i) See *Our Country, Our Culture, The Politics of Political Correctness,* by Edith Kurzwell and William Phillips. (Boston: Partisan Review, 1994).

*T*he cult of ethnicity has reversed the movement of American history, producing a nation of minorities—or at least of minority spokesmen—less interested in joining with the majority in common endeavor than in declaring their alienation from an oppressive, white, patriarchal, racist, sexist, classist society. The ethnic ideology inculcates the illusion that membership in one or another ethnic group is the basic American experience.

[However,] most Americans . . . see themselves primarily as individuals and only secondarily and trivially as adherents of a group. Nor is harm done when ethnic groups display pride in their historic past or in their contributions to the American present. But the division of society into fixed ethnicities nourishes a culture of victimization and a contagion of inflammable sensitivities. And when a vocal and visible minority pledges primary allegiance to their groups, whether ethnic, sexual, religious, or, in rare cases (communist, fascist), political, it presents a threat to the brittle bonds of national identity that hold this diverse and fractious society together. . . . The genius of America lies in its capacity to forge a single nation from peoples of remarkably diverse racial, religious, and ethnic origins. It has done so because democratic principles provide both the philosophical bond of union and practical experience in civic participation. The American Creed en-

Donna Binder, Impact Visuals

visages a nation composed of individuals making their own choices and accountable to themselves, not a nation based on inviolable ethnic communities.

51 • Legacy of Slavery: A Conservative View

EDITORS' REVIEW OF OPINIONS FROM COLUMNIST THOMAS SOWELL

*T*homas Sowell, an economist with the Hoover Institution of Stanford University, observes in *Race and Culture* that from public schools through university, U.S. students are taught that slavery was an institution peculiar to the U.S. and Western Civilization. To North Americans the word "slavery" usually connotes the enslavement of Africans, when, in fact, slavery was:

> "one of the oldest and most widespread institutions on Earth. Slavery existed in the Western Hemisphere before Columbus' ships appeared on the horizon, and it existed in Europe, Asia, Africa, and the Middle East for thousands of years. Slavery was older than Islam, Buddhism, or Christianity, and both the secular and religious moralists of societies around the world accepted human bondage, not only as a fact of life but as something requiring no special moral justification. Slavery was "peculiar" in the United States only because human bondage was inconsistent with the principles on which this nation was founded, historically, however, it was those principles which were peculiar, not slavery" (p. 186).

> "After lasting for thousands of years, slavery was destroyed over most of the planet in a period of about one century, and over virtually all of the planet within two centuries . . . [T]he impetus for the destruction of slavery came not from any of the objective, material, or economic factors so often assumed to be dominant in history, but from a moral revulsion [to it]" (p. 210).

Sowell's contention is that there is an "ideological agenda" which is being served by media intellectuals and academic liberals. This agenda is to indulge in a mindset of blaming and fault-finding, which then fuels the need for "problem solving" by a cadre of self-serving "experts," multicultural teachers, and diversity consultants (see also Sowell's column "Effrontery and Gall, Inc." in *Forbes*, February 27, 1993).

Thomas Sowell

In *Race and Culture* Sowell provides an in-depth account of the various forms and practices of slavery throughout history. In addition, he attempts to provide an economic analysis which calls into question some unquestioned "truths" about the institution. For example, he does not believe there is significant evidence to support the claim that "slavery advanced the economic level of those societies in which it existed on a mass scale" (p. 214). Sowell believes that slavery was not a particularly profitable or efficient institution, nor did it create wealth. Rather, he identifies evidence to support the notion that wealthy societies became slave-holders for a sense of personal aggrandizement, or as a consequence of their disdain for work. Further, he asserts that racist beliefs about the inferiority of other cultures did not lead to their enslavement, but that the institution of slavery, over time, led to a dogma of racism. Sowell believes current ideological passions have distorted the real history of slavery and resulted in self-serving interpretations by liberals and multiculturalists.

> "Another distortion of history is to assume a priori that social problems affecting contemporary blacks in the United States are a 'legacy of slavery.' Broken families, lower rates of marriage, and lower rates of labor force participation have been among the social phenomena explained and excused on grounds of a 'legacy of slavery.'"

Sowell cites evidence to contradict this, namely: (1) the marriage rates were higher for black than for whites in the early 1900s, (2) from 1890 to 1950 (based on census figures) blacks had higher rates of labor force participation than whites, and (3) during the time of slavery and for generations thereafter, the majority of black children were raised in two parent homes. Sowell believes that the origin of disparities and differences in behavior patterns between blacks and whites must be found in our more recent history, not historical oppression.

Sowell's opinions are an anathema to current progressive thinking and demonstrate the range among social/economic/political thinkers. Conservative voices, such as his, will need to be included and analyzed in the dialogue about diversity if innovative solutions to current dilemmas are to be found. He is clearly a "maverick," a status he enjoys, and his book distributors capitalize on his controversial status as an African American conservative in referring to *Race and Culture* by saying "if a white man wrote this book, the liberals would lynch him."

ⓘ *Race and Culture* (New York: Harper Collins, 1994, ISBN 0-465-06796-4).

Creativity in diversity initiatives abounds. For example, the National Aeronautics and Space Administration at Ames Research Center in Moffett Field, California, has found a way to encourage its people to pay attention to the diversity on a day-to-day basis. At the close of their 1995 Diversity Conference, Ross Shaw, Chair of the Planning Committee, passed out to all participants a plastic ruler punched to fit everyone's day planner with the conference logo and the reminder, "Ames Values and Nurtures Diversity in the Workplace." Placed next to one's agenda and to-do list, it reminds the user that there is a diversity dimension to every facet of one's work.

52 • Making Diversity a Way of Life

GEORGE F. SIMONS INTERVIEWS MERLIN POPE

GEORGE SIMONS: As an experienced practitioner in diversity, what do you see that is working and what's not?

MERLIN POPE: The biggest thing we see is that people do diversity training and sometimes [they and the companies they work with] think that all diversity training is equivalent—it really isn't in terms of its balance and the impact that it has on the participants. Beyond the actual training, we have come to recognize that training by itself is not sufficient to make cultural change happen. You have to put something in place that causes people to practice what you teach. For example, the area where we've been the most successful at training in organizations is that of safety. We teach safety concepts. Then we come back and we have lab practices; we have fire drills; we wear safety equipment. We make safety a way of life.

SIMONS: It's a long process.

POPE: With diversity we have to do very much the same kind of thing. But most people in the diversity business don't have a clue about how to do that. They do things like having cultural lunches, which may be nice, but they have nothing to do with changing the culture as it relates to the quality of interaction among people of diverse backgrounds. Some years ago we developed a program called "consulting pairs" where we literally take people—line people in the organization—and give them extended training in the area of diversity. They become resources to the rest of the organization about these issues. They're diverse in their background; they're diverse in their level; and they work on "joining people up," and on conflict resolution. They are relationship consultants. They devote about 10 percent of their time to this. What really makes change happen,

It doesn't matter how many times you retrain; you've got to make it a way of life.

Jim West, Impact Visuals

If you don't want to provide special treatment, then you've got to be completely committed to creating true equal opportunity. Those are really very different perspectives.

however, is not the 10 percent that they dedicate to this, but the 90 percent of the time that they're doing their job. We literally seed line change agents back into the organization.

SIMONS: A very interesting innovation.

POPE: When human resource people come around, employees change their behavior. And when human resource people leave, employees change back to how they were. If you want to achieve real change, you have to put line change agents in the organization. And it makes a difference.

SIMONS: Okay. That's good.

POPE: This is the most powerful thing that's going on in diversity and changing the culture. It doesn't matter how many times you retrain; you've got to make it a way of life. People don't do that. You have to look at systems and policies. Training deals with practices; "consulting pairs" deals with the culture; a diversity committee deals with strategy. So if you address them all, you have an organization change intervention similar to one initiated to increase quality or increase productivity. But many trainers don't have that kind of organizational development perspective.

SIMONS: You have people walking the walk and talking the talk every day and being resources for how they actually do what they do.

POPE: They actually change the environment. For instance, it has a greater impact if I'm telling a racist joke and my coworker says to me, "Merlin, I wish you wouldn't do that around me. I'm trying to grow in this area." That will change the culture. It's like smoking: you tell people not to smoke, they keep on smoking. You tell people "I wish you wouldn't smoke around me," and you get nonsmoking buildings. If I'm doing something and my male coworker pulls me off to the side and says, "Merlin, that's inappropriate around here; that's sexual harassment," it becomes a lot easier for men to hold men accountable for sexual harassment than it is for a woman to worry about "Was it?" "Is it?" "Should I say something about it?" "I really want it to stop, but I don't want to make a big deal about it."

SIMONS: Yes.

POPE: People think that it's only about leadership from the top. Well, you do have to have leadership from the top. But you also have to have leadership every day right out there where people are working together if you really want to change the environment. By using the strategy of consulting pairs we seed leadership in at every level.

SIMONS: One section of this *Fieldbook* is about Affirmative Action. What do you think will happen in this area?

POPE: I don't know where the field is going. I know where I've been. This observation's twenty years late for me. Affirmative Action, although it was necessary, will not get us all the way to equal opportunity. The problem is that we started out talking about equality of opportunity, but it was so difficult to measure we switched to equality of results, that is, the numbers game. But equality of results never guarantees equality of opportunity; sometimes it even precludes it. I listen to this discussion today, and I tell you I think of myself as a product of affirmative action. But there comes a time when you have to move beyond it. Our focus is on the numbers and what we've got to be focused on is how to create equal opportunity. It is easier to give somebody "special treatment" than it is to proactively create equal opportunity.

Managers in corporations have made a significant change in terms of the quality of their interraction with women and minorities. What they do poorly is to hold coworkers accountable for effective interaction with other coworkers, such as with a woman. The problem is we treat prejudice as though it is sacrosanct, as if everybody has a right to their own. Clearly it is a reasonable expectation of employment, not an imposition, that you will work effectively with everybody in the workplace.

We must teach managers to hold all people accountable to that standard. Because if we don't, we forfeit our right to hold anyone accountable to that standard. And therein lies an incredible opportunity for proactively creating true equal opportunity. You see, people have just missed the focus of where the intervention should be. I don't want special treatment. Special treatment undermines my development, my credibility. When I hear Newt Gingrich talk about the end of Affirmative Action, what he means is "and do nothing."

SIMONS: I agree with you there.

POPE: When I say I think we ought to get beyond affirmative action, I mean the following: If you don't want to provide special treatment, then you've got to be completely committed to creating true equal opportunity. Those are really very different perspectives. As I look at the future and at my clients, this topic is not going away.

SIMONS: When we look at today's U.S. economy, at all the organizational efforts to downsize, to become competitive, etc., at the widening gap between the top and the lowest wage earners, I'm particularly concerned that we're not paying attention to emerging class issues. True, people of all color and women may earn less per capita, but white poverty level wage earners now outnumber all poverty level people of color. There's a big proletariat out there that nobody is talking to except to label them "backlash. . . ."

POPE: . . . which is absolutely fertile ground for the Aryan Nation and other disenchanted people . . . . You used to be able to go to high school, come out, get a job, and make a good living, and it's not there anymore. People look at me and I'm a black guy who's successful, and they blame Affirmative Action for why they're not doing well. It's kind of scary that I become the object of other people's frustration.

SIMONS: Exactly. Do you see this question of class emerging?

See Nico Swaan's piece on page 225.

ⓘ This excerpt from "Different from What? Diversity as a Performance Issue," *Training Magazine*, May 1995; pp. 25–32.

POPE: Yes! The truth of the matter is that at some point race will probably not be as big an issue as it is today. Class will be more so. If you look at Europe, class is the issue, for the most part, and has been for a long time.

53 • What If It Isn't Just Lousy Facilitators?

JACK GORDON (TRAINING)

My daughter's seventh-grade English textbook is *Literature and Language,* published by McDougal, Littell & Co. of Evanston, Ill. It is a collection of short stories, poems, screenplays and nonfiction pieces by writers ranging from Alfred Lord Tennyson to Alice Walker, from O. Henry to Anna Quindlen, from Robert Frost to someone named Virginia Driving Hawk Sneve. The selections are divided into "units," with titles such as "A Matter of Perspective," "A Question of Identity," and "Scales of Justice." Each unit is further divided into two parts.

From the introduction to "Declarations of Independence," Part 1 of Unit 5: "Each of us likes to express our individuality in a different way. For some of us, it may be the clothes we choose to wear or the way we fix our hair. Others express their unique personality through their behavior. Still others express who they are by standing up for their beliefs on important social issues. . . . In these selections, note the different ways people express their own special beliefs about themselves."

From the introduction to another section called "Doors of Understanding": "We open the door to new ideas and new relationships, but close it to people we do not like. An open door suggests an inviting attitude; a closed door implies, 'Do not disturb.'"

Both of those passages easily could have been lifted from the participant handouts in any run-of-the-mill corporate diversity training workshop. The rhetoric of "differences" now forms an unbroken chain from the elementary schools to the executive boardrooms, and the material does not necessarily become more demanding as the student advances. The basic "lessons" that diversity training generally has to teach are platitudes, as banal as happy-face stickers, as unobjectionable as a bowl of lowfat yogurt. No, we shouldn't close our doors of understanding to others just because we don't know them. Yes, we should respect the individuality of everyone. We should also eat our vegetables and drink our milk.

How can training programs built around such innocuous messages backfire hard enough and often enough that a whole subclass of diversity consultants now makes a living by patching over the group antagonisms created by other consultants?

The answer is simple, answers William Daniels, president of American Consulting and Training in Mill Valley, Calif. At its center, most diversity training is about racial prejudice, gender politics or homosexuality. "This stuff is all white hot, and we don't really know what to do about it," Daniels says. "Corporations touch it and are frightened by the intensity of what they discover. You either excite things you wish you hadn't or you run into legal repercussions."

Every diversity trainer in America, including those who make the messes, will decry the legions of fly-by-night operators now selling their services as workshop leaders. They will warn that diversity training is no job for amateurs. "It requires very skilled facilitators and a very safe environment," says Sue Thompson, director of human resources development for Levi Strauss Co. in San Francisco.

But Daniels argues that the problem is more fundamental. In the first place, he says, social science research dating back 50 years has documented that putting blacks and whites together in groups to talk about discrimination, racial history, commonalities and differences is not an effective way to reduce prejudice. In fact, "talking about the problem" in this fashion is more likely to reinforce prejudiced attitudes. The evidence suggests, he says, that it is far more effective simply to put blacks and whites together to work on a common task, especially a task at which they can succeed.

Thompson disagrees, as, of course, do most diversity training supporters. She says her experience has been that encounter group-style workshops can help a great deal: "I've found it very powerful to see racism and sexism playing out in the room. In some cases I was part of it, sometimes I was colluding in it, and in some cases I was the target of it. To have that identified right when it happens—to have someone say, 'Wait, let's examine this'—is very valuable."

Daniels is not persuaded. And he has another objection. "You really can't do much of anything constructive about prejudice and stereotyping," he says, "as long as you keep talking about people in terms of groups."

That is, whenever I speak to you not in my capacity as an individual but as a representative of the group "white males," and you speak to me not as an individual but as a spokesperson for the "black female" point of view, then we are portraying ourselves as stereotypes. And we probably will just refine each other's prejudices.

That's mostly what current diversity training programs do, regardless of who's facilitating them, Daniels charges. Because for all its talk about seeing people as unique individuals, the diversity movement is firmly wedded to the notion of identity groups.

At the Midwestern headquarters of an international insurance company, a corporate diversity campaign ran afoul of Christmas. A few years ago, the traditional yuletide decorations in the lobby were deemed insensitive to the values of non-Christian employees. It is unclear whether the original indignant party actually was someone with virulently anti-tinsel religious views or merely a person taking offense on behalf of some unspecified "others" who might be offended. Regardless, the company had announced its intention to value cultural diversity, and this looked like the stuff, all right. Down came the decorations.

The following year, a group wishing to restore the holiday atmosphere came up with a multidenominational alternative. Back into the lobby went the Christmas tree and the other decorations. And in the center of it all—a menorah.

This really did offend Jewish employees, who had to explain that the menorah is a private symbol, not intended for public display in office lobbies. Down came the decorations.

Finally, this past December, Christmas was rescued. A group of Hispanic employees stepped forward to declare that *their* cultural values required the tree and all the trimmings. The Hispanics' grievance-group status trumped that of the protesters. Identity politics saved the day.

Managing diversity is cast by proponents as a performance issue. What with the global economy and the changing demographics of the national labor force, "valuing differences" is supposed to be a business imperative, not just a nice thing to do. But aside from the fact that humor in the workplace is said to enhance productivity, any performance advantages . . . are hard to spot. So is the reasoning behind claims that anything resembling the Christmas tree caper . . . will somehow encourage respect and understanding among different groups.

No doubt there are plenty of excuses for the desire to use white males as punching bags or even to take the Christmas-decoration crowd down a peg. But when these exercises are cast as educational experiences from which the males or the decorators are likely to emerge with a finer appreciation for the values and feelings of others, a question arises: What theory of the human personality are we operating from?

Further, with victimhood having become such a popular stance in the United States, the distinctions grow finer every day between "things I don't happen to approve of" and "things that oppress me, so you shouldn't be allowed to do them." Some of the complaining that goes on in the name of failure to respect diversity is about pretty trivial stuff. As one level-headed diversity trainer likes to put it: It's true that some people need to develop more cultural-sensitivity skills. But other people need to develop some "get over it" skills.
—Jack Gordon

So what happens? Daniels describes a five-day leadership program for first-line supervisors, in which one day was devoted to exploring diversity. "They brought in a black male to teach that piece. It was very rough. Some of the attendees didn't return from the first break. The other group members went looking for them and found them wandering the halls."

Why were the defectors upset? Sometimes the answer was: "This guy is telling me what I believe about black people, and maybe I do, and I'm confused." In other cases, it was: "This guy is telling me what I believe, and he's wrong. But I'm going to spend the rest of this week with my learning group, defending myself from the prejudice he has created against *me*."

Before running the leadership course again, the sponsoring company gave more coaching to the diversity facilitator. "But the second time out, things got worse," Daniels says. "There was an open explosion. The whole group voted with its feet."

The underlying problem, he suggests, was this: "The leader was operating from the assumption that 'I speak for blacks; I can tell you how we're treated and what you think about blacks.' That's the classic diversity approach: 'I have the right to speak for my group, and to tell you, from our perspective, how you people act and what you think.'"

The whites were merely antagonized and learned nothing. "And I don't doubt," Daniels adds, "that the leader went away saying: 'Well, there it is—and when you show it to them, they deny it.' So he didn't learn anything either. He's out there somewhere, still convinced he's doing good."

The real skills of "valuing diversity," Daniels maintains, involve classic communication issues, such as psychologist Chris Argyris's principle of double-loop learning. *Listen* to the other person. Don't take for granted that you share the same fundamental assumptions about the issue you're discussing. But more than that, never take for granted that you know what the other person's basic assumptions *are*.

There's diversity training's fatal flaw, Daniels says. It's good at pointing out that assumptions may not be the same. But then it lumps people into identity groups and proceeds to tell us what each group's assumptions are. Thus, it perpetuates stereotypes. And when you're trying to communicate with any individual human being, stereotypes of any sort cannot help you. "Good" or "bad," they can only get in the way.

54 • In-Basket Memo

ALAN RICHTER

Memo to: _____

From: The Executive Committee

Date: _____

Subject: Success Through Diversity Initiative

After much debate and soul-searching, our committee has decided, effective immediately, to completely drop the diversity initiative throughout our organization.

We have taken this bold, decisive action for the following reasons:

- We simply must admit that we are <u>not</u> a diverse workforce, and do not necessarily want to be.
- We are currently committed to extensive financial sacrifices over the next 18 months and simply cannot afford any expensive new initiatives that do not directly impact the bottom line.
- Diversity is not being singled out; there are a number of other initiatives that are to be cut.
- We sincerely believe in the integrity of our workforce and trust that all employees will quite naturally respect diversity without our executive support.

We apologize for having set up a task force and begun planning, but must cut out this initiative right away. We appreciate your compliance.

ⓘ This activity can be a role play or a team discussion activity. If a role play, have participants act out the roles of Executive Committee chairperson, Vice President of Human Resources, the EEO/AA Officer, two concerned employees, and the Manager for Public Affairs. If a group discussion, have participants address these questions: 1. What's your definition of diversity? 2. Do diversity initiatives impact the bottom line? 3. How do you determine whether they do or not? 4. What do you think various reactions to the memo might be?

55 · Diversity and Organization Performance

JACK GORDON (TRAINING MAGAZINE)

Hallmark Cards Inc. last year formed an ethnic business center at its Kansas City, Mo., headquarters to market special lines of holiday and greeting cards to black, Hispanic, and Jewish customers. Before the center was established, people in six or seven different units spent maybe 15 percent of their time on cards intended for minority markets, says Mary Towse, Hallmark's director of corporate diversity. "What we were hearing from Jewish customers, for instance, was: 'You don't really seem to understand Jewish culture or Jewish spirituality.'" Since the ethnic center was created, she says, sales of the lines have surged.

Not all employees in the center are black, Hispanic, or Jewish, though those groups are well represented, Towse says. Like Hayles, she is careful to explain that the principle at work here is not that only blacks can market effectively to black customers, Jews to Jews and so on. That suggestion is anathema to diversity advocates, partly because of its obvious corollary: Only WASPs can do business with WASPs.

Still, the often-heard claim that a company's labor force and its management team should reflect the demographics of its customer base is more than just a social-virtue goal masquerading as a financial argument.

Pillsbury's Robert Hayles vice president of human resources and diversity, asserts "Tons of data now show an unambiguous relationship between diversity and financial performance in business, and between diversity and agency performance in the public arena."

Hayles conducted one such study himself. He selected 10 companies in the food industry, including Pillsbury, and noted their financial performance (earnings, total return to investors) over one year, five years, and 10 years. Then he asked an independent group to rank the "diversity performance" of those companies. Measures included the number of women and minorities in the work force and in management, purchasing policies giving favored status to female and minority suppliers, the extent of diversity training for employees and managers, and external ratings from magazines such as *Prepared Foods*, *Black Enterprise*, and *Good Housekeeping*, which have ranked companies as good or bad places to work for women or minorities.

Next Hayles ran a computer correlation of financial performance with diversity performance for the 10 food companies. For one year (1993-1994), the correlation was .32—positive but not significant. For five years it was .79—highly significant. For 10 years the correlation was stronger still: .84. That doesn't prove

This excerpt is from "Different from What?: Diversity as a Performance Issue," *Training Magazine*, May 1995, pp. 25–32. For a subscription, call 1-800-328-4329.

a cause-and-effect relationship, Hayles admits. "But along with many other studies, it suggests that diversity is a strong contributor to financial performance."

What other studies? Hayles is writing a book about them. He cites one by researcher Dennis Kravitz that matched a set of companies for financial performance over a five-year period in the 1980s. Those with "progressive human resource policies," defined very broadly, showed more growth in sales and profits.

Advocates of diversity often claim that it leads to improved performance and contributes to bottom-line results. However, it is just as likely that organizations that perform well are the ones most likely to undertake diversity initiatives. Simply because there is a correlation between diversity and profitability does not link them in a cause-and-effect fashion. Conceivably, some third factor might be the reason for both results. Cause-and-effect relationships are quite difficult to prove, and optimistic thinking often takes the place of rigorous research.

56 • Free Speech vs. Political Correctness

NAT HENTOFF

A vigorous dissent from political orthodoxy on campus was made by a black Harvard Law School student during a debate on whether the law school should start punishing speech. A white student got up and said that the codes are necessary because without them black students would be driven away from colleges and thereby deprived of the equal opportunity to get an education.

The black student rose and said that the white student had a hell of a nerve to assume that he—in the face of racist speech—would pack up his books and go home. He'd been all too familiar with that kind of speech all his life, and he had never felt the need to run away from it. He'd handled it before, and he could again.

The black student then looked at his white colleague and said that it was condescending to say that blacks have to be "protected" from racist speech. "It is more racist and insulting," he emphasized, "to say that to me than to call me a nigger."

Excerpted from *Free Speech for Me—But Not for Thee: How the American Left and Right Relentlessly Censor Each Other*, by Nat Hentoff (New York: Harper Collins, 1992, $13, ISBN 0-060-99510-6); 1-800-332-3761.

Other resources from a "conservative" perspective can be found in free catalogs available from:

Hoover Institution Press, Stanford University, Stanford, CA 94305-6010, 415-723-3373, Fax 415-723-1687. They carry titles by Walter E. Williams and Thomas Sowell (both of them are included in this *Fieldbook*).

Basic Books (P.O. Box 588, Dunmore, PA 18512-0588); 1-800-331-3761 joint ventured with *The New Republic* to carry a line of political science books, many of which focus on issues related to diversity. Titles include: *Postethnic America: Beyond Multiculturalism, The War Against the Poor*, as well as *Race and Culture*.

Conservative critiques of diversity activities can be found in *The National Review*. In particular, see "Demystifying Multiculturalism" in the Feb. 21, 1994 issue, pages 26-54.

Resources from a libertarian perspective can be found in a free catalog available from Laissez Faire Books, Center for Independent Thought. They are a distributor of a variety of titles from a number of publishers and represent a free-enterprise/libertarian perspective. (938 Howard St., #202, San Francisco, CA 94103, 1-800-326-0996, Fax 415-541-0597).

See also *Kindly Inquisitors: The New Attacks on Free Thought*, by Jonathan Rauch, which reasserts the principle on which intellectual freedom depends: there is nothing wrong with giving offense in the pursuit of truth. (Chicago: University of Chicago Press, $9.95, ISBN 0-226-70576-5).

© 1993, Dick Wright. Reprinted by permission of United Features Syndicate.

NOURISHING THE HUMAN SPIRIT FOR THE DIVERSITY PILGRIMAGE

Separation of church and state was created to prevent the coercion of religious conscience that immigrants to America had experienced in many parts of Europe and Asia. This essential freedom is like any other, a double-edged sword. On one hand, it forces our religious values to emerge from our own personal convictions and those of the voluntary communities that we join. On the other hand, this separation has increasingly excluded religious discourse from our institutions while allowing full support to all sorts of world views, ideologies, and dogmas no less coercive than the feared religious absolutism. While there is often open animosity to religious values and institutions in the United States, the cultural marketplace has no such restrictions. Parents who try to share their values with their children know how challenging this is in the face of a media culture that often contradicts their best attempts.

The separation of church and state can become the equivalent of the separation of spirit and state—conducting our public policy and business affairs as if we have no spiritual resources or values. Too often, our view of justice, the economy, the business world, even affirmative action, is treated mathematically as in a zero-sum game in which there must be losers if there are to be winners. If somebody moves up, then someone else must move down. Spirit, with its proclivity for win-win solutions challenges this narrow assumption. Such elements as serenity, Christian fellowship, *mitzvah*, discipline, dharma, sacrifice, no-self, faithfulness, etc., come from our many rich traditions to challenge the cultural straitjacket of business as usual.

While many people use religion's past abuses as an excuse for not acknowledging the contributions it offers us today, our contributors do not! In this section they are telling us that spirit makes all the difference. They consciously examine formal and informal spiritual values, commitments, and "the deeper questions" in terms of what they bring to diversity. They open our eyes to what they bring to the task of shaping successful pluralism. They help us examine not only how we work together, but why we work at all. They go beneath the surface of accepted practices and ask compelling questions. Some offer personal testimony of how their tradition drives and supports their universal advocacy for human life. Others use faith and spiritual wisdom to examine our assumptions about who we are. Finally, they open new doors to who we can be.

Music is a universal language and has the unique ability to bring people together from various cultures. For centuries, people throughout the world have composed and performed music to communicate the unique harmony of their own culture. "Multicultural Music & Creative Arts for Global Harmony" is a special-interest group organized by John Arnold Smith for the purpose of:

- gathering information on the uses of music from various sources around the world
- surveying members and subscribers on forms of delivery and usage

- fostering collaborations with musicians and artists
- networking with musicians, trainers, educators, and interested parties

Reach him at: Global Interface, 487-A Beltline Rd. #246, Dallas, TX 75244; 214-416-4611, Fax 214-418-8489, e-mail: jasglobal@aol.com.

Another project that intertwines music and multicultural education is The New Spirituals Project by Redwood Cultural Work. Since 1992 Redwood has commissioned an outstanding female composer to write a major work in the spiritual tradition. The music from the project forms the basis for a high school workshop, "Unlearning Oppression: Spirituals & Other Songs or Resistance." For further information, contact: Susan Freundlich, Executive Director, Redwood Cultural Work, 1222 Preservation Parkway, Oakland, CA 94612; 510-835-1445.

See also *The Culture of Disbelief: How American Law and Politics Trivialize Religious Devotion*, by Stephen Carter (New York: Anchor-Doubleday, 1994, $14.95, ISBN 0-385-47498-9. Carter argues that the strict separation of Church and State in the American political system tends to trivialize religious belief. If religion is a central organizing principle of personal identity, he asks, must not religious citizens bring their beliefs into the public sphere in order to be fully and genuinely engaged in civic life?

Beloved: A Novel, by Toni Morrison (New York: NAL-Dutton, $5.99, ISBN 0-451-15659-5, 1987). In this profoundly moving novel set in the aftermath of the Civil War, Morrison's hero struggles to cope with the horrible legacy of her past as a slave. This intensely personal drama speaks to the larger issue of a nation struggling to come to terms with its history.

ⓘ *The Other Side*, a lively, radical, creative periodical on issues of peace, justice, and Christian faith, full of people asking questions that matter. Ecumenical in character, evangelical in fervor, surprising in scope. Sample $4 $35/year. Order from P.O. Box 2007, Hagerstown, MD 21742, phone 215-849-2178; Fax 540-372-6504.

Masters of the Dream: The Strength and Betrayal of Black America, by Alan L. Keyes (New York: Morrow, $21.50, ISBN 10-688-09599-2.) This book links spirituality to black success and argues that the loss of Christ-centered family life has been the road to ruin for black Americans.

57 • Spirituality for Men

GEORGE F. SIMONS

*M*en may not be "getting it," but most men have been hearing the message: 1) men aren't ok the way they are, and 2) women have a better agenda for how men ought to be. This "Bad News Gospel" comes from many women and some male fellow travelers. It's been repeated so often that we're telling it to ourselves — and our spirit grows weak within us.

We men aren't okay the way we are. We are the domestic batterers and the cosmic war-mongers. Obsessed with sex and work, incapable of commitment, secretive and conspiratorial, we are the absent fathers and authoritarian executives who wield all the power—badly. We are the intransigent enforcers of patriarchy and economic oppression. Biologically steeped in androgen to bring out our

TO BETTER UNDERSTAND OUR RICH CULTURAL DIVERSITY, CLASS, WE'LL STUDY HOLIDAYS OF DIFFERENT NATIONS!

WE'LL STUDY HOW CHINESE CELEBRATE THE NEW YEAR!

WE'LL LEARN ABOUT JAPAN'S GIRLS' DAY AND BOYS' DAY!

meaner side, physiologically inferior, some even see us, in the biotech long run, as superfluous—the world might be a nicer place if run by women with a large sperm bank.

Attempts at transformation of the male spirit, whether the mythopoetic men's movement (Robert Bly and drums in the woods), The Promise Keepers or the Million Man March, are attacked as exclusionary. We are yanked about by the message that we had better get our act together, but we'd better not get together to do it.

There is a women's agenda for the way men ought to be. Men must learn to share their feelings as women do and become less aggressive and more compassionate while at the same time the unexpressed message is that without remaining strong, levelheaded and in control, they will not be respected. Men often experience women's contradictory demands as "I'm wrong no matter what I do," rather than as a product of women's ambivalence, or even better, an invitation to broaden their repertoire of personal skills.

Warren Farrell, in *Why Men Are the Way They Are*, points out that men are caught in a double bind between the vocal minority of women who read MS. and the silent majority who relish Harlequin novels. It is easy to aim a sermon or an anti-porn campaign at the portrayal of women as "sex objects" in *Playboy* while missing (or even applauding) women's porn that turns men into the objects of the female quest for security. Many women's magazines continue to reinforce the demand that men be self-destructive "heroes." Unless men recognize that women's agendas for us are not, perhaps, in our best interests, our spirits will not live.

According to various estimates, 67 percent to 85 percent of counseling, personal growth programs, and products are purchased by, and reflect the agendas of, women. Where is a man to go? Does a "real man" need support, ministry, or spirituality? What might down-to-earth services to men and male spirituality (gay or straight) look like?

1. **It would address the painful crises of men's lives.** It would positively affirm male sexuality in puberty. It would assist the transition to the world of work and the decision to partner. It would be sensitive to the "petit mort" that many men associate with commitments and intimate exchange more than with orgasm.

Work and play and relationships must be addressed, along with the crises of career and separations from loved ones. For example, in the middle of a man's life his children depart for the excitement of college or first jobs and his woman partner (whether she has been at home or simply been freed by the emptying of the nest) enthusiastically resumes or begins a fresh career. While she is enjoying rebirth, he finds himself, with an aging body, at the limits of advancement in the same old job that may not have the meaning it once had. What was his way of loving and supporting his partner and children is no longer needed as much or at all.

Single and gay men have their own version of these crises of meaning as they age. The lack of an adequate response to such crises leaves men prey to despair, divorce, and reactionary behavior.

2. **It would provide a spirituality that values the lives and promotes the health of men.** The expendibility of men in a "women and children first" society demands that they be tough to survive and then invites them to use their machismo to destroy each other. Men are the cannon fodder of politics and economics, as well as of the military machine. Viewing their countless violent deaths boosts the box office take. Brutality seems noticeable only when women or children become its victims. We have a justice system that punishes cruelty to animals more severely than cruelty to men. From my perspective, until the well-being of a single grown man is given the same value as that of a woman or a child, most right-to-life protests will be futile and look hypocritical.

What begins when Daddy says to Sonny, "You take care of Mommy while I'm gone," ends in battlefield "glory" with the "ultimate sacrifice." As many women now insist on being caretakers of others only when they choose rather than by default, men are right to question their automatic assignment to being society's protectors and its weaponry.

3. **It would reinvigorate the meaning of work.** In *The New Male-Female Relationship*, Herb Goldberg shows how powerful forces in our language about men and women conspire to make a perpetual "child" of a woman while making the man into a "machine." Men's competitive survival and success has depended on their capability to develop a "repeating swing" at the tee of life. Men are to get their excitement from their work, "the game," and enjoy winning. It is hard for them to see the long term cost of "the game" until they are sidelined or carried off the field. A functional spirituality of work for men will have to open men to other satisfactions, not just wag a finger at the ones they are supposed to be enjoying now.

4. **It would revitalize or transform symbolism, particularly that of fatherhood which has become destructive and deadly.** From Santa Cruz to Bar Harbor women are exploring alternative sources of theology. Neo-witchcraft, eastern philosophy, and Native American shamanism are tapped for inspiration, sometimes spun out of whole cloth, either to supplement or to replace the Judeo-Christian heritage. Now it's men's turn to wonder if they can find adequate spiritual myths and symbols in traditional sources.

In the past some men lived on the fringe of religion because they saw it as a women's thing to begin with. Men smoked on the church steps while the women listened to priests in skirts. Today, thinkers in the academe and on the streets must reexamine religious patriarchal imagery in the light of what it conveys to men. It is disconcerting that pivotal stories of both Judaism and Christianity echo the theme, "the father is willing to sacrifice his son."

Finding Our Fathers, the title of a book by Sam Osherson, is also the theme of numerous support groups, where men grapple with the pain and loss caused by the absence of their fathers and their alienation from them. This pain according to Ken Druck, is one of the *Secrets Men Keep*, which is also the title of his book. Not only is personal healing important, but understanding our fathers pain and grief would withdraw many men from the insatiable search for father's approval by endlessly proving our manhood.

Men may be as orphaned from their spiritual forebears as they are from their natural fathers. For example, a useful image of Jesus is difficult for many Christian men. Was he a "man's man" who hung out with the guys? Or, a proto-feminist who defended women's rights long before women articulated them? Iconography, from the most maudlin Sacred Heart to abstract crucifixion scenes, gives us little to identify with that is not stereotypical. Symbols that require too much commentary to work for us are not symbols at all. They tell us not to trust our experience.

Men's growth in consciousness about their own condition at this moment in time has de facto been stimulated by women's strident articulation of their own concerns. Women's anger can be a gift of self-recognition for men who don't get mired in guilt over it. In its heat we can begin to mold ourselves after a pattern of our own design and not simply capitulate to women's perceptions and demands.

Despite the fact that men are shaped and buffeted by many of the same social systems as women are, it is important that we not see or talk about ourselves as victims. Women have already done that. Many of them are using blame and resentment to dig themselves a hole that they may never climb out of. We don't need men's books with titles comparable to *Men Who Hate Women and the Women Who Love them*. Women are not to blame for the present situation, nor are we. Blaming is a trap and we have a much bigger agenda for our spirit.

"Mans inherent nature is to be curious, gentle, intimate, responsible, enthusiastic, sensual, tolerant, courageous, honest, vulnerable, affectionate, proud, spiritual, committed, wild, nurturing, peaceful, helpful, intense, compassionate, happy, and to fully and safely express all emotions. When will we stop training him to be otherwise?" Gordon Clay, Founder and Director, National Men's Resource Center.

The National Men's Resource Center (P.O. Box 800, San Anselmo, CA 94979-0800, voice mail 415-453-2839, e-mail gordonclay@aol.com) is a nonprofit organization dedicated to addressing men's issues through working with organizations public and private and with educational institutions to provide information and referral resources to men. It sponsors the Browsers™ bookmobile, containing over 1,200 men's titles, which travels the country visiting rural communities, schools, and bookstores.

58 · A New Vision of Livelihood: Where Does Our Work Fit in the Cosmos?

MATTHEW FOX

et me tell you a story. Three years ago, I was speaking in Port Huron, Michigan, and they had just that week closed down a car factory—four thousand workers thrown out of work within a week. Now speaking in a church to about seven hundred, eight hundred people and before I began, I said to myself, "Am I going to tell the whole truth or part of the truth?" and I said, "Well, I leave town tomorrow so I'll tell the whole truth." So I got up in front of these people and I said, "First I want to extend my empathy to everybody here who has been affected by this layoff and of course the community has to band together and create the safety net, the retraining and the compassion for these people, and so forth. However, I want to say this: Maybe something bigger is happening here than just the closing down of a particular family's livelihood. Perhaps we have to ask the question today whether we need a lot more cars on the planet. There are already 600 million automobiles and they are a cause of a lot of our troubles, and the same is true for the defense industry. We are going through the same thing in California. You might say, "Well we've always built cars in Port Huron or we've always had military bases in California." We have to go deeper and say yes, but what work does Gaia ask of our generation today? What work [is it that] future generations [are] asking of us today? And frankly, I don't think it's a lot more cars or a lot more military bases. . . .

Let me share with you what Studs Turkel says about work. He says, "Work is about daily meaning as well as daily bread. For recognition as well as cash; for astonishment rather than torpor; in short, for a sort of life rather than a Monday through Friday sort of dying. . . . We have a right to ask of work that it induce meaning, recognition, astonishment, and life. . . . "

The *Tao Te Ching*, the Chinese scriptures, says, "In work do what you enjoy." There's a difference between job and work. A job is something we often do to pay our bills. Work touches your heart and it has to touch other people's hearts. If there's one question I would ask to awaken us to spiritual work it would be "How does your work touch the joy in you and what joy does your work bring out in others? . . ."

Lester Brown, head of Worldwatch Institute, whose job it is to go around the world collecting all the scientific data about the earth, said we have 20 years left to

*Gaia refers to the mythical Greek goddess who is the personification of the spirit of the earth. "New age" philosophers as well as credentialed scientists have asserted that the planet earth is truly a living organism with consciousness.

ⓘ An intriguing and insightful view of diversity from a Christian perspective can be found in *The Wolf Shall Dwell with the Lamb—a Spirituality for Leadership in a Multicultural Community*, by Eric Law, (ISBN 0-8272-4231-X; 1-800-366-3363) available from Chalice Press, Box 179, St. Louis, MO 63166-0179.

bring about the environmental revolution. The environmental revolution will be just as basic as the Industrial Revolution. It will affect our relationships for everything—work, business, banking, farming—just as the Industrial Revolution did 200 years ago, or the agricultural revolution did 10,000 years ago. Imagine how moving from hunting/gathering to agriculture changed everything. It made cities possible. It made specialists in raising food possible so others were free to do other things. Tremendous human revolution. Now Brown says the environmental revolution will be just as all-encompassing a change, a transformation, but the difference is that we only have 20 years to pull it off. So every one of us, no matter what our age or what our task and job and gifts, is part of this environmental revolution. It's the real work that needs to be done. He said the number one obstacle to bringing this environmental revolution off is human inertia.

Inertia is a sin of the spirit. It's what our ancestors called one of the sins of the spirit, "acedia." Saint Thomas Aquinas said acedia is a lack of energy to begin new things. Being a couch potato. And it's rampant in our culture and it's about lack of energy. And so what would be the opposite of acedia? Zeal. Energy. There's the cure. There's the medicine for what's holding back the environmental revolution. If inertia is the correct analysis that Lester Brown is giving us, where do we find zeal? Aquinas has an incredible statement on that. He says that zeal comes from an intense experience of the beauty of things. To overcome the inertia that is overcoming us, that is contributing so substantively to the demolition of this planet, we have to fall in love again. We think falling in love is about finding a mate once or a couple of times in one's life. It's bigger than that, folks. You can fall in love with the galaxy. There are 10,000 species of wildflowers to fall in love with. And there are trees and forests and whales and fish. . . .

59 • Involving Culture: A Fieldworker's Guide to Culturally Appropriate Development

HELGI EYFORD

*T*he World Conference on Cultural Policies (Mexico, 1982) has defined culture as: the whole complex of distinctive spiritual, material, intellectual, and emotional features that characterize a society or social group. It includes not only the arts and letters, but also modes of life, the fundamental rights of the human being, value systems, traditions, and beliefs. (UNESCO)

"Whole complex" culture is not one or two things in isolation. It is a whole way of thinking and feeling about the world. While culture is manifest in a particular value system, a certain way of doing things, a distinctive style of dress or food, it is much more than the sum of these things. Culture is an integrated, synergistic whole.

Clifford Geertz (*The Interpretation of Cultures*. New York: Basic Books, 1973, p. 5) describes culture as the "webs of significance that man has spun for himself." Culture is the code that allows us to interpret signals in a meaningful way, it is the filter through which we strain the world. As such, culture defines for us what is real and important and what is noise and superfluous.

Language is an integral part of culture. "All human societies without exception are enclosed in an envelope of culture, of certain social, religious, legal, and other practices, and most of this cultural envelope consists of words."* The words in a language and how they are used often illustrate a unique perspective on reality that a culture has developed to make sense of the world. We can learn much if we take the time and trouble to learn the words—not just the casual, everyday words but the deep, metaphorical words used in songs and ceremonies.

*Northrup Frye, *The Educated Imagination* (Toronto: CBC, 1963), p. 192.

Because language embodies a perspective, an approach to reality, it also helps to determine our sense of identity, who we are, what we can be, and what we can do. Freire views the ability to name the world as the very essence of being human. "Human existence cannot be silent, nor can it be nourished by false words, but only by true words, with which men transform the world. To exist, humanly, is to name the world, to change it.**

We need a new breed of change agents who, first and foremost, care for people as human beings, who treat them as subjects and not objects or recipients of change, who steep themselves in the aspirations, problems, and the wisdom of their own people, and who therefore actually follow the people—like Mahatma Gandhi who said, "There go my people and I must follow them for I am their leader."

**Paulo Freire, *Pedagogy of the Oppressed*, p. 76. This classic adult education text by famous Brazilian educator outlines in scholarly prose how poor and oppressed people learn to accept their condition and how the rich and powerful conspire, sometimes unconsciously, to keep the poor in their place.

TALKING CIRCLES

Talking circles are useful when the topic under consideration has no right or wrong answer or when people need to share feelings. The purpose of talking circles is to create a safe environment for people to share their point of view with others. It is a technique for allowing authentic and uncensored participation, which is a prerequisite to culturally appropriate development. This process helps people gain a sense of trust in each other. They come to believe that what they say will be listened to and accepted without criticism. They also gain an appreciation for

(i) The Talking Circle idea comes from the work of the Centre for Development Learning, Calgary, Alberta, which can be contacted at 1-403-270-8098.

points of view other than their own. This is one of the most effective ways to overcome the natural barriers to equal sharing between privileged development worker and community people.

The basic rule of talking circles is that the groups sit in a circle and each person gets a chance to say whatever is on their mind without being criticized or judged by others. The talk flows around the circle and nobody talks twice until everyone talks once. Sometimes groups pass around a feather, stone, or talking stick. Whoever has the object has the floor. Talking circles usually need a facilitator to ensure that the guidelines are followed. These guidelines include:

- All comments should be addressed directly to the question or issue not to comments by other participants.
- Only one person speaks at a time and no cross-talk, i.e., talking out of turn, is allowed.
- Comments that put down others or oneself are not allowed.
- Speakers should feel free to express themselves in any way that is comfortable: personal stories, metaphors, analytical statements, etc.

60 • Jewish Sources of Inspiration in Doing Diversity Work

ELLEN HOFHEIMER BETTMANN

The most useful advice my mother ever gave me was to always leave the campsite a little cleaner than when I found it. As an adult I have come to realize how big the campsite is, and how hard it is, sometimes, to accomplish this task. The clarity of my mother's expectation has been a guiding force in my life as a human rights activist.

When I was growing up, the United States was devoted to the "melting pot" theory, and my family was doing its very best to be American, still Jewish, of course, thank-God-we-have-religious-freedom-in-the-new-country, but not "too Jewish." I have had to work hard as an adult to reclaim some of my heritage.

The year I turned twelve my family moved to a new neighborhood. One day, one of our new neighbors shouted at my mother, "Get your Jew dog off my lawn!" I remember wondering how that woman knew that my dog Harry was Jewish. From my perspective, Harry was just a dog, and, like my family, well assimilated into mainstream American life.

My parents' response to the incident was to give Harry away. In protest I ran away from home. I returned with knowledge about my new neighborhood I wished I didn't have, and an understanding that sometimes Jews try very hard to gain acceptance. I knew that getting rid of Harry wouldn't make our new neighbor like us, but, it must have, at the very least, given her a satisfying feeling of power. While she couldn't stop our moving into the neighborhood, she could make sure that we didn't feel welcome.

I missed Harry, but more than that, I missed my lost innocence about being Jewish. I tied this event up in an invisible knot and swallowed it. It went down but it still sits like a lump inside me.

Jewish teaching, like all cultural knowledge, is transmitted both formally and informally. Although I didn't know it then, my mother's advice to think of the campsite has a Jewish counterpart: *tikkun olam*, Hebrew for "repairing the world." I think of *tikkun olam* as God's shorthand message to me: just do it! I am not free to say, "I didn't make this mess, therefore it has nothing to do with me." My task is to discover what needs "repairing" and use my God-given gifts to set it right. While finding the appropriate tasks may seem confusing, we Jews are helped in this process by the concept of *mitzvot* (plural for *mitzvah*). *Mitzvah* is sometimes translated as a "good deed," however it goes beyond the meaning of a kindly act because Jews are commanded by God to perform these deeds.

Among the 613 mitzvot are several commandments that are central to my life. "Do not stand idly by" reminds me that it is my job to notice suffering, to care, and to act. The literal translation is, "Don't stand on your friend's blood." Just as I learned to expand my concept of "campsite" I have spent my adult life discovering the broadest interpretation of "friend." It is often hard not to feel overwhelmed by the enormity of the task. On one occasion I called my rabbi during a week-long training workshop. "It's so slow!" I complained. "The workshop is going well, but there is so much more to do, and this is only one group, and I'm only one person, and I don't have enough time. . . ." He let me finish my lament before he told me a saying from *pirkei avot* ("Wisdom of Our Ancestors"): "Yours is not to complete the task, but nor are you free to desist from trying." The fact that I cannot possibly end racism and all forms of bigotry in my lifetime should not, cannot be used as a reason for my not making the attempt. When attempting what often feels impossible, it is crucial for my sense of balance to have a statement of faith that acknowledges the enormity of the task and the possibility that I might not be completely successful, but refuses to consider abandoning the effort.

When attempting what often feels impossible, it is crucial for my sense of balance to have a statement of faith that acknowledges the enormity of the task and the possibility that I might not be completely successful, but refuses to consider abandoning the effort.

Key to Judaism is remembering our history as slaves. It is so basic it is a part of a daily prayer. *Yom Hashoah*, the Holocaust Day of Remembrance, is a twentieth century version of remembering; we vow never to forget the six million Jews murdered by the Nazis, and we say "Never again! Never again!" As a Jew it is important for me to know the Jews' history of oppression, so I can use our experience of suffering to understand the pain of others.

I am sustained regularly by the words of many Jewish sages living and dead. From my mother's aunt Lily, I learned the importance of setting priorities and dealing with the conflict of having more than one thing to do at a time. "With one *tuchus*"(Yiddish for "behind"), Lily proclaimed, "you can't dance at two weddings!" Daily I face more demands for my time and energy than I can possibly respond to, and Lily's words comfort me.

"If I am not for myself, who is for me?
If I am only for myself, what am I?
If not now, when?"

Rabbi Hillel wrote those words in the first century C.E. When I lose my urgency about creating a more equitable society, "If not now, when?" is like the sound of the shofar, the ram's horn, blown in the synagogue at the new year. It calls me back to my work on this earth. Jewish work, human work: timeless and timely.

61 • Rúmi Poem

TRANSLATED BY JOHN MOYNE AND COLEMAN BARKS

Sometimes visible, sometimes not, sometimes
devout Christians, sometimes staunchly Jewish.
Until our inner love fits into everyone,
all we can do is take daily these different shapes.

Mevlána Jaláluddín Rúmí

(i) This poem appears in *Unseen Rain: Quantrains of Rúmí*. Available from Threshold Books, RD 4, Box 600, Putney, VT 05346; 802-254-8300.

In the Name of God, Most Beneficent, Most Merciful

62 • Islamic Universalism

RABIA TERRI HARRIS

Diversity is a divine tool for the furtherance of human consciousness.

The great saint Jeláluddín Rúmí tells this story. A Turk, a Persian, and an Arab were traveling together. They had pooled their little money, and had only enough for a single purchase. They were all hungry, and each knew exactly what he craved. "I want *uzum!*" said the Turk. "No, no, we must have *angur!*" insisted the Persian. "It's *'inab* or nothing," declared the Arab. They had almost come to blows when a fourth man, a wise man, came down the road and interrupted them. "If you will entrust your money to me," he proposed, "I promise to satisfy you all." With no other resolution in sight, they nervously agreed. And the fourth man, who was a knower of languages, went off to the market and bought them grapes—which is what they all had asked for.

The Muslim community, we believe, was intended to play a universalizing and reconciling role—to take, as it were, the position of the wise man in the story. "Thus have We made you a middle community," God informs us in the *Qur'an* (*Surah Baqarah,* 143) and the thoughtful Muslim will consider seriously the requirements of such mediation. There are many episodes in history that reveal its results: the *convivencia* of Southern Spain in the Middle Ages, where Muslims, Christians, and Jews came together in a great cultural flowering, is only the most famous of them. In circumstances where passions rule, the social responsibility ordained for us may all too easily be forgotten. This in no way, however, changes the fact of its institution.

"O People of the Book! Come to what is common among us," the Holy Prophet was told to invite the other religious communities of his time." That we worship none but God; that we associate no partners with Him; that we do not set up from among ourselves lords other than God" (*Surah Al-i 'Imran* 64). This call was not a summons to take up his own practice, to receive the immense gift he had been given to distribute; it was a call to the shared understanding of all the children of Abraham. Even so, it was generally refused. Yet Muhammad (peace and blessings be upon him) was never authorized by God to exert any pressure, under any circumstances, upon those who did not respond to his invitations. Fighting was permitted him for the defense of the community, but was never, ever, to be employed for

Rabia Terri Harris is an assistant editor for *Fellowship,* the magazine of the Fellowship of Reconciliation, an international interfaith peace organization. 6 issues at $15 per year from FOR/MPF, P.O. Box 271, Nyack, NY 10960; 914-358-4601, Fax: 914-358-4924.

Sharon Stewart, Impact Visuals.

This is Houston, Texas, not Mecca. A gathering of about 5,000 Muslims praying in a city park during Eid, a ceremony celebrating the end of Ramadan.

"conversion by the sword." Do not be misled: in all of Muslim history, trying to spread religion through violence has been the rarest of aberrations.

"No compulsion in religion: truth stands out clear from error" (*Surah Baqarah*, 256) is an exalted doctrine from which the Holy Prophet never in his life departed, and it remains an immovable cornerstone of the Muslim point of view. Unity cannot be imposed by force—nor is there any point in attempting it. Oneness exists, has always existed, and will always exist. But who will be able to see how much of it, and from what perspective, is wholly in the hands of God. "The goal of you all is God: it is He that will show you the truth of the matters in which you dispute" (*Surah Ma'idah*, 48).

Since individuals differ necessarily in their points of view, so also must groups. The human community is singular, according to Revelation, but human communities are plural, and there is no mistake in that: that is the way it is supposed to be. "We created you all from a male and a female and made you into nations and tribes [so that you may recognize one another" (*Surah Hujurat*, 13). Diversity is a divine tool for the furtherance of human consciousness. It ensures that we can never escape some knowledge of the full range of our possibilities, which habit and inertia continually work to confine.

If the fact of you did not challenge me, if the fact of me did not challenge you, what would save either of us from complacency? What would induce us to grow? Were it not for the variety ordained by God, what would become of us here? The divine richness is not served by homogeneity. And we would be so bored!

"If God had so wished, He could have made you all one community, but His plan is to test you in what He has given you. So vie with each other in good works" (*Surah Ma'idah*, 48). The secret of difference, the verse intimates, is that it incites us to display our best, to bring what is unique to each of us into the presence of all. But the full realization of God's wish requires us to agree to what He has done — to accept that He has made all of us, equally, participants in the constant outpouring of creation, recipients of the endless divine gift. If we seek to be fully human, rather than just the biggest bully on the block, then there is no alternative to doing as we are told: we must recognize both the divine unity, and each other. Islam, in this sense, cannot be "just for Muslims." It is desperately needed by us all.

63 • Work and Serenity

RALPH G. H. SIU

Lao Tzu lived in China in the sixth century B.C., and Buddha lived in India decades later. Some of the basic concepts of these two gentlemen apply to the present day circumstances of work from the standpoint of the individual's own welfare. I am not saying that such behavior is necessarily preferable to the way of life emerging from other traditions, studies, or carefully conducted research. As a matter of fact, this advice might be construed as subterfuge by some strong-willed executives. All I am suggesting is that such a different way of looking at the meaning of work may provide an additional ingredient to a discussion of work's purpose.

ⓘ Excerpted from "Work & Serenity," *Occupational Mental Health* (Fall 1971). The full text is included in *The Balanced Living Kit* available from ODT, Inc., at 413-549-1293.

TWO BASIC PRINCIPLES

The followers of Lao Tzu operate from a number of basic principles of behavior. One of them is known as the yin-yang. Roughly encapsulated, the

All through the night, Rejeb could not sleep. He sat up in bed looking at the weather-beaten back, the sunburned neck, and the sad face of his wife, breathing heavily with an occasional groan. He seemed to be oppressed by a heavy heart. So he got up and walked around the village. The beets had been planted, the animals taken care of, and people friendly. He could not find a reason for his uneasiness, as he dozed off on the damp ground. When he awoke, he found that his wife had watered the cattle and prepared fresh dough. After breakfast by himself he had nothing to do but visit the coffee-houses and play cards. But still he could not shake off the disturbing feeling. He decided to visit the fields.

The sun was beating down fiercely, when he finally reached his wife, digging away at the parched earth. When he inquired about the progress, the lady replied that there were still twenty acres to be planted. "What?" shouted Rejeb. "What have you been doing the last ten days? Answer me!" But the tired lady was too frightened to answer. She trembled like a leaf and panted like a dying animal. Her eyes were inflamed from the glaring sun and reflected all the misery of mankind.

Rejeb suddenly felt crushed and confused and realized the cause of his heavy heart. It was the sense of pity for his poor wife. So he dropped his eyes out of remorse, slowly turned around, and solemnly decided to do something about it. The next evening, Rejeb came back from the market with two lanterns. He looked

concept states: Things go in cycles. When the sun reaches the meridian, it declines. When the moon becomes full, it wanes. Everything is made up of these opposites of ups and downs, plus and minus, light and dark, and so on—of the yang and the yin. The pendulum, however, never reaches the point of complete exclusion of one or the other before it reverses in direction, providing continually varying mixtures of yin and yang. There is no stasis and there are no absolutes. These constitute the underlying bases for reasonableness in human situations.

The second basic principle is offered by Buddha. It teaches that the minimizing of suffering rather than the maximizing of happiness constitutes the good of living. If work is to have the best of meanings for living, it must contribute to decreasing misery, grief, anguish, or pain. Increased suffering on the part of one person cannot be justified as a desirable trade-off for augmented happiness on the part of another. Furthermore, since suffering can only be experienced by individual persons and not by organizations, suffering to individuals cannot be justified by gains to an organization—regardless whether it be in terms of enlarged profits for a corporation, increased converts for a church, or enhanced power for a nation.

An organization is often interested in decreasing suffering or mental anguish on the part of its members, because in so doing it is able to achieve its organizational objectives more effectively. But this does not alter the fact that the minimizing of suffering per se is seldom the immediate objective of an organization. The first practical purpose of an organization is always to survive as an organization and the second is to grow. The distinction of concern over mental health per se and concern over mental health as an ancillary consideration has been illustrated very well in a short story in the margin by the Turk writer, Hanjarlioglu.

SPECIFIC ADVICE

Observe the cormorant in the fishing fleet. You know how cormorants are used for fishing. The technique involves a man in a rowboat with about half a dozen or so cormorants, each with a ring around the neck. As the bird spots a fish, it would dive into the water and unerringly come up with it. Because of the ring, the larger fish are not swallowed but held in the throat. The fisherman picks up the bird and squeezes out the fish through the mouth. The bird then dives for another and the cycle repeats itself.

The neo-Taoist would say to the American worker: "Observe the cormorant. Why is it that of all the different animals, the cormorant has been chosen to slave away day and night catching fish for the fisherman? Were the bird not greedy for fish, or not efficient in catching it, or not readily trained, would society have created an industry to exploit the bird? Would the ingenious device of a ring around its neck, and the simple procedure of squeezing the bird's neck to force it to regurgitate the fish have been devised? Of course not."

Greed, talent, and capacity for learning then are the basis of exploitation. The more you are able to moderate and/or to hide them from society, the greater will be your chances of escaping the fate of the cormorant.

Let us discuss greed. How much is enough? There is an old proverb that says: "One day eat three meals, one night sleep in eight feet of space." Obviously, that is not sufficient for modern day living. So we will be reasonable about it and raise the ante.

In trying to arrive at a minimum threshold, it is necessary to remember that the institutions of society are geared to make society prosper, not necessarily to minimizing suffering on your part. It is for this reason, among others, that the schools tend to drum it into your mind the high desirability of those characteristics that tend to make society prosper—namely ambition, progress, and success. These, in turn, are to be valued in terms of society's objective. All of them gradually but surely increase your greed and make a cormorant out of you.

You can observe this magnet at work in the various social rules of thumb. You are told that you ought to afford a home worth about two and a fourth times your annual income. The United Giver's Fund suggests one percent of your salary for donation. The church says ten percent for its share. The Internal Revenue Service takes its hefty portion. The Alma Mater presses for its 1,000-dollar club. If you ever take the time to add all of these increments, you will wind up with quite a pretty penny. To lull you into hock, the various organizational pitch-men have come up with narcotic arrangements of credit cards, installment buying, lump-sum loans, and pledges.

Once you subscribe to society's guide to affluent living, you are trapped like the cormorant. You will never meet your minimum requirements, simply because crouched underneath all of the fancy words is the subtle rhythm of "more."

at his wife compassionately and said, "It is too hot for you to work under the scorching sun. It is too much of a strain. Take these lanterns. From now on, you can work during the cool nights instead."

When an organization speaks of occupational mental health, more often than not, it thinks like Rejeb. Getting the job done comes first. Getting it done more efficiently comes next. Mental health comes third as part of the calculations on efficiency.

—Ralph G.H. Siu

See also "Us Versus Them" by Siu in *The Cultural Diversity Sourcebook* available from ODT, at 1-800-736-1293.

64 • Dialogue with Myself: My Emotional, Intellectual, Spiritual, and Physical Selves

YU-LIANG HUANG (SALLY NISSEN)

Reach up to the lofty goals of global harmony   **1**
Reach down to lift the human spirit and hope   **2**

142   CULTURAL DIVERSITY *Fieldbook*

To use ourselves as instruments of change in promoting the value of diversity, we must constantly seek to maintain a balance of all parts of ourselves.

Reach up to highest human potential   **3**
Reach down to give a hand to those who have fallen   **4**
Open my **HEART** to feel the compassion for those who are unaware   **5**
Open my **MIND** to allow for perspectives different from my own   **6**
Open my **eyes** to see the injustice and human suffering   **7**
Open my **SOUL** to absorb the inexplicable human complexity   **8**
Find the balance between giving and taking   **9**
The balance between speaking about goals   **10**
And taking action toward reaching them
The balance between my need for individual achievement and
My need for family closeness, and interpersonal relationships
Reach up and out to people of diverse backgrounds   **11**
Estsablish a coalition of forces in realizing our common goals
Reach down to build a solid foundation for interdependence   **12**
Rotate the energy from all sources   **13**
Store them in my **BODY** to generate synergy
Direct this synergy into passion, purposefulness and sense of urgency
Push out and up all the negative energies from others
Transform them into purity of stream water
Wash away any residue of envy, jealousy, hunger for power
Use this same stream water to cleanse myself thoroughly
So I can be free of the burden of human frailties and
Be nourished, renewed and ready to branch out, yet still
Rooted firmly on the foundation of good will
I extend my arms to the universe
Collect the energy from everyone and everywhere
Bring it all back to my Dantien✶, and establish   ✶See margin note on page 143
A center for caring, justice and freedom to choose
Collectively we can make the society better, freer,
More compassionate, less antagonistic
Where relationships among multicultural people can flourish
Friendships and collaborations can be initiated and continued
Where everyone's life is enriched because of our differences
Free from the burden of bigotry, alienation and segregation
My world, and our world, will then celebrate our differences as
The sky, the earth, the fire, the water, the wood, and the gold
Crystallize all the elements of nature into beautiful and sustainable
Human Diversity

Two rich U.S. traditions provide tools for diversity quite different from those found in most organizational training programs. "Dialogue with Myself" is whole-person learning from the Chinese tradition of Tai Ji. "The Peace Vision" is a driving force for "pow-wows" sponsored by Native American groups to share culture and create peace and reconciliation with people of all backgrounds and classes.

Dantien is the field or reservoir of vital energy, the gut force in the belly, the centered and contained power-feeling inside and around the lower abdomen.

65 • The Peace Vision

ELAYNA REYNA—BLUEBIRD WOMAN

One Earth One People
The Original Plan of Creator:
We are One People on One Earth.
All Life is sacred. The Earth is sacred.
We must cherish and protect our Mother
Earth, Father Sky, and Sacred Waters.
The Generations of humankind from the
Four Directions must live in Harmony and
Balance with each other and all living things.
We all are related. As we respect and honor the
Sacredness of all Life and of all Creation,
So Seven Generations to follow each Gen-
eration our Future Generations will live.
Seven eagle feathers represent Future
Generations in sacred ceremonies.
They carry our prayers to Creator.
We pray that Mother Earth and
All of Her Children will live.
It is One Prayer *Peace.*

66 •   Norman, the Barking Dancing Pig

ROBERT FULGHUM

A kindergarten teacher I know was asked to have her class dramatize a fairy tale for a teacher's conference. After much discussion, the children achieved consensus on that old favorite, "Cinderella." The classic old "rags to riches" story that never dies. "Cream will rise" is the moral of this tale—someday you may get what you think you deserve. It's why adults play the lottery with such passion.

"Cinderella" was a good choice from the teacher's point of view because there were many parts and lots of room for discretionary padding of parts so that every child in the class could be in the play. A list of characters was compiled as the class talked through the plot of the drama: There was the absolutely ravishing Cinderella, the evil stepmother, the two wicked and dumb stepsisters, the beautiful and wise fairy godmother, the pumpkin, mice, coachman, horses, the king, all the people at the king's ball—generals, admirals, knights, princesses, and of course, that ultimate object of fabled desire, the Prince—good news incarnate.

The children were allowed to choose roles for themselves. As the parts were allotted, each child was labeled with felt pen and paper, and sent to stand over on the other side of the room while casting was completed. Finally, every child had a part.

Except one.

One small boy. Who had remained quiet and disengaged from the selection process. A somewhat enigmatic kid—"different"—and because he was plump for his age, often teased by the other children.

"Well, Norman," said the teacher, "who are you going to be?"

"Well," replied Norman, "I am going to be the pig."

"Pig? There's no pig in this story."

"Well, there is now."

Wisdom was fortunately included in the teacher's tool bag. She looked carefully at Norman. What harm? It was a bit of casting to type. Norman did have a certain pigginess about him, all right. So be it. Norman was declared the pig in the story of Cinderella. Nobody else wanted to be the pig, anyhow, so it was quite fine with the class. And since there was nothing in the script explaining what the pig was supposed to do, the action was left up to Norman.

As it turned out, Norman gave himself a walk-on part. The pig walked along with Cinderella wherever Cinderella went, ambling along on all fours in a piggy way, in a costume of his own devising—pink long underwear complete with trapdoor rear flap, pipe-cleaner tail, and a paper cup for a nose. He made no sound. He simply sat on his back haunches and observed what was going on, like some silently supportive Greek chorus. The expressions on his face reflected the details of the dramatic action. Looking worried, sad, anxious, hopeful, puzzled, mad, bored, sick, and pleased as the moment required. There was no doubt about what was going on, and no doubt that it was important. One look at the pig and you knew. The pig was so earnest. So sincere. So very "there." The pig brought gravity and mythic import to this well-worn fairy tale.

At the climax, when the prince finally placed the glass slipper on the Princess's foot and the ecstatic couple hugged and rode off to live happily ever after, the pig went wild with joy, danced around on his hind legs, and broke his silence by barking.

In rehearsal, the teacher had tried explaining to Norman that even if there was a pig in the Cinderella story, pigs don't bark. But as she expected, Norman explained that *this* pig barked.

And the barking, she had to admit, *was* well done.

The presentation at the teacher's conference was a smash hit. At the curtain call, guess who received a standing ovation?

Of course. Norman, the barking pig.

Who was, after all, the *real* Cinderella story.

Word of a good thing gets around, and the kindergarten class had many invitations to come and perform Cinderella. Sometimes the teacher would have to explain what it was about the performance that was unique.

"It has a pig in it, you see?"

"Oh, really?"
"Yes, the star of the show is . . . a *barking* pig."
"But there's no barking pig in 'Cinderella'."
"Well, there is now."

From Robert L. Fulglum's *Uh-Oh*. Reprinted by permission of Villard Books a division of Random House, Inc. Copyright © 1991.

67 • Who's in a Name

RUSSELL MEANS FROM AN INTERVIEW WITH JOHN EDGAR WIDEMAN (MODERN MATURITY)

come from the Horse clan, which gives you a name for each stage of human life: child, young adult, older adult, elder. You're supposed to try to

Prize-winning novelist and playwright Gloria Naylor comments on how ". . . a Black woman [is] . . . the only legitimate Cinderella in modern America, complete with head rag, broom, and being left to make your own damned dress for a ball you'll have to crash . . . I know about the feelings of a stepchild in someone else's home of the brave."

Essence, November, 1982.

Piet van Lier, Impact Visuals

Russell Means

One particularly simple yet eloquent activity any size group can do is the exercise "What's in a Name?" Have the participants divide into groups and ask each person to take a few minutes and explain what their name means, where they got it from, or a family story about either their first, last, or nickname. This is both an effective group "ice-breaker," and a simple team building exercise that begins to help get people to learn more about one another, including their cultural backgrounds.

live up to each name. I was given a name when I was born, *Wanbli Ohitika*, which means Brave Eagle. So, of course, I was always running around taking dares, getting in lots of mischief. Being a pain, sometimes, I bet. I really took the name to heart.

My second name was *Cio* (pronounced SHE-oh), a bird from the prairies, the plains, that does a beautiful dance during mating season. The white man calls *cio* "prairie chicken." A lot of imagination there, you know. But we call it *cio* and the word describes the dance and gives you a picture. Indigenous languages always give you pictures. When I was a young man I was given the right to dance and became a champion fancy dancer at some of our traditional Indian dances.

I was given my third name in 1972 at a July 4th celebration at Porcupine, South Dakota, on the Pine Ridge Reservation three years after joining the American Indian Movement. *Oyate Wacinyapi*. Works for the People.

You receive your fourth name when you become an elder, and hopefully I'll get there. I already know my community, the name of respected, wise and patient leader from the past. When I reach the time when I'm considered an elder and worthy, the name will be conferred on me and again I'll have to live up to it.

Copyright © 1995, John Edgar Wideman. Appears by permission of the author, John Wideman and *Modern Maturity*.

68 • Affirmative Action and Racial Harmony

PETER GABEL (TIKKUN)

*U*nless there is an unforeseen upsurge of emotionally compelling support for affirmative action by a cross-racial coalition in the near future its demise appears likely to be the next nail in the New Deal coffin. Should we understand this as being the result of a new wave of mean-spiritedness or even racism that is sweeping the white population of which the first indication was the anti-immigrant Proposition 187 in California?

No.

No more accurate is Secretary of Labor Robert Reich's economic explanation that non-college-educated white males are facing declining real incomes—or the more conventional Left economic analysis that ruling elites are shoring up their own power by pitting white and minority sectors of the working class against each other.

The reason for the success of the assault on affirmative action is that the idea of affirmative action has largely lost its idealistic meaning, emanating from a vision of true racial equality, of inclusion of all people in a loving and nonexploitative human community, which emerged from the spirit of the civil rights movement. That idealistic meaning was part of a larger challenge to the alienation that pervades American society, to the selfishness and individualism that is fostered by the competitive marketplace and that makes the creation of loving human relationships and cooperative human community so difficult.

This idealistic meaning of affirmative action has been replaced by its virtual opposite, a meaning that actually defends the legitimacy of the competitive marketplace and the alienation that it engenders while claiming that Blacks and other minorities should be given preference over "more qualified" whites for jobs and for admission to college and professional schools. The justification for this special treatment is that past discrimination resulting from the history of slavery and legalized segregation has created an unequal playing field that favors whites and denies minorities "equality of opportunity" in their effort to make it in the marketplace—therefore, minorities should be given a leg up in spite of their relative "lack of merit" until the effects of the past discrimination are eradicated.

When Martin Luther King, Jr. cried out that he had been to the mountaintop and was never coming down, he wasn't talking about making it in the competitive marketplace. He was talking about transforming our cruel and alienated world so that people would recognize, respect, and love one another across the richness of their racial differences.

But it was precisely the failure of progressive forces to make this idealistic vision of a transformed human community the centerpiece of its political and legal claims that in significant part led to the erosion of the transformative appeal of this century's social movements, including the civil-rights movement.

The consequence of this despiritualization of the meaning of affirmative action has been to make it rational for whites and even many Blacks and other minorities to oppose it. Affirmative action today implicitly affirms the idea that the goal of life is to make as much money and get as much status as possible in a market of scarce opportunities, and that people generally succeed in this competitive struggle according to their own merit, measured by more or less objective criteria. This is the background framework of social meaning against which people are expected to measure their success in life, their ultimate sense of self-worth. The theory then assumes that objectively less-qualified minorities should be allowed to deprive their white competitors of deserved success, recognition, and money because of past discrimination of which their current white competitors are not guilty.

Except in the most narrow legalistic sense, I think it is impossible to defend this impoverished market-based meaning of affirmative action.

The reason for the success of the assault on affirmative action is that the idea of affirmative action has largely lost its idealistic meaning, emanating from a vision of true racial equality, of inclusion of all people in a loving and nonexploitative human community, which emerged from the spirit of the civil rights movement.

First of all, it is an approach to law and social policy that legitimizes the very competitive and individualistic social reality that has to be changed if people are to begin to lead meaningful, socially connected and humane lives. However they express it, most people know this at a gut level. Why would they be motivated to fight for a program that, in its despiritualized form, is basically an affirmation of the status quo?

Second, most white people do not feel "privileged" in this society—they feel isolated, disconnected from any consistent sense of social validation, and like failures according to market criteria of success and worth. Why should they give up the modicum of potential recognition and success that affirmative action tells them they have won fair and square in order to help someone else "less qualified" whom they have not personally injured? Most white people are secretly enraged that nobody seems to care about them, and they blame themselves for not having made it on their own. You can't tell them they have a moral responsibility to sacrifice their hopes of escaping their humiliation for the sake of helping others because of sins they believe were committed long before they were born.

Third, just as market-based affirmative action implicitly legitimizes the competitive marketplace, it also legitimizes meritocracy (by making an "exception" for minorities). As it operates in the United States, meritocracy is an evil because it denies people unconditional acceptance for who they are—each of us is made to feel we must achieve something to "merit" recognition, worthiness, and love. Instead of eliciting people's talents and capacities in a climate of trust and support for their intrinsic value as fellow human beings, we have created a system in which people chronically feel they are about to be "found out" as lacking. They spend their lives frantically trying to measure up to some external criteria of merit, while often dreaming of failure.

As someone who has been a law professor for more than twenty years, I feel confident in saying that the Law School Admissions Test, and then the Bar Examination, measure value-laden skills of this type that are neither "objective" measures of merit to be an attorney, nor do they measure in the slightest degree the ethical and empathic capacities or the sense of justice that one ought to demonstrate to become a lawyer. These tests breed injustice because they tell whites they objectively merit things that they do not objectively merit, and they breed racial hatred because minorities know this to be true, but they cannot influence the negative judgments imposed upon them.

Why should we support a market-based theory of affirmative action that legitimizes meritocratic judgments that are evil in themselves and that breed injustice and racial hatred?

Fourth, market-based affirmative action is often humiliating to Blacks and other minorities because it treats them as unqualified and defective, as if they do not "really" deserve their admission to college or professional school or their job. This is one reason that almost 50 percent of minorities are currently opposed to

> Instead of eliciting people's talents and capacities in a climate of trust and support for their intrinsic value as fellow human beings, we have created a system in which people chronically feel they are about to be "found out" as lacking.

affirmative action (ABC/*Washington Post*, March 24, 1995). It is unjust for them to be made to feel this way because it is not true that they are "less qualified except on the basis of (usually) idiotic non-objective criteria that are utterly stacked against them. In the case of legal education, this injustice is made worse by the fact that law schools for the most part value the same shallow, detached, verbal manipulations that the tests measure (compassion and a sense of justice are largely irrelevant to success in law school, although they are essential to a morally significant legal practice).

This structural humiliation inevitably leads Blacks and other minorities to act out their rage at being disrespected and humiliated, often in the form of politically correct, victimizer denunciations of whites that frighten most decent white people, who, after all, believe they have done nothing wrong. Contrary to the charges often levelled against them, most of these whites are not racists, and, in addition, they have been told by the society (through policies like affirmative action) that they "deserve" whatever they've managed to achieve. When they are attacked, guilt-tripped, and threatened with losing even the patina of self-worth that they might gain from becoming a professional, they are even less able to hear the echo of idealistic meaning that affirmative action once had, and further lose hope that they can be part of an effort to bring about the kind of community that would embody true mutual recognition and racial justice. Although these whites would prefer to be part of just such an effort to build a society based on transcendent meaning and high ethical purpose, they settle for a retreat into private life and for the crumbs of professional recognition. And they move toward a conservative politics that validates both their anger and their retreat from hope, because the alternative seems so unsafe and crazy.

Although I will vote against any attempt to abolish affirmative action, I don't see any real promise of salvation in supporting a market-based approach to it that seems so clearly ridden with contradictions and assumptions that we are opposed to. I think we must recognize that it may well increase rather than heal societal racism. But what is the alternative?

Think again of the original impulse behind affirmative action, the impulse to go beyond the mere removal of barriers ("overcoming discrimination so we can all be free to compete in the marketplace") and instead to take affirmative steps to achieve true racial justice and equality. The key point about this idealistic meaning is that far from appearing to exclude whites, it served to connect whites to a higher sense of purpose, something that would give our lives meaning in part by freeing us from the so-called privilege that is actually an empty prison. That idealistic meaning of affirmative action also connected us to Blacks and other minorities rather than separating us from them.

Redeeming that impulse today means developing a cross-racial strategy that, instead of pitting whites and Blacks against each other (threatening one group or

Reprinted from *TIKKUN* MAGAZINE, A BI-MONTHLY JEWISH CRITIQUE OF POLITICS, CULTURE, AND SOCIETY. Subscriptions are $31 per year from *TIKKUN*, 251 W. 100th St., 5th Floor, New York, NY 10025.

the other with invalidation and social exclusion), unites them in a challenge to the phony meritocratic criteria that historically have divided them.

69 • When Politics Fails, What Comes Next? The Case for Voluntarism

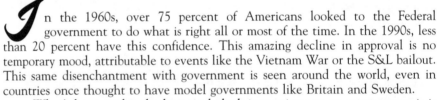

JAMES L. PAYNE

For an extended treatment of voluntarism, see James L. Payne, *The Promise of Community: Local Voluntary Organizations as Problem-Solvers*, published in 1994 by The Philanthropy Roundtable (320 North Meridian St., Indianapolis, IN 46204; 317-639-6546). See also the issue of *The Freeman* devoted to voluntarism (October 1994) published by the Foundation for Economic Education (Irvington-on-Hudson, NY 10533; 914-591-7230). Other organizations promoting voluntarism include the Acton Institute (161 Ottawa NW, Suite 301, Grand Rapids, MI 49503; 616-454-3080) and the Capital Research Center (727 15th St. N. W., Suite 800, Washington, D.C. 20005; 202-393-2600).

*I*n the 1960s, over 75 percent of Americans looked to the Federal government to do what is right all or most of the time. In the 1990s, less than 20 percent have this confidence. This amazing decline in approval is no temporary mood, attributable to events like the Vietnam War or the S&L bailout. This same disenchantment with government is seen around the world, even in countries once thought to have model governments like Britain and Sweden.

What's happened is the historical clock is running out on government: it is increasingly out of step with modern values. Specifically, 1) it is a coercive institution in an age that questions the use of force; and 2) it is a centralized system in an era that values diversity.

The possible demise of government disturbs many people, because they see it as the only way to address public problems. Who, they ask, will put out fires or run libraries if government doesn't? Fortunately, there is an alternative approach already in wide and successful use. It's called voluntarism.

Voluntarism is based on the premise of not using force or the threat of force to solve problems. Instead, it relies on generosity, on persuasion, on the desire to make a better world. Let's suppose there's litter in your street. In the governmental approach, you would appeal to politicians to set up a tax system to force people to contribute money to fund a bureaucracy to pick up the litter. Under voluntarism, in its simplest version, you would go out and pick it up yourself! If there was more than you could handle, you would start a voluntary group and persuade your neighbors to donate time—to work as volunteers—or money—to hire someone to pick up the litter.

Notice the advantages. No one is forced to contribute, so we avoid the resentment of those who don't believe in the project. And because people can stop contributing whenever they see their money being wasted, voluntary organizations are prompted to be efficient. Imagine what would happen to corruption at the Federal Department of Housing and Urban Development if we could simply decline to donate to it until it cleaned up its act!

Finally, voluntarism offers what democracy always promises but cannot deliver: citizen control. In government, a citizen is only an infinitesimal fraction of a sprawling electoral and bureaucratic system. As a result, everyone feels powerless. With voluntarism, small groups of friends and neighbors can actually carry out the delivery of public services.

A shining future awaits us as we abandon the prevailing system of trying to force our neighbors to do good, and start cooperating with them on a friendly, voluntary basis.

For further information on the breadth and scope of the not-for-profit sector and voluntary organizations within the United States contact Independent Sector, 1828 L. St., NW Washington, D.C. 20036, 202-223-8100. Independent Sector publishes a compendium of information on voluntary activity in its *Nonprofit Almanac: Dimensions of the Independent Sector* and *Giving and Volunteering in the United States*.

70 • What's in a Date?

AMHERST EDUCATIONAL PUBLISHING

The Gregorian Calendar, of 12 months varying in lengths from 28–31 days, with the new year starting on January 1, is the most familiar calendar to most of us. It reflects an agreement about how major components of time will be defined and allows for interaction and communication across every religious, cultural, political, and geographical boundary. It provides a framework that allows us for those interactions to behave as one community.

However, for many cultural, religious, and ethnic groups, it is not the only calendar, nor even the primary one, that defines the year and the days to be observed and celebrated. In order to capture the important occasions for millions of Americans who belong to varied ethnic, religious, and cultural groups, other

Contact: Amherst Educational Publishing, 30 Blue Hills Road, Amherst, MA 01002-2220; 1-800-865-5549; Fax: 413-253-7024.

ⓘ Amherst Educational Publishing has created the Multicultural Resource Calendar which contains listings and descriptions of birthdays, historical/cultural events, days of religious observance, and days of special observance for more than 35 cultural, religious, and other groups. The illustrations below are from the calendar.

calendars are used, based on other assumptions both about how the components of time are defined and about what occasions are to be observed and celebrated.

From the perspective of specific cultural and religious groups, the simple question, "What year is it?" and the critical components of that year become more complex. In what year is September 1996 for an observant Jew, a Muslim, or for traditional Chinese, Vietnamese, and Koreans? For the Jew, September 1, 1996 is in year 5756 and on September 14, 1996 it becomes year 5757. For a Muslim, January 1, 1997 is in year 1417 with the new year occurring on May 9, 1997. For Asian cultures that follow the Chinese lunar calendar, the new year does not begin on January 1, 1997 but on February 7, 1997 and is the year 4695.

Thus the answer to the question, "When does the year begin next year?" does not have the same answer every year. Many cultural and religious groups base their calendars on calculations of the phases of the moon or a combination of moon and solar calculations resulting in the days for particular events, such as the beginning of the year, moving each year. The beginning of the Chinese New Year, for example, can vary from mid January to mid-February of the Gregorian Calendar. Long-range planning that takes into account days of special meaning to many different cultural groups, therefore, becomes much more complex than simply consulting a perpetual Gregorian Calendar.

The key times of the year to celebrate, moreover, can also vary for cultural, religious, and ethnic groups. While the differences may not be as sharp, various ethnic groups in the United States may emphasize different dates as important to observe and celebrate. For example, Kwanza, which is more a cultural than religious occasion, has become as important, and to some more important, than Christmas for many African Americans. Celebrating Martin Luther King's Birthday has become the most significant day in the year for African Americans' historical and cultural remembrance. Many Mexican Americans prefer to celebrate the traditional religious Day of the Dead holiday from the evening of October 31 through November 1 instead of Halloween.

For any individual, therefore, the calendar becomes a way of connecting to the particular ethnic, cultural, or religious group of which they are a part. For those not part of that group, understanding and knowing the calendar that defines the year and the critical days of demarcation of a particular group helps to provide a way of understanding and connecting with that group. Simple gestures of recognition and respect for important celebratory events can help to build connections among different individuals and groups which can also lead to participation in those events and the further breaking down of barriers that often separate us.

In planning occasions as part of an organization, or in our everyday interactions, that involve people from varied cultural, ethnic, and religious backgrounds, we need to take account of what days are important from their perspective as well as from our own. Understanding the different calendars that shape time for different people also helps to create the complex positive bonds in an increasingly diverse society that maintain our common community while at the same time respecting and acknowledging the ways in which we are different. Just as wishing family, friends, and acquaintances a "Happy New Year" on January 1 is one of the social bonds that makes us one community, greeting those whose new year is celebrated on different day, and perhaps at a very different time in the "Gregorian" year, is also a small, but significant step in creating harmonious connections that make all relationships more positive, meaningful, and satisfying.

71 • Playing Straight With a Mixed Deck

BOB ABRAMMS AND DIANE JOHNS
(SUPERVISORY MANAGEMENT)

*T*ry to imagine a sharp, responsible, effective manager today who has somehow been able to avoid learning anything about computers . . . Not too easy to picture, is it? We have all had to learn, most of us starting at an awkward "0," at least a little about computers because of the tremendous impact they have had on our work life.

Now, try to imagine this same sharp and effective manager trying to pretend that if he stays in his office long enough, his suddenly very diverse workforce will somehow go back to being comfortably white and male. At which time he can come out of his office and start communicating again.

Yes, it's true. Despite the clearly changing face of the workforce, some otherwise impeccable managers are forgetting that their responsibility for communicating means communicating with *everyone*.

GLOBAL CONNECTEDNESS

We have always lived in a world of diversity. Irish, Jewish, Black, Polish, Hispanic, Asian, and Italian groups were all highly visible contributors to the early growth of our nation. It is only now that we are accepting the challenge to respond more expansively and sensitively to what Marshall McLuhan has called "the global village." Technological advances and the increasing electronic "connectedness" of

ⓘ See "Working with People from Diverse Backgrounds: Some Tips for Relating," by C. Vázquez & D. Johns. Also, "Black Boss, White Boss . . . Listen To Me." Both available from ODT at 1-800-736-1293.

Two excellent newsletters for up-to-date information on diversity are: *Cultural Diversity at Work*, 206-362-0336 or Fax 206-363-5028 and *Managing Diversity*, 716-665-3654 or Fax 716-665-8060. Call or fax either for a free sample copy.

the last 50 years have brought us closer to other parts of the globe than ever before. The world, in its great variety, is now spilling into our schools, our neighborhoods, and being more accurately reflected in our workforce.

For managers, this new mission of taking responsibility for communicating across differences is a particularly challenging invitation to growth. For just as flexibility in management styles (situational leadership) has become a widely used tool for increasing workplace effectiveness, flexibility in *styles of communication* is a further step in the same direction.

MANAGEMENT FOR THE FUTURE

Now more than ever, learning to draw upon the richness of a kaleidoscopic workforce, expanding to be able to help all team members bring out their best efforts, is an astute managerial decision. In fact, the predicted workforce shortage will see broader utilization of immigrant and handicapped workers within even the next 3 to 5 years.

White, male managers who continue to try to fall back along traditional and comfortable "white" communication patterns may be doomed in the domestic economy as well as in the global marketplace. Findings have shown that there is a definite physiological basis for the experience that women think, communicate, and act very differently than men do. Even if a woman is of the same race and class as a man, he shouldn't be fooled into thinking her communication styles and frame of reference at work are the same as his.

Add to this the fact that many minorities do not feel their position in the organization has really improved much over the past few years, and it seems clear that the lack of alternatives to the white male club's management/communication styles has made it difficult for minorities and women to progress beyond the mid-range of corporate hierarchies.

SO WHAT'S A SHARP MANAGER TO DO?

First of all, acknowledge that learning to communicate flexibly has benefits you want to obtain—personal, professional, or organizational enrichment among them. Having access to the much wider range of problem-solving skills, solutions, perspectives, approaches, and input that a diverse workforce brings is significant among those benefits.

Next, you can start to take a look at *you*. Where do you fit in the mosaic? What is your ethnic or cultural background, social or economic class/status, education level (and favorite learning mode—do you like to read and see, listen, or *do*?)? What interests you, what inspires you and gives you a sense of fulfillment?

Answering these questions can put you in touch with an essential reality—a touchstone for communication with others—that everyone else that you work and

ⓘ See, for example "Gray Matters" by Sharon Begley, *Newsweek*, March 27, 1995; "Sizing Up the Sexes" by Christine Forman, *Time*, Jan. 20, 1992; or the classic *Sex and the Brain* by Durden-Smith & de Simone (New York: Little Brown, 325 p.)

play and deal with is as complex, contradictory, talented and vulnerable as you are—all in ways that come in different colors, packages, and speech patterns.

Pretty basic stuff, but so easy to forget.

ACTION STEP—FIND OUT!

So how does this translate to daily interactions at work? Apprising yourself of some of the main traits of, or communication pitfalls with, the people that you work with is a commendable next step. Finding out, for example, that the uncomfortable "closeness" you may feel with your Italian or Arabic colleagues may have everything to do with how those cultures experience physical space between people—the closer the better in those cultures, to express interest, enthusiasm and loyalty. People with northern European backgrounds tend to find this proximity invasive or unpleasant.

With the sharp increase in international business, there is a wealth of material available on these kinds of cultural differences. Your local library can be a good place to begin looking. Remember too, as you read about cultural differences, that even second and third generation members are still influenced by family environments pervaded by these same subliminal cultural styles.

BACK AT THE OFFICE

On an interpersonal level, you can plunge in by simply expressing honestly your concerns and confusions:

"I get uneasy when you don't look at me when we speak. Is something wrong that I need to know about?" (*Direct eye contact, especially for some Asian cultures, is considered rude.*)

"I'm never sure how much feedback to give you. I'd like to support your work performance but I can't tell if my suggestions are helpful or even welcome. Can you tell me?" (*Many times black/white speech patterns lead whites into unnecessary "over- explaining" to blacks.*)

"I just don't know sometimes if I should open the door for you or not. I'd like to be helpful, but I don't want to offend you. Would this have been an appropriate time to help or not?" (*A concern for many around people with limited physical ability. Sometimes perplexing as a gender issue, too!*)

Treating another person naturally and affirming the innate human dignity that we all share, goes a long way towards opening up communication.

THE GOLDEN ACE

And, along those same lines, we have a golden ace up our sleeve–a technique that's fast, relatively easy, and it works:

Treat the other person as though she or he were you in disguise.

The level, friendly, honest encounter that can happen as a result of maintaining this perspective can override a myriad of cultural details.

Acceptance, good-will, and respect are the cornerstones of successful communication and exchange—ones that cross *all* barriers of class, gender, race, and ability.

This article is not copyrighted. You have permission to reproduce it in any form.

Models that Work—Alternative Views and Best Practices

Activities that work and ideas that break new ground—that is what our contributors bring to this section. Cultures, left to themselves, tend to implode and self-destruct by reinforcing their best ideas to the point where they become intractable dogmas. These societies or groups depend upon their strengths to the point that they become weaknesses. This is as true of the diversity culture as it is of any other group, movement, or profession.

Renewal comes out of diversity. Rejuvenation occurs when we cross boundaries, learn from other disciplines, change paradigms, and think the unthinkable. It means using a computer to teach a dying language and reinforce a threatened culture, as one contributor reports. Other writers tell us it comes from learning from those we mentor or redrawing the map of the world.

Alternatives come from searching out best practices—finding out who's doing what in our organizations, whatever their credentials. It comes from questioning established practices in law, criminal justice, customer service, marketing, economics. Here is a multitude of new ideas and activities to stimulate your own imagination and creativity.

A new technique in the communication field is increasingly being applied to cultural diversity interventions in organizations. It is called dialogue and was inspired by the late David Bohm. In dialogue, time is set aside for open conversation under guidelines that foster candor, reflection, and respect for all participants. The objective is not to arrive at a fixed endpoint, but rather to increase a group's understanding of underlying issues.

When practiced by a group or team, dialogue lifts into vivid relief the underlying cultural assumptions standing in the way of a more inclusive culture. In time this leads to higher levels of collaboration and partnership—critical for organizations wanting to take full advantage of their diversity.

For more information about various forms of dialogue groups, contact Linda Teurfs, a principal in The Dialogue Group, who conducts public and inhouse programs on the facilitation and practice of dialogue at 909-244-6626, or her partner Glenna Gerard at 714-497-9757. Also contact Sally Huang-Nissen (see Contributors section) A meditation on the dialog process by Sally can be found in Section 6.

72 • The Invisible Helping Hand: How Profit-Making Firms Help the Poor

JAMES L. PAYNE
(THE AMERICAN ENTERPRISE)

*I*n Dallas, Texas, there's an unusual organization that serves the needy and homeless. It takes shabby street people and gives them a bed in a warm, safe place to sleep, a hot shower, and doughnuts and coffee for breakfast. It finds them jobs, provides transportation to and from the work site, gives them a sandwich for lunch and a five-dollar advance on their pay.

The organization is not a federal job-training program or a church-run charity. It's a private, profit-making company that gets no government aid of any kind and, indeed, pays $1.4 million in taxes to federal, state, and local governments.

The Dallas branch of Industrial Labor Service Corporation is the largest employer of temporary manual laborers in the city. On a typical day it sends out 650 workers, bussing them to and from job sites in its vans. It also operates a shelter named the Bunkhaus which accommodates up to 180 men per night. It pays its workers an average of $4.70 per hour and collects $7.50 per hour from the employers who use them. From this $2.80 spread, it pays dispatchers, van drivers, salesmen, security guards, rent, utilities, and so forth. After all these expenses, ILS still makes a profit—of about 17 cents per hour of labor contracted.

Yet ILS's success in the marketplace is not its greatest achievement. It is, almost without knowing it, an effective social welfare program. This comes as a surprise. The down and out are supposed to require charity—handouts and compassion—not capitalists who are trying to make money from them. Yet a close look at ILS operations reveals that the theory of the invisible hand, whereby profit-seeking can unintentionally serve the public good, applies even to the needy.

GIVING LODGERS WHAT THEY WANT

To learn about the ILS operation, I entered the system for a few days, sleeping in the Bunkhaus and taking jobs through the hiring hall. It was uncanny to see how, on point after point, the pressure to make money produces a socially constructive result.

The Bunkhaus charges five dollars a night, and covers its costs with this income. Since it is demanding something from its customers, the company has to give something in return. Its biggest service, I felt, was security. Most of the men

> *i* See "From Underclass to Working Class" by James L. Payne in *The American Enterprise* (Sept./Oct., 1995), pp. 24-28, for a full-length version of this approach. This issue of the magazine also contains a number of other perspectives on community- and church-based alternatives to government welfare.

ⓘ Also see "History's Solutions" by Marvin Olasky, *National Review* (Feb. 7, 1994), pp. 45-48.

staying in the Bunkhaus have done time in prison. Yet somehow, just one manager and one security guard keep good order among this rough humanity. These staffers know how to screen out the worst troublemakers, exclude drugs, and cool off altercations before violence breaks out.

Part of their strategy is allowing the workers considerable freedom, and finding ways to accommodate their needs. Smoking is permitted (there are many chain smokers in this group), and beer is allowed, although it cannot be brought in after 10 PM. These concessions to human weakness respect the worker's dignity, and they also result in a more relaxed atmosphere. The workers, while predominantly black, are racially mixed, yet there is little sign of racial hostility. As I walked around the Bunkhaus one evening during a televised Dallas Cowboys football game, half a dozen blacks cordially offered me, a white stranger, a beer.

REAL JOBS FOR REAL SELF-ESTEEM

The hiring hall is located just around the corner from the Bunkhaus. Social policy today emphasizes self-esteem, but treats the concept mechanically, as if it were a substance to be given out like a pill. But it's not enough to tell someone "You're the greatest!" To raise self-esteem, the individual has to know he has done something worthwhile. Many government agencies will give someone money under the guise that he is "working" for it, but the clients know this is a sham. They see the time wasted in long breaks, in watching "instructional videos," and participating in "orientation sessions." These signals reveal that no one really cares whether this work is done.

In a real job, where an employer selfishly demands productive labor in exchange for money, the worker can hardly escape gaining a sense of accomplishment. This applies to manual labor, perhaps especially to manual labor. When you've unloaded a 60-foot trailer truck, you know you've accomplished something that sets you apart from, and somewhat above, the soft, unproductive sectors of society.

But meaningful jobs don't grow on trees, and they cannot be dreamed up by administrators twiddling pencils at their desks. They come from the world of commerce and production. The most important staff members in a work program are therefore not trainers or counsellors, but the salespersons who find the real work opportunities. In a charitably-focused agency this aspect is easily be overlooked, but in a private firm it will not be. ILS has a sales force of five employees who toil to link the men under their oversight to employers, so that ILS workers have as shot at a meaningful, dignity-enhancing job.

LABOR DISCIPLINE

Workers at the bottom of the social scale commonly lack good work habits. Arriving on time and doing what they are told can be problems. Government jobs programs have difficulty inculcating good work habits because they are funded according to the number of people the program serves. Administrators have an incentive to tolerate poor performance to keep clients in the program. The result is that, too often, a government jobs program condones, even teaches, bad work habits.

In the profit-making world, the incentives are reversed. Employers' output depends on good workers, so they systematically discourage bad work habits. For example, on my first day six of us were dispatched to a construction project in the Dallas suburb of Plano. After 15 minutes on the job, two workers were at the bus stop with their brooms and shovels, waiting for a ride back to Dallas. The foreman fired them because, among other things, they failed to stand up when he began to give instructions, and because they failed to put on their hard hats after he told them to.

The following day I too felt the lash of labor discipline. I had collected my job ticket and equipment to return to the same construction site and was waiting under an awning during a heavy cloudburst when my van was called on the loudspeaker. I figured I could wait a few minutes until the shower passed, but I figured wrong. By the time I reached the van, I had been replaced. This meant I dropped back into the newcomer's labor pool and didn't get another job for the rest of the day.

TREATING WORKERS WITH DIGNITY

Many manual laborers, with their shabby dress and poor grooming, are not socially impressive, and this tempts those in higher positions to be inconsiderate. I was surprised to discover that at ILS, the staff treats all workers with a professional courtesy. At the Bunkhaus, on the loudspeaker we were addressed as "gentlemen." At the dispatch windows and equipment counters, I saw no instance of a worker being treated roughly or unhelpfully.

There's an economic pressure for courtesy. No matter how grubby and unimpressive they may appear, these workers are necessary for the success of the business. They are customers, and the company needs to keep them coming back, for an empty labor hall spells trouble. The pressure to treat workers well comes from the highest level. "That was one thing Charles really came down on us about on his last visit," reported assistant manager Eric Veblen. "In the day-to-day rush, you know, you get careless about how you treat the workers, and it's good for someone to call you out about it." He was referring to the principal owner of ILS, Charles Joekel, who drops by the Dallas branch office from time to time. Again, one is struck by the contrast with government. One could hardly imagine a senator or mayor visiting a tax-funded job center and reminding staff to be courteous.

What lesson can we learn about welfare programs from the ILS operation? Perhaps it is the idea of exchange, to expect something in return for assistance rendered. Commercial transactions automatically include this feature, and that is why they have a healthy, constructive thrust. Government practices unilateral giving, and that is why its welfare programs have been singularly unsuccessful.

ILS (Industrial Labor Service Corporation) is currently operating under the name of Pacesetter Personnel Service. For further information contact the manager, Paul Moreno, at 1818 S. Ervay, Dallas, TX 75215; 214-565-1133, Fax 214-428-2866.

INROADS is a national nonprofit career development organization whose mission is to place talented minority youth in business and industry and prepare them for corporate and community leadership. One of the corporate sponsors who has made a success of INROADS is the Chubb Group of Insurance Companies. Starting with 19 interns in 1986, the yearly intake of interns now well exceeds 100, many of whom have become full-time Chubb employees. For more information, contact National INROADS Coordinator, Chubb Group of Insurance Companies, Human Resources Planning Department, 15 Mountainview Rd., Warren, NJ 07059.

73 • Multicultural Community Efforts— Tips for European Americans

BO SEARS

Examining actual success stories in cross-cultural and multicultural community experiences is vital. So much of what passes for deep thought in the cross-cultural and multicultural area has nothing to do with the real world.

Since most of the members of Resisting Defamation are European American, my ideas are presented as those of a European American. I do not speak for members of other ethnic groups. But the following remarks are intended to help European Americans participate effectively in cross-cultural ventures.

Active members of Resisting Defamation have engaged in several cross-cultural community projects, including a Mexican-Irish coalition to defeat regional government proposals that would have diluted newly gained voting strengths by recently empowered ethnic and national origin groups in San Jose; an Irish-Mexican-German coalition to welcome a new Superintendent to the most troubled high school district in San Jose; a Portuguese-Mexican-Irish-German-Italian coalition to resist the city's take-over of a community garden for a professional hockey ice-skating practice rink; and a Mexican-Irish-German coalition to assail certain practices by the county Registrar of Voters.

We learned a number of things in this process.

1. There is a critical need for matching voice levels. For example, a Caucasian-Vietnamese coalition (race on one level with national origin on another level) could never be developed. But European Americans who are of Irish ancestry can easily help to develop a coalition of Vietnamese-Americans and Irish-Americans. If the group with which you wish to develop a coalition is speaking from a racial voice (e.g., Black) then European Americans need to join their voices to that coalition on the same racial level.

If the group with which you wish to develop a coalition is speaking from a continental/cultural voice (e.g., African American or Asian American), then European Americans need to join that coalition on a similar level (i.e., European American). If the group with which you wish to develop a coalition is speaking from an ethnic voice (e.g., Latino), then European Americans need to join that coalition on a similar level (e.g., Celtic American or Germanic American). If the group with which you wish to develop a coalition is speaking from a national origin voice (e.g., Cambodian), then European Americans need to join that coalition on a similar level (e.g., Italian).

This is probably the most overlooked requirement when European Americans seek to join with other groups. To succeed in cross-cultural coalitions, European Americans must tailor their participation to match the voice level of the others already interested. Our experience has shown that European Americans seeking to help out as "Americans" working with racial, continental/cultural, ethnic, or national origin groups, are almost always seen to be so condescending as to amount to racism—a most unfortunate outcome for an initiative built around the most high-minded intentions!

2. We do not believe in many other kinds of tailoring. For European Americans to speak from a sense of guilt ("We're so sorry.") from a sense of historical dominance ("We know it is time for us to step back.") or from condescension ("We're here to help you.") is to undermine the entire enterprise. These attitudes reek of insincerity and cast doubt on the genuineness of participation by European Americans.

After determining the correct voice level for the cross-cultural venture, European Americans need to forge ahead with a firm understanding that they belong IN the multiculture (not behind it, above it, off to one side, or under it) and that they are members of a warm-hearted, generous, and very diverse continental/cultural umbrella ethnicity. To approach a cross-cultural venture with negative attitudes toward one's own ethnicity speaks of hypocrisy and weirdness to the other groups with which the cross-cultural enterprise is sought.

European Americans need to gently rebuke any negative stereotypes and racial/ethnic slurs directed at them. The rebuke should be done in a way that

(i) Resisting Defamation is a media watchdog group of diverse ethnicities and religions based in San Jose, Calif. (408-937-1518, e-mail ResistDef@aol.com) In the past they have offered seminars dealing with "Sensitivity to European Americans." They have an on-going commitment to combatting ethnic slurs, wherever they may occur.

Our experience has shown that European Americans seeking to help out as "Americans" working with racial, continental/cultural, ethnic, or national origin groups, are almost always seen to be so condescending as to amount to racism—a most unfortunate outcome for an initiative built around the most high-minded intentions!

reflects the candid and open embrace of the principle that ALL negative stereotypes and racial/ethnic slurs need to be put away in our cross-cultural and multicultural society—no matter at whom such stereotypes and slurs are directed.

We attended a city Human Rights Commission meeting during which an African American diversity trainer remarked that the strangest thing about "whites" was that they needed to be told when they were insulted! We believe such slurs against European Americans are counterproductive.

There is nothing wrong or destructive about rebuking negative stereotypes and racial/ethnic slurs encountered in the course of a cross-cultural enterprise. Not to rebuke them will cause the perception that the silent European Americans have failed to actually embrace full participation in the cross-cultural venture. That is, not to speak out politely and in an even tone against negative stereotypes and racial/ethnic slurs directed at ANY group (including one's own) signals bad faith to any observer.

A well-mannered rebuke will not break up a cross-cultural venture, it will strengthen it.

3. Learn the proper and accepted names and labels for other participants in cross-cultural groups. It is not too hard, after asking, "How are you?," to ask, "What name would you prefer I use in talking about the ethnic group with which you identify?" And this means that European Americans who are involved need to know what they want to be called, too, and be willing to explain what it is.

4. Watch out for European Americans who are genuine self-loathers. These people flock to cross-cultural enterprises in order to demean their own umbrella ethnicity, and are very destructive. The only European Americans who can form effective cross-cultural coalitions with other groups are those who have a firm and dignified sense of themselves as being part of a warm-hearted, generous, and diverse umbrella ethnic group. Anything less will lead to failure in the cross-cultural venture.

5. Temporary coalitions with one limited purpose are best. Once a successful cross-cultural venture has been achieved, the participants will know more people to contact when the time comes for another venture. Then get on the phone and work out the details: who, what, when, why, and where.

6. European American participation in cross-cultural ventures will not be reported in the local print media, so don't look for public education in this way. The *San Jose Mercury News* (a Knight-Ridder paper) had reporters cover each of the four examples listed in the third paragraph above and, in each case, the reporting deliberately excluded the Irish, German, Italian, and Portuguese participation, and outlined the situation as one in which embattled Mexican Americans were fighting (with no community support outside their own ethnic group) against the oppressions of a vicious and racist "white" establishment— when the paper bothered to cover the coalitions' efforts at all.

This smothering of European American involvement was the biggest surprise to us, and it means that the residents of San Jose have no knowledge of this history of very practical and local cross-cultural cooperation! It may be that there are other examples of cross-cultural ventures going on at this very minute in San Jose about which we know nothing because of a very real hostility to presenting factual data about such alliances. The *Mercury News* will report on cooperative efforts by the Vietnamese and Japanese communities, for example, but will never report similar efforts by the Vietnamese and Irish communities and include mention of the Irish participation.

Mixed Blood Theater is a theater group offering EnterTRaining: using the language and traditions of live theater, music, dance, comedy, satire, monologue, and dialogue to clarify issues of race, culture, gender, disability, age, sexual orientation, or other life experiences. Customized theater uses client-specific issues, terms, buzzwords, and locations. Reach them at The Mixed Blood Theater Company, 1501 South Fourth St., Minneapolis, MN 55454, 612-338-0937, or call EnterTRaining at 612-338-4509.

A Tale of "O" by Dr. Rosabeth Moss Kanter is the world's best-selling video on diversity. Using symbols rather than words, it avoids references to specific groups but looks at the group dynamics and natural human behavior around the phenomena of sameness and difference. The new revised video includes both animation and live vignettes and comes in both a long and short version along with an Instructor's and User's Guide, including course handouts on diskette. Available for $695 each from Goodmeasure Direct, Inc., One Memorial Dr., Cambridge, MA 02142, 617-621-3838, Fax 617-225-2015.

The Cultural Ambassador program originated in 1991 as an Alberta government training program that develops resource people to assist Albertans of all ethnocultural origins to participate fully in Alberta society. It allows people to experience the cultural diversity of the province in a structured, nonthreatening way by bringing people together who otherwise might never have talked to each other. The program contributes to the three goals of the Alberta Multiculturalism Act (1990):

1. Awareness—by enhancing Albertans' understanding and appreciation of the benefits and positive values of a culturally diverse society and demonstrating how that contributes to a strong province
2. Access—by assisting public institutions, businesses, industries, and organizations to develop operations and services that are available and appropriate to the needs of all Albertans
3. Participation—by assisting Albertans from cultural and racial minorities to integrate effectively and participate fully in society

For more information contact Carolyn Pinto at Alberta Community Development, 901 Standard Life Centre, 10405 Jasper Ave., Edmonton, AB T5J 4R7, Canada; 403-478-3352, Fax 403-457-4437, e-mail: pinto@freenet.edmonton.ab.ca.

Paved with Good Intentions: The Failure of Race Relations in Contemporary America, by Jared Taylor (New York: Carroll & Graff, $22.95, ISBN 0-7867-00254) documents the cover-up in the handling of racial information in the media and in particular assaults the universal assumption that "white racism" is entirely to blame for the deteriorating situation of much of black society.

74 · Becoming Allies

AMY J. ZUCKERMAN AND GEORGE F. SIMONS

*O*nce you become aware of the challenges and issues created by differences in background of the people you live and work with, you can begin to value them in new ways. You are also ready to learn how to become an ally for people different from yourself, and to let others be allies for you, if you are to benefit from the full diversity of your group, organization, or community.

WHO IS AN ALLY?

An ally is someone who is willing to stand up and support you. Allies might have some things in common with you, but typically they reach across difference in order to help achieve mutual goals.

WHAT KIND OF PERSON IS AN ALLY?

Allies know that their lives are richer for supporting others. They aren't threatened by people who "accuse" them of pandering to outsiders or culturally "unacceptable" groups or spread rumors, because allies are secure in who they are. They know that being different is not bad and they seek to effectively diffuse attempts to malign or slander. They are able to draw on their own experience of prejudice and unfairness to help others. They are able to see that if one group is treated unfairly, it makes it easier for another group—one they might belong to—to be mistreated. They are not allies because it's "the right thing to do," or because they take pity on anyone. We want to be equals and peers with those whose allies we are, and we don't seek to "champion the cause."

WHAT DO ALLIES DO?

Allies often play the valuable role of talking to people who wouldn't listen to a member of a specific group. For instance, allies are often effective with people who wouldn't knowingly be in the company of gay people. Allies get the same message of fairness out, but sometimes in words that others can better understand. Current and future allies are already positioned in organizations where they can create change. Allies are essential to the peaceful, productive presence in the workplace and community of groups who differ from the dominant culture.

    Things you can do to be an effective ally in your organization:

1. Confront prejudiced remarks, jokes and behaviors.
2. Encourage efforts to institute company policies that are inclusive of the concerns of groups who would otherwise be left out.
3. Treat people you are allying with as peers.
4. Maintain a sense of humor that degrades no one.
5. Reach out to individuals and groups to build community and coalition.

BEING ALLIES WHEN YOU ARE A MEMBER OF THE DOMINANT OR PREVAILING CULTURE

Being an ally is serious work. In some environments, it can mean becoming a target of physical threats and violence. Remember the legacies of courageous people who took on struggles that did not directly affect them, because to do anything less was not enough. The following list will help you to develop your skills as an ally.* Reflect on them and use the space below to record your thoughts either for yourself or to discuss with others.

- No matter who you are, you are the perfect person to be an ally.
- Recognize the fears people have of people they do not understand and develop creative strategies to diffuse it.
- People different from you are experts on their own experiences and you have much to learn from them. Ask, listen, and learn.
- Help where, when, and how you can.
- Be willing to take risks and make mistakes. Trust the people you are trying to support to let you.
- Learn the stories of those you are an ally to, their values and history, their hopes and aspirations. Help people to honor and celebrate the past and the present.
- Don't expect gratitude. Remember, you are an ally because you choose to be, and because it is in your best interest to be. Be their ally even if they're not willing to be yours.
- Give yourself credit for the ways in which you are able to help your current and future coworkers.

My thoughts on being or becoming an ally _____

_____

Once you become aware of the challenges and issues created by differences in background of the people you live and work with, you can begin to value them in new ways. You are also ready to learn how to become an ally for people different from yourself.

* This list and the one on the following pages were developed in part by San Francisco diversity trainer Charles Seltzer.

HAVING ALLIES WHEN YOU ARE NOT A MEMBER OF THE DOMINANT OR PREVAILING CULTURE

You may be proud of your culture, history, and contributions, but sharing perspectives with others can be difficult because of past experiences of misunderstanding, bias, and mistreatment. However, when you have the courage to trust others to help, both their lives and ours are that much richer and we are collectively stronger. The following items are good to keep in mind when working with allies. Reflect on them and use the space below to record your thoughts either for yourself or to discuss with others.

- You and members of your group deserve to have allies.
- Your issues are important to, and usually affect, all the people in your group. In addition, you are the expert on your own experience.
- Some potential allies have been hurt by bias and prejudice themselves, and sometimes this (temporarily) prevents them from being your ally.
- Expect your allies to be perfect allies, but know they will make mistakes. Trust that they are able to deal with "difficult" issues. Tell them what you need from them.
- Many members of your group may be survivors of difficult ordeals because of who they are. Know the history of your group's challenges and resistance, and let it inspire your present challenges.
- Remember to be an ally to your allies and provide them with the information they need to continue to be effective.

My thoughts on having an ally _____

75 • Enhancing Diversity Fairness with the Multisource Assessment Approach

ANN J. EWEN AND MARK R. EDWARDS

That's not fair!" This charge is not confined to the elementary school playground. It is also heard in organizations. In particular, it's often leveled against the performance appraisal system. When true, which is often the case, employees are demotivated and productivity is lost.

For an appraisal system to be perceived as equitable, it must enable the managers (raters) to accurately distinguish among various levels of employee performance. It must also entail a system for appropriate distribution of rewards and developmental opportunities.

A revolutionary change is occurring in the performance development and appraisal arena. Driven by dramatic organizational changes, we see a greater number of employees reporting to each manager, more team-based structures, and higher employee expectations. Traditional top-down feedback models where the boss collects the performance information and renders a verdict do not make sense in light of these changes. A multisource assessment process (MSA) is being increasingly used as an alternative to traditional single-source, or MBO-type, appraisal processes.

Traditional single-source or supervisor-only appraisals often fail the fairness test. They are not accurate, credible, or even useful to employees or to leaders. Such measures often do not distinguish between performers, resulting in high appraisal ratings for nearly everyone. This creates false expectations that performance will be rewarded. We find that most organizations are plagued by the interrelated problems of "undifferentiated appraisals" and "rating inflation." Organizations clearly have limited resources with regard to merit pay. The fact that these dollars are often allocated without a clear link to the appraisal system causes a host of problems. Are there any alternatives?

(i) A full report with empirical data on over 20,000 multisource assessments (MSAs) is available from TEAMS, Inc. 4450 S. Rural Rd., S. A200, Tempe, AZ 85282; 602-413-9773.

A "NEW" ALTERNATIVE: MULTISOURCE ASSESSMENT

Multisource assessment captures evaluations from the "knowledge network," those in the circle of influence around each performer. The feedback comes from a team generally of 6 to 9 people. The basic MSA process includes the following:

- Assessment on critical skills or key behavioral competencies
- Training for participants before and after receiving feedback
- Multiple evaluations are independent and anonymous
- Assessment occurs from knowledgeable work associates
- Safeguards are used to insure process fairness to all participants

MSA systems without safeguards are likely to multiply instead of reduce error, because traditional statistical assumptions do not hold. Each small sample contains the probability that a highly peculiar response may occur due to intentional or unintentional bias, resulting from friendship, competition, jealousy, or other factors. Safeguards that moderate distortion and maximize user fairness are necessary in MSA systems to moderate these predictable errors.

> By expanding the evaluation team from one person to a group of 6 to 9 members, the quality and accuracy of the performance rating is enhanced and perceived to be fairer.

THE IMPORTANCE OF FAIRNESS

If the performance appraisal is not viewed as fair, organizations lose. If litigation occurs due to employees' charges of unfairness, the organization loses opportunity costs as well as the goodwill of other employees even if it "wins" the lawsuit. Productivity may also be lost.

ETHNICITY

The results across the organizations we have worked with indicate that MSA neutralizes discrimination based on ethnicity. In many organizations where single-source appraisals are used, Caucasians receive higher scores than people of color. Data show that regardless of ethnicity, employee scores on performance are neutralized when an MSA process is used.

Additionally, the multisource assessment was rated as fairer than supervisor-only appraisals by women, older employees and people of color

SUMMARY

Fairness is substantially improved with a multisource assessment approach over traditional top-down appraisals. By expanding the evaluation team from one person to a group of 6 to 9 members, the quality and accuracy of the performance rating is enhanced and perceived to be fairer.

Management theorists and practitioners have been calling for performance measurement processes that are color-blind, and an MSA system delivers exactly that result. Furthermore, our research indicates that MSA systems also create increased fairness on dimensions of gender and age. We believe that MSAs are a necessity if organizations are committed to achieving diverse, high-performing employee populations.

76 · Diversity in Law
Letter to the Editor (The New Yorker)

ANDREA BAKER

When I came from Idaho to attend school near Philadelphia last fall, West met East like two trucks on a one-lane mountain road. Chenoweth, a Representative from

Idaho, is right when she says that "our way of life out here is something that in the East they can't fathom." However, the opposite is also true. It wasn't until I ventured east of Yellowstone that I learned that the unadulterated Idaho land I love exists precisely because the federal government owns the majority of its acres; that good things are sponsored by the N.E.A.; that loose gun laws and decreased welfare can be destructive for the inner-city poor. It is clear to me now that laws that are unnecessary (and even harmful) for some parts of this country may be necessary for others. But I balk at giving the states more autonomy. The legislative wisdom of people who are seeing only one facet of a very big diamond is doubtful.

Andrea Baker
Haverford, PA

77 · Take Back the Charter

PAUL HAWKEN (UTNE READER)

*a*t present, the environmental and social responsibility movements consist of many different initiatives connected primarily by value's and beliefs rather than by design. What is needed is a conscious plan to create a sustainable future, including a set of design strategies for people to follow. One of the first I will suggest is to take back the charter.

Although corporate charters may seem to have little to do with sustainability, they are critical to any long-term movement toward restoration of the planet. Read *Taking Care of Business: Citizenship and the Charter of Incorporation*, a 1992 pamphlet by Richard Grossman and Frank T. Adams (Charter Ink, Box 806, Cambridge, MA O2140).

Corporations are chartered by, and exist at the behest of, citizens. Incorporation is not a right but a privilege granted by the state that includes certain considerations such as limited liability. Corporations are supposed to be under our ultimate authority not the other way around. The charter of incorporation is a revocable dispensation that was supposed to ensure accountability of the corporation to society as a whole. When Rockwell criminally despoils a weapons facility at Rocky Flats Colorado with plutonium waste or when any corporation continually harms, abuses, or violates the public trust, citizens should have the right

One of the ways in which new models must be created to respond to our social needs is to hold individuals and corporations accountable for their actions. Hawken's bold proposal is both realistic and responsible. Where corporations abuse the public, the response should be swift and harsh. The fact that white collar crimes (like the S&L scandal) are punished with such leniency is just one more example of the double-standard of justice based on class in the U.S.

(i) Hawken outlines eleven other "Strategies for Sustainability" in his article "A Declaration of Sustainability," in *Utne Reader* (Sept/Oct 1993), pp. 54–61).

to revoke its charter, causing the company to disband, sell off its enterprises to other companies, and effectively go out of business. The workers would have jobs with the new owners, but the executives, directors, and management would be out of jobs, with a permanent notice on their resumes that they mismanaged a corporation into a charter revocation. This is not merely a deterrent to corporate abuse but a critical element of an ecological society because it creates feedback loops that prompt accountability, citizen involvement, and learning. We should remember that the citizens of this country originally envisioned corporations to be part of public-private partnership, which is why the relationship between the chartering authority of state legislatures and the corporation was kept alive and active. They had it right.

78 · A Model Prison

ROBERT WORTH (ATLANTIC MONTHLY)

*A*ll prisons, according to Luther [Dennis Luther, now retired warden of McKean Federal Correctional Institution, Bradford, Pa.], have a culture of some sort, but it is generally violent and abusive, based on gangs. Prison staffs are aware of this culture, but they are helpless to change it.

The root of Luther's approach is an unconditional respect for the inmates as people. "If you want people to behave responsibly, and treat you with respect, then you treat other people that way," Luther says. McKean is literally decorated with this conviction. Plaques all over the prison remind staff members and inmates alike of their responsibilities; one of these plaques is titled "Beliefs About the Treatment of Inmates." There are twenty-eight beliefs, the product of Luther's many years as a warden, and they begin like this:

1. Inmates are sent to prison *as* punishment and not *for* punishment.
2. Correctional workers have a *responsibility* to ensure that inmates are returned to the community no more angry or hostile than when they were committed.
3. Inmates are *entitled* to a safe and humane environment while in prison.
4. You must believe in man's *capacity* to change his behavior.
5. Normalize the environment to the extent possible by providing programs, amenities, and services. The denial of such must be related to maintaining order and security rather than punishment.
6. Most inmates will respond favorably to a clean and aesthetically pleasing physical environment and will not vandalize or destroy it.

79 · Survival Styles

LEONARD LOOMIS

*W*hy should peace-keeping organizations like the Armed Forces, police and sheriffs' departments, and probation departments apparently suffer high levels of internal conflict? Why should they seem to be very non-receptive to diversity and conflict resolution training? A possible answer is that "survival style" is a key barrier to intramural harmony and new ideas about diversity.

Survival style begins in the old brain. It is a mechanism which operates automatically to keep humans alive when they are in life-threatening situations or what appear to be life-threatening situations. Just as the old brain is susceptible to programming over a relatively long period of time, survival styles are capable of being programmed into soldiers, police officers and the like. In fact, survival style programming is often purposively done to keep these people alive. Sometimes, survival depends on the absolute imposition of one's will on another. Probation officers in the largest department in the world (L.A. County) use this technique to control hardened juvenile offenders in maximum security situations.

The crudest examples of survival styles in unintended operation are soldiers or police who duck or take on defense/self-defense postures when they are not in a threatening situation. Survival styles can come into unintended operation, for example, when two probation officers accustomed to imposing their wills on others, begin to argue about very minor issues. Survival styles also leave the work place and cause interpersonal problems between probation officers and their spouses.

Survival styles have previously been treated as if they were a dysfunctional aspect of a person's make-up. These styles are not dysfunctional and shouldn't be approached as such. They keep their possessors alive in extreme circumstances and facilitate instantaneous decision-making when it is called for. Survival mechanisms are virtually the last thing a human gives up. Attempting to train survival styles out of people just won't be successful.

Rather, survival styles as exemplified in military and quasi-military organizations should be accepted as any other cultural parameter would be. Then successful training can begin to take place.

80 • Subject to Debate

KATHA POLLITT (THE NATION)

PARIS: August 14, 1995— If you read your newspaper, you know that Jacques Chirac, France's new conservative President, has proposed raising the minimum wage and increasing the national arts budget. Still, it's the little things that suggest how far the United States has diverged from the rest of the West. Here in Paris, for example, the unemployed get into museums and movie theaters at reduced rates, as do those on various forms of social assistance and those belonging to a *famille nombreuse*. It's a small enough offer, dismissed by Georges and Sylvie, leftist friends, as an effort to fill up empty theaters or as a meaningless gesture, since the unemployed—officially 11.6 percent of the work force—and other down-and-outers are too depressed to take advantage of it: When they leave the house it's to battle the police in the dreary high-rise banlieue to which the poor have been exiled from the gentrified city center.

Maybe so, but imagine a mother with five little ones in tow sailing into the movies at half price in Atlanta, or an out-of-work bicycle messenger flashing an official unemployment ID card at the Guggenheim Museum. There'd be a riot: Hey, buster, how come you're not out looking for work? What'd you have all those kids for if you can't support them? Why should my tax dollars pay for you to watch Sharon Stone undress?

The idea that the state should subsidize people so they can be part of mainstream society is as foreign to the U.S. way of thinking as the notion that moviegoing and museum hopping are part of what it means to be a social being. Significantly, the French equivalent of our general assistance—the welfare benefit available, in places that haven't abolished it yet, to childless singles—is called the Revenue Minimum d'Insertion, the minimum a person needs to "insert" himself into society. It's about $500 a month, plus help with the rent—more than a mother with two children gets ($366) on average in America.

ⓘ *Transcultural Leadership: Empowering the Diverse Workforce,* George Simons, Carmen Vázquez, and Philip Harris. A collection of current, practical ideas, and tools for those who must manage today's diverse workforce in a global business environment. (Available from: George Simons International, P.O. Box 7360, Santa Cruz, CA 95061-7360, $28.95, ISBN 0-87201-299-9; 408-426-9608, Fax 408-457-8590, e-mail: gsintaz@aol.com).

81 • Diversity and Organizational Change

GINGER LAPID-BOGDA

*T*he action research method illuminates the steps which must be taken for effective change to occur. There must be a *contract* for the diversity effort which defines the goals, roles, expectations, resources, and scope of the intended change. Many diversity initiatives start with a focus which is too narrow to be

Diversity initiatives require the organization to constantly take stock of how it is doing and to be flexible enough to shift paradigms and change direction as needed.

effective (i.e., a mentoring program only) or a focus which is too broad to accomplish and too vague to measure ("We're going to change the work environment"). Other diversity change efforts begin without serious consideration of the required resources. Are the organization's leaders truly committed to the effort? Do they have proficiency in the skill-sets they need to support the implementation of this effort—and, do they have the authority to obtain and spend the time and money on what they are trying to achieve? Contracting helps resolve the above issues at the front end.

A diversity *assessment* is just as essential to a successful diversity effort as a systemic organizational assessment is to any organizational change initiative. Without an assessment, how can an organization know what issues exist and what their various underlying root causes might be? If the organization's decision-makers do not know this, how can they know where to put their scarce time and resources? Perhaps they do need a training program—but what type, by what time, and for whom? On the other hand, training may not be the most effective approach. For example, holding senior managers accountable for achieving diversity goals, as well as for changing organizational practices, may achieve more diversity success, in less time and at a lower cost. And, how will the organization know whether diversity-related progress has been made over time unless they have a baseline against which to compare the change? An effective assessment process will address these concerns.

The action research emphasis and technology related to *evaluation and renewal* are particularly important in the area of diversity. Organizations frequently find diversity difficult to measure for two reasons. First, diversity changes generally occur over a long term; consequently, sponsors must be patient because efforts to measure success can only occur over time. Second, many diversity outcomes (except numeric outcomes such as hiring or retention statistics) are more *qualitative* than quantitative. The variety of evaluation tools supplied by the behavioral sciences can be extremely useful here. In the area of renewal (continuously reassessing the change effort), successful diversity initiatives require the organization to constantly take stock of how it is doing and to be flexible enough to shift paradigms and change direction as needed. There are some "best practices" when it comes to diversity,[1] but there is no clear template that any organization can follow in every situation. No organization is like any other organization.

[1] Ann Morrison, *The New Leaders: Guidelines on Leadership Diversity in America* (San Francisco: Jossey Bass Publishers, 1992).

Achieving & Managing Diversity Series is a four-part video diversity series with discussion guides. It includes:

1. The Vortex Vision: The Executive Vision. This video is designed to enrich a top-to-middle-management training program on corporate vision and changing corporate culture.
2. Hidden Conversations. Communication across cultures improves when workers recognize and explore the unspoken cultural conversations each of us has with ourselves when speaking and listening.
3. Chaos in Beta Sector. This video about the importance of developing diverse employees explores some of the common pitfalls in searching for, hiring, and retaining nontraditional workers.
4. The Team Dream. This video explores the challenges of building a multicultural team. It is ideal for training both those who set-up and lead workforce teams and those who participate in them.

Available in English and French. Unit price $395, all four videos $1,495. George Simons International, P.O. Box 7360, Santa Cruz, CA 95061-7360, 408-426-9608, Fax 408-457-8590, e-mail: gsintaz@aol.com.

82 · A Mentoring Dilemma

H. VINCENT FORD

Sixty-one percent of African-American, Asian, and Hispanic/Latino managers and employees feel that a major mistake that senior management makes in dealing with diversity is: *making decisions about minorities in the executive suite without consulting or conferring with them.*

African-American Woman
It seems to me that they (Caucasian males) are very uncomfortable with me. If I do have any contact with them it is always in a group. I can't seem to get any private time to discuss sensitive or career issues.

I am tired of all this concern about my virtue. White men do not interest me nor am I attracted to them. But they seem to think that sex or romantic encounters are all we are good for—what an awful stereotype. How can I ever advance without the "boys" believing that I slept my way up? It is ridiculous.

I'm married. I have two children. My husband is a Wall Street financial analyst. I have my MBA and MS in Microbiology. Yet I am seen as a Black vixen. I dress very conservatively and avoid any behavior that might even remotely be perceived as flirtatious. Yet I get comments about my eyes, my hair, my perfume. Meanwhile, I

Role play each of the parts described here. Then brainstorm ways to move beyond these impasses.

have not advanced at the rate of my counterparts. I can't get the assistance I require from my boss to discuss career opportunities. This needs to be addressed because I am sure that it is not just happening to me.

Caucasian Manager

I feel uncomfortable going out to lunch with one of them (African-American women). I think everyone will suspect that the relationship is other than business, that certainly isn't good for either of our reputations. So I avoid them.

I work with several attractive, very attractive, women. I make sure that my door is always open, and that everyone knows why we are meeting. Whenever possible, I invite two or more at the same time to avoid any appearance of sexual intentions. All we (men) need is a suggestion of sexual harassment—and there goes the career.

For a particularly creative view of the thoughts and perspectives of the lives of African-American women see *Proud Sisters, The Wisdom and Wit of African-American Women* Diane J. Johnson, editor, (White Plains: Peter Pauper Press, 1995, ISBN 0-88088-472-X) $8.50 plus shipping and handeling. Available from: Mmapeu Consulting, 183 Bridge St., Suite 2R, Northampton, MA 01060-2404, 413-586-5905.

83 • Health Care: 10 Communication Tips For Improving The Effectiveness of Interpreters

SUZANNE SALIMBENE AND JACEK W. GRACZYKOWSKI

Tip 1: Brief the interpreter first. Summarize what you will say to the patient to select the treatment option and emphasize the key information you wish to impart.

Tip 2: Explain information/ask questions in 2 or 3 different ways. Don't be afraid of repeating yourself. Try to choose different words and expressions with each explanation or question. This will help rule out misunderstanding.

Tip 3: Avoid long or complicated sentences. Be concise and try to avoid superfluous words or ideas.

Tip 4: Keep it short! Don't talk for more than one or two minutes without stopping to allow the interpreter to explain what you have said to the patient.

For a free copy of "Three Tips for Translated Training" send a SASE to Box 134-Tips, Amherst, MA 01004.

Tip 5: Allow the interpreter "thought time." The professionally trained interpreter will try to capture the essence of what you mean rather than simply translate word-for-word. Sometimes it takes a bit of time to convey the same meaning in a language with an entirely different structure and communication pattern.

Tip 6: Don't interrupt! Interrupting the interpreter while he/she is talking to the patient may cause him/her to "lose face" in the patient's eyes, to lose the trend of thought, or even to forget some vital information.

Tip 7: Don't be impatient. Permit the interpreter to use as much time as is necessary to clarify a point.

Tip 8: Allow for the "directness of English." Don't be concerned if the interpreter takes 5-10 minutes to "summarize" what you have said in 2 minutes. Don't be concerned if the patient talks for 5-10 minutes and the interpreter tells you what has been said in 2 minutes!

Tip 9: Utilize gestures and facial expressions. Arrange yourself so that you, the patient, and the interpreter are visible to one another. Use lots of gestures and facial expressions when you speak through the interpreter. Watch the patients eyes and facial expressions—both when you speak and when the interpreter speaks. Look for signs of comprehension, confusion, agreement, or disagreement.

Tip 10: Remember that "culture" may even cause a professional interpreter to modify what you or what the patient has said. Clarify with the interpreter whether it's O.K. to discuss sexual or other "delicate issues", give bad news to the patient, etc. Ask the interpreter the best way to broach these subjects with the patient or family.

Copyright © 1995, Suzanne Salimbene and Jacek W. Graczykoski. All rights reserved.

See *Giving a Cultural Context to the Clinical Encounter: An Intercultural Sensitizer for the Health Professions,* by Rena Gropper, a medical anthropologist with a lifetime of experience in health care with diverse cultural groups. She has developed a remarkable product for health professionals: an intercultural sensitizer. A series of clinical situations representing twenty-three cultures are presented as critical incidents. Each involves a cultural misunderstanding between a health-care practitioner and a patient. The reader is offered four possible answers and is asked to choose the most appropriate. The answers and explanations appear in another chapter. Order from Intercultural Press (see Contributors section).

84 • The Terminology of Diversity

NIELS AGGER-GUPTA

Aboriginal—"The native inhabitants (of North America) and existing from the earliest times"—*Webster's Dictionary.* Other terms used by non-aboriginals are:

"First Nations peoples," "indigenous peoples," and in the United States, "Native Americans." The specific nation is usually the best choice, e.g. "Cree," "Blackfoot," "Ojibwa," "Inuit," etc. Even better are the preferred terms by the people from the Nation themselves, usually in their language—e.g., "Tsu' Tina" or "sarcee"; "Kainaiwa" or "Blood"; etc.

This listing of preferences is made somewhat complicated by the usage by Aboriginal people themselves of the term "Indian," the term that has historically been in use since the European colonizers of North America mistakenly thought they were in India.

Third World — There are now *several* usages for this term.

1. It has been used over the last thirty years (or so) to refer to the "developing" countries who are neither part of the "first world" (Europe and the Middle East), nor the "second world" (North America). A problem with this is the ethnocentrism inherent in assuming that all countries aspire to the same kind of lifestyle as in North America.
2. It is now being used as a self-identified euphemism for "person of color" particularly among people with a strong analysis of neo-colonialism, structural racism and paternalism within North American society. The use of this term helps create an affiliation with other "third world" men and women who see themselves as separate and outside North American society.

85 • Impetus to Awareness

WARD L. KAISER

*L*et's set the scene: You are one of a group of people asked to draw—from memory alone—a map of the world. You have paper, a pencil and time.

How tough will the assignment be for you? What will the result look like? What parts of the world will you get right . . . where will your map turn fuzzy . . . what outright errors will show up? How will you assess your product?

I've conducted this experiment many times. So has Thomas F. Saarinen, Professor of Geography and Regional Development, University of Arizona.

Saarinen and a group of colleagues gave the same instructions to students in 75 universities in 52 countries, analyzing 3,568 hand-drawn maps of the world.

Saarinien's findings, based on work with first-year college students, closely correlate with my own, though my sampling focuses on people in mid-career responsibilities: corporate executives, high school teachers, peace activists, clergy, professors. The findings vary from predictable to surprising. Three findings are set out here.

Finding #1: Most "personal maps" enlarge the northern hemisphere and downplay areas near the equator. Europe, Greenland, and Canada are regularly shown larger than actual size, with Greenland sometimes more than 600 times its actual size, suggesting the continued dominance of the Mercator projection, which, as it moves from equator toward the poles, progressively exaggerates size. People who know maps long ago rejected the Mercator as a general purpose map; yet it still informs—more precisely, misinforms—the world picture of large numbers of otherwise sophisticated persons.

Finding #2: People know their own vicinity best. A predictable result, to be sure. They may magnify the importance of their area by drawing it more than life-size, and, almost invariably, give it the most detail in the accuracy of coastlines, the location of rivers, lakes and mountains, and the presence of cities. This finding needs to be seen in relation to number 3.

Finding #3: Saarinen found that people of every continent and background tend to exaggerate the size of Europe and to reduce other areas. My own experience is only slighty different: both Europe *and North America* get the super-continent treatment. Interpreting his findings at the International Geographic Congress in Washington, D.C., Saarinen noted, "The results were astounding. In some cases Europe is even bigger than Africa."✳

So what's the problem? First, it's highly inaccurate. Europe measures 3.8 million square miles; Africa weighs in at 11.6 million . . . a miscalculation of more than 300 percent!

In addition to mathematical imprecision, however, the results strongly suggest a cultural bias, carrying overtones of white dominance in the world, a continuing colonial mentality. If Europeans alone enlarged Europe, and other test-takers enlarged their own areas, that would say something quite different. The results would be consistent with finding number 2. But when people of varying ages, occupations and nationalities overwhelmingly see Europe as big and important, something more than personal preference is operative. Some of us call this a Eurocentric, or North-centered, view of the world.

Such a view no longer matches reality. Europeans and North Americans can no longer relegate the rest of world to positions of inferiority. We are linked together in an interlocking economy in which whatever happens anywhere matters everywhere. Business is more likely than ever to have a global reach. Even an enterprise that is totally conducted in North America—if it exists at all—lives in

✳ Quoted in "The Warped World of Mental Maps" by Richard Monastersky, in *Science News*, Oct. 3, 1992, p. 222.

Peters Map Controversy: While the editors find the Peters Map invaluable for teaching about diversity, it is important to point out that the approach has its detractors in the cartographic world. Basically, any projection of a round surface onto a flat plane creates a number of distortions. The question becomes, "Which distortions do you prefer?"

Those fascinated by the politics of picking a map (and the values that are associated with that choice) will enjoy the critique found in *Drawing the Line: Tales of Maps and Cartocontroversy* by Mark Monmonier (New York: Henry Holt & Co., 1995, ISBN 0-8050-2581-2), pp. 9–44.

Peters Projection World Maps and training modules are available from ODT (1-800-736-1293).

What's *right* with this map? Many are finding it a stimulus to developing awareness of international, intercultural realities in today's global community.

a dynamic, intercultural environment. The plain truth is that, in such a world, we can't function effectively while being misled by distorted geographic perceptions.

The task is to develop a new, more realistic world view that will give proper attention to all parts of the world, all peoples, all contributions, all cultures. Fortunately, help is at hand. One tool that many are finding valuable in reshaping our world image is the Peters map of the world. It presents each land mass—whether on the equator or far from it, in Europe or Africa or Vietnam, in true proprtion. It is known therefore as an *equal-area projection*.

It "doesn't look right" to people on first sight. Yet that is precisely its value in an intercultural context. It shocks. It shakes loose our preconceptions. It forces us to confront certain realities, some of which may be uncomfortable. It can free us to ask, "If we have accepted a distorted view of the world all this time, what other ideas do we hold that need to be rethought?"

Presented to the world by Professor Arno Peters, a German historian, in 1974, with the first English-language version published in 1983, it has sold millions of copies worldwide. Agencies of the United Nations, educational institutions and Protestant and Roman Catholic churches are among its major users.

Among the greatest advantages of the Peters map is its "fairness to all peoples." In contrast to the support traditional maps give to a seriously skewed view of the world, the Peters gives every land mass, every nation, every people its own rightful place.This, then, provides an objective basis for new understanding and action.

"The Peters Projection breaks new ground in our understanding of ourselves as Americans, and in relation to the human family around the globe," says Bob Abramms of the management consulting firm ODT Incorporated. "It is immensely valuable for the information it presents about our geographic neighborhood. Morover, the map represents a stunning visual metaphor for thinking about change and our 'traditional' views of the world. When managers and executives first see the map in our seminars, they are shocked into recognizing the limiting assumptions of their 'old' view of the world. Many say, 'If all that I *thought* was true about the earth's shape and land masses is now found to be distorted . . . then maybe many of my *other* assumptions about the world must become suspect as well.' "

And that, surely, is a healthy condition for us all: not to have answers imposed on us by some external authority, but to question, to probe, to discover, to live in openness to new truth in this wonderfully diverse world.

KEY DILEMMAS IN THE SEARCH FOR A WORKABLE FUTURE

One's imagination can picture the "dilemma" as a mythical beast with two horns, while "being on the horns of a dilemma" is not knowing which way to turn. Dilemmas are the "stuff" of diversity. Our starting point is difference, and to resolve a dilemma we must both respect and reconcile differences in order to meet the needs of people and the situations they find themselves in.

Some deep dilemmas repeat themselves in a variety of ways throughout this section as well as surface elswhere in this *Fieldbook*. Here are some of the dilemmas and questions that the editors have seen echoing through diversity conversations.

ASSIMILATION AND ACCULTURATION VERSUS TRIBALISM AND ISOLATION

It is a natural tendency of people living and working together to develop a common culture in the form of thinking patterns and solutions to their environmental challenges. The term "melting pot" is much disparaged in diversity circles today. Yet, no matter how disliked the phrase has become, it is important to remember that it was created by earlier immigrant populations. It reflected how much they wanted to leave behind the enmities, rivalries, and the national and ethnic violence that characterized "the old country."

The contributors to this section discuss immigration, acculturation, forms of separatism, and group flight from one environment to another. A community and a nation need some commonalities. Yet, unless enriched by a steady stream of outside influences or environmental changes, over time cultures tend to stabilize into rigid monocultures. Diversity provides that needed stream. At certain seasons, it also may turn into a mad rushing river that carries us far downstream to shores where we may or may not want to live. Many North Americans are feeling that turbulence today.

Being with others, we know we will inevitably change. Sometimes we vociferously disagree about if, how much, and how fast we want to change. We are uncertain about how to incorporate or adapt to the culture of those around us. There is a limit to how much we can resist the cultural forces around us. At either extreme we fear loss—loss of identity or loss of opportunity. Do we accomplish our objectives best as insiders or as outsiders to a group or system? Do we change ourselves, influence others, change systems, or all three, and how do we do that? How do we fight the system without attacking people or injuring innocent bystanders?

US VERSUS THEM

In discussing diversity we quickly reach the question of membership. How does one belong to any group? Whom do we hold as belonging to our group? How

"An African-American employee at an East Coast Company took the day off to celebrate Martin Luther King Jr. day. Upon returning to work, he discovered a note that had been scribbled on his desk calendar: 'Kill four more, get four more days off.'" From "Keeping Hate Out of the Workplace," by Charlene Marmer Solomon, July 1992, *Personnel Journal*. A thorough and well-written collection of advice and anecdotes about hate crimes that occur in the workplace. Despite recent efforts to promote diversity, companies are finding that the workplace isn't immune to the racism that exists in society at large.

far do the boundaries of acceptance, inclusion, tolerance reach? What key indicators do we use for excluding and including: class, physical appearance, use of language, performance, ideology, manners? Why do we choose the indicators we do? Is, "You cannot understand me because you're not a . . . !" the ultimate defense one has to resist the power of another or of another's culture? At what point is one's individuality, the I, exchanged for the us? And what motivates the shift?

IS JUSTICE JUST? IS FAIRNESS FAIR?

Historically, the values of justice, fair play, and democratic process, etc., are enshrined as basic North American civic ideals. Favoritism, nepotism, and class distinctions are considered foreign and inimical to these civic ideals. We both have and have not practiced what we have preached. Detractors contend that the ideals themselves are flawed, a product of male dominance and patriarchy. Others insist that these ideals are imperfectly carried out and in need of deeper commitment. They hold that without sharing such virtuous ideals and practicing them, our society will no longer be viable. The trials of the Los Angeles police involved in the Rodney King beating and that of O.J. Simpson highlight this dilemma.

IS ALTRUISM POSSIBLE?

Under what circumstances is "doing good" for others the imposition of one's own cultural standards on them? What is the nature of "the helping contract"? How do we serve others in ways that empower them? What do we do that is disempowering? Is there any bottom line other than the marketplace? Is diversity about anything but power? In the Pandora's box which diversity seems to open, is there still a creature called hope? Conservatives claim that the desire to do good represents a personal agenda and is not an appropriate province of government. Some liberals would assert that "doing good" is a form of cultural imperialism. The question is a deeper one: How do we get our society to work?

CLASS VERSUS MERITOCRACY

The politics of identity, the struggle to restore value and legitimacy to people and groups, is considered a human right. Is the ideal that one is rewarded solely on the basis of performance actually true? Is good performance under the control of the individual or a result of genetic, environmental, or cultural endowment? We often speak of the haves and the have-nots in our society. Do we have because we merit or do we merit because we have? Must we have privilege in order to have access or must we have access in order to have privilege? It seems that self-esteem can be supported from only two sources, both social: the

THIS SOCIETY DOESN'T VALUE *CHILDREN* ANYMORE! YOU WOMEN WOULD RATHER PURSUE A SELFISH *CAREER* THAN STAY HOME WITH YOUR KIDS!

(i) "Community and Equality in Conflict," *The New York Times*, September 8, 1985. Lukas examines a central conflict in defining what it means to be American. Using both historical and contemporary examples to illustrate his point, he maps the conflict between demands for equality as universal principles enshrined in America's founding documents and what Madison called "the spirit of locality." Lukas examines how this conflict is played out in a contemporary problem, such as school desegregation.

unconditional love of others and pride in our own accomplishments. How much longer can we insist on a culture that believes in meritocracy without social responsibility?

DEMOCRACY AND HUMANISM VERSUS DARWINISM

To what degree in the "real" world of business and politics (whatever the group, society, organization, or institution) are the rules and values of democracy actually held or acted upon? Will the myths of the free market—of laissez-faire capitalism and of individualism—take us where we want to go? Is "survival of the fittest" the only rule that really counts? Warfare of all kinds including corporate competitiveness has become relentless and constant. It seems incomprehensible to today's "civilized" world that soldiers in medieval times stopped fighting to have lunch and rested on weekends.

PUBLIC VERSUS TRIBAL VERSUS LOCAL VERSUS PRIVATE RIGHTS

How much control may social groups exercise over their members? Over outsiders? How much should the state interfere with the family? When intact and functional cultures break down in pluralistic North America, how much of their function must the state undertake? We seem enmeshed in a struggle in which groups vie for favorable legislation to benefit their own group. We depend on the state to settle our differences and disputes instead of negotiating for what we need from each other. Are we giving up on becoming a community, or, are we simply doing the "tough" talk needed to resolve the issues? Can we find better and more direct ways of talking to each other about our rights and expectations than the intermediary of the state?

ALLEGIANCES AND ALLIANCES

If I belong to one group, can I belong to another? To what degree? Sometimes this dilemma creates painful choices. For example, as a black woman activist, why am I made to choose between my race and my gender? Do I stand with my black brothers in racial solidarity or with other women to protest sexism? As a white female how can I be heard when I see white males falsely accused of sexual harassment by female activists in the workplace? In North America today most of us are an amalgam of our social identity and our experiences. How can we be forced to be only part of ourselves?

FAITH VERSUS ANTI-FAITH

The country is divided by acceptance and rejection of values that come from religious traditions. It often seems like each side would like to assimilate or eliminate the other. How can we learn of others' religious traditions and explain our own without being accused of attempting to impose them as we explain? In a truly pluralistic country both sides should be able to respectfully coexist.

WHO'S IN CONTROL HERE?

How do we view power in North America? Is power inherited, appointed, elected, self-appointed? How much law and order do we need? How much ambiguity can we tolerate? Can we expect people to be inner-directed without giving them external directions? How do we value our own culture? When is it best for us? Under what circumstances are the values that come from another culture best, or useful? How are we inclined by our own culture to adopt some solutions over others? Can I feel comfortable when I realize that virtually nothing that I do is "culture free"—including how I approach diversity?

OTHER QUESTIONS

Many other questions and dilemmas surface in what our contributors offer us throughout this book. For example, diversity itself is a North American cultural construct that is currently being marketed to other parts of the world. We are starting to critique the culture of diversity as a culture, to look for ways to change it, improve it, and even find alternatives. One thing is certain, these are ongoing questions, with no final answers. They are questions that we answer for ourselves and our communities and our organizations day after day, decision after decision. We sometimes believe that we ourselves know the right answers, but history will tell us what answers we gave to the future, and future generations may decide to write history differently.

86 · Assessing Diverse Employees— A Multicultural Quagmire?

BARBARA DEANE
(CULTURAL DIVERSITY AT WORK)

" *I*t is no longer appropriate to assess managers who are women and people of color using norms traditionally taken from one reference group, mostly white males." Bob Abramms, Senior Associate, ODT, Inc. in

Amherst, Massachusetts, strikes a sharp blow to "normative" tests and instruments that American companies love to use to assess their employees.

Remember that a normative test attempts to measure a whole population and then compares each person's individual performance or rating to that of peers or colleagues.

According to Abramms, the old model of management practices is based on the "mythic white male manager," but that "archetypal ideal" no longer fits the multicultural workforce. He says the old management theories assumed certain "optimal styles" for managing effectively. Today, that assumption no longer holds. The management style or practice that works with an African-American employee may be entirely different from what works with an immigrant employee from India.

Are we caught in a multicultural quagmire? How do we assess managers and employees today? According to Abramms, the better approach is "non-normative." With a non-normative instrument, a person's results are no longer compared to anyone else's. "People get feedback that is unique to themselves," he explains.

Abramms believes ODT offers one of the best, non-normative assessment instruments around. It is available in three versions: PRIME Search for managers, PRIME Match for employees, and a recently introduced PRIME Peer for team members. PRIME stands for Practices In Managerial Effectiveness.

Let's take a look at the manager's version. "PRIME Search provides a very confidential way of getting feedback about how you're doing as a manager," asserts Abramms. Managers ask those who report directly to them to fill out a questionnaire that rates the manager on 50 behaviorally-specific management practices spread across 10 functions. Here's one example: "My manager makes sure his/her expectations about my performance are written down, clear, specific and, whenever possible, measurable." The employee answers two questions about this practice: "How much emphasis [am I getting from my boss]?" and "How much do I want?" This particular question falls into Function One, "Establishing and Communicating Expectations."

Employees mail out their questionnaires to be scored and analyzed by a computer. Their individual questionnaire responses remain confidential. The results, after combining all the employees' responses, are returned to the manager. The employee ratings, as well as the feedback to the manager, are displayed in a two by two grid indicating how well the manager's practices match the desires of his/her workers. (See Figure 1.)

"As you can see," Abramms explains, "two of the boxes are 'on-target' and two are not." He says when a manager gets results scattered all over the grid, it may mean that gender, race, ethnicity, or culture is operating and the manager may not be tuned into handling the demographic differences effectively.

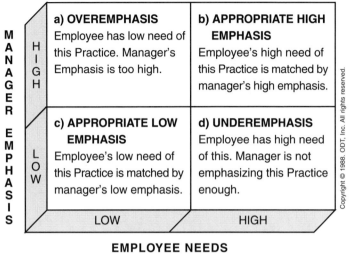

		EMPLOYEE NEEDS	
MANAGER EMPHASIS	**HIGH**	**a) OVEREMPHASIS** Employee has low need of this Practice. Manager's Emphasis is too high.	**b) APPROPRIATE HIGH EMPHASIS** Employee's high need of this Practice is matched by manager's high emphasis.
	LOW	**c) APPROPRIATE LOW EMPHASIS** Employee's low need of this Practice is matched by manager's low emphasis.	**d) UNDEREMPHASIS** Employee has high need of this. Manager is not emphasizing this Practice enough.
		LOW	HIGH

Figure 1

This is the intriguing aspect of PRIME Search—it can reveal substantive data about how a manager is doing with diverse people.

"If we get underemphasis on what we call three 'trigger' questions, a red flag goes up immediately," says Dianne LaMountain, Senior ODT Associate who has major responsibility for debriefing managers on their results. She says the "trigger" questions involve the perception that an employee is not being treated fairly in comparison to other people.

LaMountain tells about one manager in a large corporation. The diversity of his group centered around varying education levels. When he received his PRIME data, the evidence was very clear; 12 people were happy with his management practices, but five were not. When LaMountain created a special profile of the "overemphasis" and "underemphasis" boxes, it was a real eye-opener. The manager didn't realize how differently his actions were perceived by the two groups.

In the 1990's, however, employees don't want to wait until their managers are ready to be enlightened. The PRIME Match version is available to help an individual employee appraise her/his relationship with the boss. The "Match" version serves as a self-help kit containing a questionnaire, a "Scoring Matrix" and an "Action Planning Workbook". The workbook is comprehensive and even walks the employee through the decision whether to share the employee's

ⓘ PRIME Search, PRIME Match, and PRIME Peer are available from ODT, Inc, a management consulting firm and publisher of multicultural materials for human resource professionals. Subsequent to this article's first appearance, other paperless feedback programs have been introduced, providing a savings of 50-85 percent over the previous paper and pencil versions of these tools. Free catalog available. Write: ODT, Inc. Box 134, Amherst, MA 01004; 413-549-1293, Fax 413-549-3503.

discoveries with his/her manager. Abramms says this module "can sensitize employees to differences and how they may affect the relationships with their managers."

PRIME Match is poised to answer an important question, says Abramms, "What is it that people need, and they're asking for, to do their jobs well?" He claims no other instrument can answer this question.

With the advent of so many team-based work structures, ODT also just introduced a peer-feedback tool, PRIME Peer. One of the interesting things they discovered in developing the tool is that peers want (and need) very different behaviors from their co-workers than they want (or need) from their boss! Abramms cautions there is no magic here. "These 50 management practices have been available and honed for 20 years—we know what managers need to do well." If they do "it" well, it works with whatever the target group is demographically. If managers do "it" in a mediocre way, it has mediocre consequences for white males, but it may have quite negative results for women and people of color. However, if managers do "it" poorly, white males may experience "inconvenience," but women and people of color suffer "tragedies and career calamities—they become the walking wounded of incompetent management practices."

87 •   ¡Ya Basta! (Enough Is Enough!)

CHRIS SANDOVAL

Knowing people's boundaries and recognizing the triggers in the diplomatic minefield can be a useful beginning for a group of dissimilar people brought together to focus on a similar mission. "**¡Ya Basta!**" is an exercise that helps people to look at those issues.

Eight people representing two sides of an issue, organizational layers (e.g., management and labor), or cultural groups are asked to form a "fish bowl." A fish bowl is a panel that is formed in the middle of a large audience so that their behaviors and dialogue may be observed by the larger group. Each side is represented by four individuals. A leader or facilitator then asks one panel group to complete the following statement by discussing it for about 5 minutes:

> In order to build trust and relationship, you must never, ever _____ and you must always, always _____ to maintain that trust and relationship.

Then the leader or facilitator asks panel group 2 to respond to the same statement. What the facilitator and larger group generally observe is that both groups frequently have similar responses, expectations, and boundaries.

88 • We say O.J. <u>si</u>, they say O.J. <u>no</u>!

ANTONIO REY

Following the arrest of O.J. Simpson, white people thought him guilty. Most national polls showed from a third to three fourths of white people said he was guilty. In contrast, people of color and African Americans especially in about the same proportions refused to say O.J. was guilty.

Both white people and the rest of us know why. White people say there is a mountain of evidence. We know it is just what we call racism. We do not see racism the same way white people do. When white persons say racism, they mean bias based on race. We mean they rig the game so that white people win.

The mountain of evidence white people claim against O.J. is fantasy. What we call racism is fantasy. Beneath the fantasies we have unconscious awareness. Culture produces our collective unconscious awareness. We live in different worlds based on unconscious cultural archetypes. White people know O.J. did it. We do not! We know white people will do anything to maintain their dominance over people of color. White people say they don't do that anymore. We say they do not do it any less. We and white people view the history of North America differently.

Justice to white people is repression of crime. Justice to us is freedom from white oppression. White people want to punish O.J. They judged him guilty before his trial. We know the presumption of innocent until proven guilty is a lie. We all prejudge. White people think us guilty when we are not—far more often than we can tolerate.

So we say O.J. *si* and they say O.J. *no*!

89 · Jury Nullification

RICHARD MORAN
(NPR MORNING EDITION, OCTOBER 10, 1995)

*L*ike America itself, I'm of two minds when it comes to the verdict in the O.J. Simpson case. On the one hand, it violates my sense of justice. On the other hand, what the jury did by disregarding the ton of evidence against O.J. was in keeping with a long and proud tradition in American law. Let me explain.

Jury nullification—the right of the jury to return a verdict of "Not Guilty" despite the evidence—was regarded by the founding fathers as the cornerstone of American justice and democracy.

The framers of our constitution believed that in order to protect the ordinary citizen from the tyranny of government, the ultimate power to punish those accused of criminal wrongdoing must rest in the hands of the common people.

John Adams, the passionate sage, believed that it was not only the right of a juror, but his duty, to reach a verdict in accordance with his own "best understanding, judgment, and conscience."

Jurors bring their own life experiences to the evaluation of courtroom evidence—that's what they're supposed to do if they are to act as the conscience of the community. Blacks and Whites have different life experiences, especially when it comes to the police.

Research has shown that Black and White jurors are predisposed to evaluate evidence differently. Whites tend to trust the police and believe the prosecution, while Blacks tend to be much more skeptical of law enforcement.

It's possible that the jury honestly decided that the prosecution did not meet its burden of proof—and that the decision was racially guided or directed. Just as it's possible that O.J. Simpson was guilty and that Mark Fuhrman planted the bloody glove.

No one, regardless of skin color, thinks murder is O.K. If the jury did nullify the law, it was probably protesting against the way the police and prosecution conducted themselves, not just in this case, but in the treatment of minorities in general. They weren't saying it's O.K. for Black people to kill White people.

The verdict was a combination of distrust for the Los Angeles police and a long standing anger at the criminal justice system.

90 ·   Let the Dead Bury Their Dead

THOMAS SOWELL (FORBES)

*a*t the time of the 50th anniversary of Japan's attack on Pearl Harbor, the Japanese parliament considered apologizing to the United States, but decided not to. Meanwhile, President Bush apologized to Japanese Americans for their internment during World War II. Spain . . . apologize[d] to the Jews who were expelled *en masse* from that country 500 years ago.

These collective apologies for historical actions taken by others may be seen as grand moral gestures by some, but in fact they exacerbate the already dangerous tendency to obliterate the crucial concept of personal responsibility. What possible meaning does it have, either logically or morally, for someone to apologize for what someone else did to a third party?

Are all people of Slavic ancestry to apologize to all Jews for the centuries of brutal anti-Semitism in Eastern Europe? And are all Jews to apologize to all Slavs for those Jewish slave-traders who, in earlier centuries, sold Slavs into bondage from Spain to the Ottoman Empire? What about all the atrocities of the Christians against the Moslems, or the Moslems against the Christians, during their centuries of warfare?

The list could go on and on. Historic wrongs can be found all over the globe. In fact, much of history consists of those wrongs. If all of us started to apologize to each other for all the wrongs of history, the noise would be deafening.

Many of those who emphasize the wrongs of history have a highly selective list of those wrongs, geared toward contemporary ideological politics. Thus, the wrongs of European imperialists against various Third World nations are to be kept alive as enduring grievances and—more to the point—enduring entitlements to largesse. However, the wrongs of any of these nations against each other, or against their own peoples, are passed over in silence, no matter how much worse they might have been.

Sometimes the argument is that we need to correct the contemporary effects of past wrongs. Seldom is any evidence either asked for or given to show that we know what those effects are. It is certainly not easy to know.

In many parts of the world, groups clearly mistreated historically have emerged better off educationally, economically, and socially than those who mistreated them. The Chinese minorities in various Southeast Asian Countries have seldom had equal rights, but they have typically risen from initial poverty to a position where they are better off economically than the majority populations of Malaysia, Indonesia, or other countries in the region.

Much the same story could be told of immigrants from the Indian subcontinent who settled in East Africa or in Fuji, or of immigrants from Lebanon in West Africa, Italians in Argentina, and many others around the world. In a number of countries and a number of periods of history, it has been common for particular groups to take over substandard land left idle by others as "waste land"—and to become more successful farmers than others around them who were farming more fertile land.

We have barely scratched the surface in understanding why some groups prosper, even under bad conditions, or why others fail to utilize much better opportunities. Indeed, a whole tendentious vocabulary has arisen to obscure or bury such questions. Those who fail are said to have been "extended" or denied "access." Those who succeed are said to have been "privileged." Again, evidence is neither asked nor given. This formula leaves out achievement—or even luck.

Would anyone (other than ideologues or intellectuals) say that Babe Ruth had more "opportunity" to hit home runs, when in fact he was the most walked batter in history?

This strange way of talking is not confined to a few fringe ideologues. It has caught on across the spectrum, and is now part of the mainstream mind-set, at least among academics. Retired Harvard President Derek Bok, for example, said that to apply the same admissions standards to minority students as to others would be to "exclude them from the university." This was said more than a century after blacks began attending Harvard, entering and graduating without double standards during most of that time.

Much contemporary discussion of historic guilt is more than moral mushheadedness. Some of it is exploited quite skillfully by people whose careers depend on it. A whole class of "diversity consultants" or race relations specialists has come into existence to promote guilt among students, faculty, and administrators at leading colleges and universities across the country.

At the University of Wisconsin, for example, an itinerant race relations specialist evoked "the repentant sobs of white students" at one of his workshops, which promoted the theme that virtually all whites were racists. Similar themes and similar techniques have been widely used from large universities like Harvard and Tulane to small colleges like Oberlin and Whitman.

Historic wrongs can be found all over the globe. In fact, much of history consists of those wrongs. If all of us started to apologize to each other for all the wrongs of history, the noise would be deafening.

Achieving justice in our own time is a task that takes the resources of even the best societies. We should leave the past in the past.

91 • The Farrakhan Phenomenon

RON DANIELS (Z MAGAZINE)

What is the appeal of Louis Farrakhan? The answer may lie in a perspective put forth by Professor John Bracey of the University of Massachusetts in his book *Black Nationalism in America*. Bracey contends that

Louis Farrakhan

throughout the history of Africans in America, Black sentiment has swung like a pendulum between various forms of integrationist and nationalist strategies. While neither of these tendencies ever quite disappears from the spectrum, Bracey postulates that there are factors which determine which of these tendencies will be dominant in any given period. According to Bracey, whenever conditions appear to be favorable for a better life for Black people in this country, optimism translates into an ascendancy of integrationist thought and strategies. Whenever conditions appear unfavorable for Black people to achieve a better life, nationalist tendencies and strategies gain ascendancy.

Impact Visuals

92 • ADR—Putting More Clout in Your Diversity

SYBIL EVANS (TRAINING MAGAZINE)

Alternative Dispute Resolution (ADR) is the term for a variety of ways in which a dispute can be resolved outside of the formal justice system. Internal ADR processes include the following:

diversiRISK™

Four birds are sitting in a tree. If you shoot one, how many are left?

A. Three
B. Two
C. One
D. Zero

Open Door: Open-door policies allow employees to bring their complaints directly to higher-level management with the complaints generally aired on an informal basis.

Peer Review: A peer-review panel consists of rank-and-file employees and managers who are trained in reviewing grievances that are raised by their fellow employees. The panel holds a hearing and rules on the grievance. The panel has no power to change corporate policy and can only review whether policy was followed properly.

Ombuds: An ombuds is an employee who acts as a confidential source and facilitator. The ombuds hears and investigates problems and concerns which are not readily resolved through other channels. The ombuds attempts to influence management to act on the complaint and can recommend changes in systems and processes.

Mediation: Mediation is a nonbinding process in which a neutral third party facilitates negotiations between the disputing parties in an effort to reach a resolution. The mediator has no power to impose a resolution on the parties. Sometimes the mediator may give non-binding evaluations of the case.

Conflict Management System: Such a system involves training of diverse personnel in resolving issues through a variety of techniques such as counseling, mediation, and team intervention. The goal is to resolve conflicts constructively before they escalate into full-blown disputes. ADR has been described as the "last best hope in our litigious society."

Can there be a system to deal with employee concerns that not only repairs damage and prevents litigation but *prevents* damage and enhances employer—employee relationships? This is where the principles and benefits of ADR and Diversity are in harmony. Diversity and ADR are like two sides of a coin—the diversity side values differences and enhances communication and collaboration; the dispute resolution side develops systems that take over if the communication breaks down. By working together, diversity and ADR advocates can have more clout.

Copyright © 1995, Sybil Evans. All rights reserved.

93 • Immigration & Acculturation

CARMEN VÁZQUEZ AND DIANE JOHNS

STRESS OF IMMIGRATION

When working with others who are fairly new to your own culture, there are a number of unspoken elements that can significantly affect both their behavior and their performance at work. Consider that they:

- Are often not able to relax or feel fully "at home" here for a long time.
- May not have wanted to leave their homeland but may have been forced to for political, religious, or economic reasons.
- May themselves be the victims of oppression, famine, torture, murdered or lost families, or other atrocities of war.
- May have been highly educated or with professional standing in their own country; or may have been working class or poor.
- May be learning English with the extra pressure of having to "succeed" at work. Hearing a new language, trying to understand it and constantly translating in your head for 8 hours or more a day is exhausting and stressful in itself. Add the extra tension of trying to "make it" in a new job in a new country and the stress can be overwhelming.
- May be confused by tone of voice, gestures, joking behavior toward them, physical distance between people, customs around food or drink, behavior with supervisors or with the opposite sex. Things we take for granted as "communications" are not so obvious to newcomers.

Note: This last point can also be kept in mind when working with people who may be developmentally delayed (mentally, physically or emotionally), as they may not have been exposed to and able to absorb and practice the standard social conditioning of the "majority" culture.

PHASES OF ACCULTURATION

If you work with people from different cultures who have immigrated here, you may also find it helpful to know that at any given time they are going through one or more of the specific stages of acculturation to their new life here. This process of acculturation has four phases/components:

1. "America is great"—Ethnic person tries to become very Americanized. Wants to absorb all the fashions, foods, learn slang and be very much a part of the American "in group." Their eager willingness can sometimes be misunderstood as being "fresh" or "pushy."
2. "America stinks"—Characterized by complete rejection of American values. When "reality" strikes, the underside of the American Dream surfaces— prejudice, rejection, inability to "fit in" easily lead to natural feelings of hostility, anger, frustration, depression.

ⓘ Excerpted from *Working With People from Diverse Backgrounds: Some Tips for Relating*, by Carmen Vázquez and Diane Johns, 1990. All rights reserved. This handy tip-sheet includes a self-quiz, a chart comparing Asian and Hispanic values to North American White Urban Corporate Values, information on racial identity versus ethnic identity. Six pages on card stock. Available in a 10-pack for $30 from ODT, Inc. at 1-800-736-1293.

 diversiRISK™

Answer to the DIVERSOPHY®

The best answer is D. If you shoot one, the others will fly away. This question is an interesting test of cultural values. People from individualistic Western cultures tend to see this as an abstract mathematical problem and are likely to answer A. 3, whereas more people from collective cultures tend to focus on the situation's outcomes.

3. "Getting along"—Gradual acculturation to American ways, with a compromise of certain ethnic values and norms and an absorbing of others from the American culture. More stability, satisfaction and relaxation.
4. "Body sense"—This element is threaded throughout the other three stages and has to do with the physical process of adjusting to another culture—things having to do with hours of daylight, temperature, seasonal shifts, noise level, quality of sound . . . etc.

94 • Immigrants In, Native Whites Out

WILLIAM H. FREY & JONATHAN TILOVE
(NEW YORK TIMES MAGAZINE)

Three years ago, Marilyn Yarosko moved to Las Vegas; she was feeling out of place in her native Southern California. The Asian population in her hometown of Torrance, just south of Los Angeles, had doubled to 22 percent in the 1980's. The pastor and most of the parishioners at her Roman Catholic church were now Vietnamese. Most of her fellow nurses at Charter Suburban Hospital, she says, were Filipino, super-hardworking and, she thinks, a bit cliquish. Yarosko, whose parents were Canadian and paternal grandparents were from the Ukraine, is not a xenophobe. She is not bitter or looking for someone to blame. "We took it from the Indians: who are we to complain?" she says. But, she acknowledges, "I began to feel like an outsider.

"For every white person who leaves," she says of Los Angeles, "a foreigner takes their place."

Her remark is not merely an anecdotal insight. A new analysis of the 1990 United States Census discloses that some of America's largest metropolitan areas are experiencing something statistically very close to Yarosko's observation: For every immigrant who arrives, a white person leaves. Look collectively at the New York, Chicago, Los Angeles, Houston and Boston metropolitan areas—5 of the top 11 im-

BOSNIA-HERZEGO USA

migration destinations. In the last half of the 80's, for every 10 immigrants who arrived, 9 residents left for points elsewhere. And most of those leaving were non-Hispanic whites. Of the top immigrant destinations, only metropolitan San Diego was attracting more whites from the rest of the nation than it was losing. The places that whites were bound for were metro areas like Tampa-St. Petersburg, Seattle, Phoenix, Atlanta and Las Vegas, all of which attract relatively few immigrants.

The trend constitutes a new, larger form of white flight. Unlike in the old version, whites this time are not just fleeing the cities for the suburbs. They are leaving entire metropolitan areas and states—whole regions—for whiter destinations. And new census estimates indicate that this pattern of flight from big immigration destinations has become even more pronounced in the 90's.

This combination of concentrated minority immigration and distinctly white dispersal is reshaping America more and more into two nations. One is the rapidly changing, intensely diverse America represented by the coastal ports of entry from San Francisco to Houston in the West, and Boston to Washington plus Miami in the East, along with the premier Middle Western destination of Chicago. The second is the rest of the country, experiencing this new diversity in modest numbers or not at all. In other words, the old image of immigrant assimilation is being supplanted by a new one—Balkanization.

The force behind all this change is a decade of greater immigration, and greater minority immigration, than any in American history. According to the Urban Institute, a research organization in Washington, some 10 million legal and illegal immigrants entered the country in the 80's, exceeding the previous high of 5 million recorded in the first decade of the century. The relative rate of immigration is obviously much lower now; the population is also now three times as large.

Nevertheless, today's geographic concentration of immigrants is much higher. More than three-quarters of immigrants in the 1980's settled in just six states, and more than half of those immigrants were in just eight metropolitan areas.

Moreover, unlike past eras of immigration, this new wave is more than 80 percent Latin American and Asian. Most immigrants arrive to discover that they are officially classified as members of a racial group—usually Hispanic or Asian. Legally and culturally, they are all defined as minorities—just as blacks have been, even though most blacks originally came to America as slaves. In California, this pattern has altered the dynamics of affirmative action in ways that go unrecognized in the currently raging debate on the subject. Because of immigration, in the 30-odd years since the dawn of affirmative action, blacks have gone from more than two-thirds to less than half of America's minority population.

Those who leave are not just switching neighborhoods. Consider California. It will be less than half white within a decade because of a massive influx of minority immigrants and a disproportionately white exodus, mostly to neighboring states, which are among the whitest in the nation. In Las Vegas, most of Marilyn Yarosko's neighbors and co-workers are white. Gone is any sense of identity or

Borderlands/La Frontera: The New Mestiza, by Gloria Anzadua. (San Francisco: Spinsters/Aunt Lute, 1987), $10.95, ISBN 1-879960-12-5. In prose and poetry, Anzadua examines the experience of being caught between two cultures and feeling alien in both. She looks at the history of the Southwest and the contemporary condition of illegal and legal immigration in a style that forces the reader to recognize the multicultural and multilingual realities of contemporary society.

community Yarosko had with those she left behind. For now, when someone like Yarosko flees Los Angeles for Las Vegas, she is not just leaving one state for another, she is leaving one America for another.

See *Still An Open Door? U.S. Immigration Policy and the American Economy*, by Vernon Briggs, Jr. and Stephen Moore (Washington, D.C.: American University Press, 1994). Anti-immigrationist Briggs sees today's immigrants as largely unskilled workers who settle disproportionately in cities (which tends to harm blacks), have less schooling than previous generations, and get on welfare more. Moore counters with data showing immigrants as entrepreneurial job-creators, who are better educated, who contribute significantly to U.S. companies (e.g., computers, electronics, pharmaceuticals) and who, by virtue of their youth, have helped bail out the Social Security and pension system. A lively debate!

95 •   A Socially Engineered Head Start

JAMES S. ROBB (*NATIONAL REVIEW*)

" . . . Millions of immigrants and foreign visitors are eligible for—and many are actually using—affirmative-action benefits to get a head start on U.S.-born minorities, not to mention white Americans. In effect, they are getting off the plane and moving right to the head of the line. . . . The fact that foreign citizens routinely get special consideration as if they shared a history of U.S. discrimination with blacks and select other native minorities does not distress sociologists and most affirmative-action bureaucrats.

Congress has made barring immigrants from affirmative action *illegal*. . . . The immigration Reform and Control Act of 1986 made it illegal to bar immigrants from employment solely on the basis of their nationality.

The great irony is that the immigrants have not asked for this special treatment. Most immigrants come to this country to get a fair chance, not a socially engineered head start. . . . A short executive order could end affirmative action for immigrants—the entitlement nobody planned and hardly anyone wants."

© 1993, Mike Thompson, The State Journal Register.

96 • Immigrants, Memories, and Trash

ANDREW LAM (IN CONTEXT)

I took a countryman from Vietnam for a tour of the Berkeley campus where I once studied. San Francisco's skyscrapers gleaming across the bay seemed more formidable than Berkeley's Greco-Roman style buildings. But when we walked past a large garbage bin filled with papers and carton boxes, he suddenly paused. Pointing to the heap of trash he exclaimed, "Brother, in Vietnam, this stuff is all money!"

I, of course, know this. But in America how easy it is to forget. What I throw away today would have astounded me years ago.

This young man is not an environmentalist; he understands little about the world's ecology or the greenhouse effect. His comment simply reflects his own Third World background. He is, therefore, frugal and practical. What's more he has a great

The Society for International Education, Training, and Research (**SIETAR International**) is a dynamic international professional association of diverse individuals and institutions concerned with promoting interaction. Through conferences, workshops, and other participatory programs held at various locations throughout the world, along with Society publications, members increase their competence and create mutually beneficial networks within and across disciplinary, professional, and cultural boundaries. (For a listing of chapters and events around the world, contact SIETAR International at 808 17th St., NW, Suite 200, Washington, D.C. 20006; 202-466-7883, Fax 202-223-9569, e-mail 75250.1275 @compuserve.com, Internet web page http://aspin.asu.edu/provider/communication/sietar.htm).

respect for the materials we Americans discard as refuse, as waste. His family in Vietnam could live for a week recycling these papers, he tells me, and it pains him still to see so much wasted.

"I can't believe you throw this stuff away." He shakes his head, and I feel a slight tug of guilt—

diversiSMARTS™

Which of the following people are not U.S. citizens?

A. Puerto Ricans living in New York.
B. Puerto Ricans living in Puerto Rico or the Virgin Islands.
C. Children of naturalized citizens born outside the U.S.
D. People from Guam living in Japan.
E. Irish living in Boston.

my garbage is filled with junk mail, newspapers, empty bottles, leftovers (what used to be his living).

At my parents' home my extended family gathers over a letter sent from a cousin living in Saigon. The letter itself is flimsy thin—it threatens to dissolve with a single teardrop. Recycled for who knows how many times, the dark material reflects the poverty of the country from which it came. "The poor country is condemned," says one uncle haughtily. He now drives a midnight-blue Mercedes Benz.

A sure sign, then, of a Third World immigrant's successful assimilation into an overdeveloped society is when he casts a snobbish glance back towards the impoverished world he left behind. We sit and ponder as to how we ever managed to live in that malaria-infested place, where the sewer turns the river black as night. The green bottleflies the size of your toe; the unpaved road with potholes; the heat; the stench—didn't it all seem like a bad dream, my dear?

The cousin came back from two weeks of frolicking in Vietnam complaining of bad hotels. They have no street lights, he says, they still wrap food in newspapers, they smoke hand-rolled, filterless cigarettes. To the pedicab driver who was once an ARVN officer, my cousin gave a 20 dollar bill. It's equivalent, you know, to that old man's monthly wage.

But it was also these same relatives who, on one winter night some 15 years ago, dragged a carton full of day-old food across an empty Safeway parking lot near the one-room apartment where three families lived. I was with them when we were stopped by the police. Indignant, my uncle offered to return the food to its trash bin but the officer demurred. "Help yourself," he shrugged, and walked away.

diversiSMARTS™

Only E. Irish living in Boston, are not U.S. citizens. Estimates of the numbers of Irish illegally taking up residence in the US are as high as 10,000 annually. Because they are largely white and speak English, they are less likely to be singled out as violators of the immigration laws of the country.

A world and only 16 years away, I look back to my homeland and admit how much I and others have forgotten—as if along with the pile of papers and uneaten food, we have carelessly tossed away our memories. In our material success in America, we have forgotten what it was that sustained us—our attachment to the land, our old identity.

In search of old wisdom, I visit my grandmother in her convalescent home. She is the one least influenced by America's opulence. With her wrinkled hands she meticulously wraps a piece of apple in a napkin and stuffs it in her pocket. "To throw food away is a waste of God's gift," she tells me.

To throw memory away is also a waste of God's gift. My grandmother survived the starvation year when the Japanese burned most of the rice fields in North Vietnam during World War II. And so, no matter how many times we tell her not to save, she won't listen. "They won't have these many things for long," she predicts.

Isolated in her convalescent home, forgotten by the outside world, she gathers bits of our identities, scattered pieces of our soul.

97 • The Subtle Forms of Bias

ALAN WEISS

Many of us are convinced that there isn't a biased bone in our entire body. That's because we are sensitive to the more obvious forms of bias and discrimination, and try hard not to participate in any of them. However, we are often unconsciously involved in the subtler forms of bias, which can lead to a narrow, homogenous workplace.

Here are some of the less obvious forms of discrimination which can occur. Determine for yourself if any exist in your environment, and whether you play even an inadvertent role in perpetuating them:

- **Ageism.** Older workers (sometimes as young as those in their mid-40s, and sometimes those whose physical characteristics, i.e., gray hair, meet a stereotype) are systematically excluded from office parties, high-pressure assignments, opportunities involving relocation, client conferences, etc. Merely because of age, these people are assumed not to be able to contribute creatively or energetically.
- **Salary grade elitism.** One's salary grade (i.e., Hay Points or some other classification system) is used to determine how intelligent people and their

> Most bias is not the blazingly obvious bigotry we can all readily condemn. It is more often a case of well-intentioned people making inadvertent judgments of obvious and not-so-obvious groups.
>
> —Alan Weiss,
> Rejoicing in Diversity

ideas are. Similar ideas and approaches are given far different weight, depending upon whether a high salary grade or a low salary grade suggested them.

- **Non-exempt condescension.** Because one is an hourly worker, salaried workers assume he or she has a lower intelligence level, can't be relied upon or trusted, and can be excused for vulgarity, crudeness or lack of ethics. None of these traits is a result of income or education, and the dangerous converse is that salaried people "automatically" have higher ethics, integrity, intelligence, etc.
- **Family focus.** The dual discrimination which occurs here is that those with families, or with the potential to begin families, are excluded from assignments involving travel, relocation, long-term commitments and generally pressurized situations. Conversely, those without families and unlikely to have families are expected to work longer hours, work on weekends, travel excessively and undertake other assignments infringing on personal time because their interests are not of the same priority as those with families.
- **"Positive labeling."** In this case, perceived positive attributes actually cause a narrowing of opportunity. For example, managers may comment that an ethnic group is particularly strong in technical and research areas, and therefore does not tend to produce very good managers because "they would rather be sole contributors than have to confront people as a manager." Entire mobility paths are blocked due to this kind of "positive stereotyping."

98 · Seccession of the Successful

TIM VANDERPOOL (*UTNE READER*)

HOMEOWNERS' ASSOCIATIONS TURN NEIGHBORHOODS INTO ISLANDS

More than 32 million Americans now live under the rules of homeowners' associations. Not to be confused with neighborhood groups, these organizations—alternately referred to as residential community associations and *common interest developments*—are initiated by developers to supervise budding, generally upscale villages, and membership is usually mandatory. These quasi-democratic institutions provide amenities from trash pickup to landscape design. The highest concentration of these suburban regimes is in the Sun Belt. Nationally, the statistics are stunning: Since their debut in 19th century Boston, and a tremendous boost during Florida's 1960s condominium boom, the number of associations has swelled to 150,000—and it's growing at the rate of 10,000 every year.

Critics deride communities represented by homeowners' associations as walled-off worlds where the well-heeled can collectively ignore problems like crime and fiscal despair. Many association members consider their rules repressive and needlessly complex.

Nonetheless, these community organizations continue to spring up in unprecedented numbers. This privatization of government functions raises a host of vexing societal questions.

"I call it secession by the successful," says Evan McKenzie, a political scientist at the University of Illinois and author of *Privatopia* (Yale University Press, 1994), a book dissecting the blissful illusions associations proffer. "When we think about citizenship in our communities, we think of some concept of rights and responsibilities. But *common interest developments* encourage secessionist mentalities. They give people a variety of incentives for not seeing themselves as belonging to their city or county, since they belong to associations that provide services such as recreation centers, swimming pools, and parks. Meanwhile, those cities and counties shrivel from neglect."

(i) For an evocative look at the process of organizational change and how to effectively change resistance into support, see Rick Maurer's *Beyond the Wall of Resistance, Unconventional Strategies that Build Support for Change.* (Austin, Texas Bard Books, 1996, ISBN 1-885167-07-5). To order *Beyond the Wall*, call 1-800-945-3132. The book shows why the conventional ways of dealing with resistance actually increase opposition and includes assessment tools that encourage immediate application.

99 · Government, of and by the People . . .

WALTER E. WILLIAMS

The first principle of natural law holds that each person owns himself. In the state of nature, without government, all people are free and equal but insecure. That insecurity derives from the fact that other people may not respect our self-ownership rights and, through intimidation, threats, and coercion, wrongly confiscate our property and violate our persons.

Because of this insecurity, people form governments granting them certain limited powers. For example, in the state of nature, we all have the right to protect ourselves, family, and property from encroachment by others. When our rights to life, liberty, and property are violated, we have the right to be prosecutor, judge, jury, and, if need be, executioner. When we form governments, we grant these rights to the state in exchange for the guarantee that the state will perform these security functions. We give up only the rights necessary for government to perform its only function—protecting our security.

Through numerous successful attacks, private property and individual liberty are mere skeletons of their past. Thomas Jefferson anticipated this, saying, "The natural progress of things is for government to gain ground and for liberty to yield." An easy measure of how government is gaining ground is to look at the time spent earning money for which we have no claim. The average taxpayers works from January 1 to May 6 to pay federal, state, and local taxes. Each year we work a day or two longer to satisfy government. We should not forget that a working definition of slavery is that one works all year and has no claim to the fruits of his toil.

Liberty is threatened today not because of its failure but, somewhat ironically, because of its success. Liberty's counterpart in the economic arena, free markets, has been so successful in eliminating traditional problems like disease, pestilence, hunger, and gross poverty that all other human problems appear both unbearable and inexcusable.

The desire by many Americans to eliminate the so-called unbearable and inexcusable problems has led us astray from those basic ideals and principles on which our prosperous country was built. In the name of other ideals, such as equality of income, sex and race balance, orderly markets, consumer protection, energy conservation, and environmentalism, just to name a few, we have abandoned many personal freedoms. As a result of widespread control by government in an effort to achieve these so-called higher objectives, people have been subordinated to the point where considerations of personal freedom are but secondary or tertiary matters. The ultimate end to this process is totalitarianism, which is no more than a reduced form of servitude.

The primary justification for the attack on liberty and economic freedom can be found in people's desire for government to do good. We say government should care for the poor, the disadvantaged, the elderly, failing businesses, college students, and many other "deserving" segments of our society. However, we must recognize government has no resources of its own; in other words, members of Congress and senators are not spending their own money for the programs. Furthermore, there's no tooth fairy or Santa Claus who gives them the resources. The recognition that government does not have any resources of its own forces us to recognize that the only way that the government can give one American one dollar is to confiscate it from another American through intimidation, threats, and coercion.

Reconsidering the Tools of Justice— Whither AA/EEO?

A man protesting affirmative action at an NAACP pro-affirmative action rally protesting the "Contract with America." The man's sign had earlier been ripped apart by demonstrators angry at his presence at their rally.

Class, race, and gender are inextricably intertwined in the North American experience. All are necessary perspectives for understanding any one of them. However, in the United States, what we call diversity efforts started with attempts to rectify *class* distinctions stemming from racial, gender, and ethnic bias and prejudice. From these efforts to mend our flawed social fabric, we were awakened to the changing demographics of the workplace (largely due to the *Workforce 2000* report, which dominated thinking in the late 1980s and early 1990s). Finally we were faced with the imperative of becoming culturally competent in order to compete in the global marketplaces. These dynamics and challenges (see the ABCD model in the Preface) constitute the full-blown model of diversity.

This vast, now international, diversity enterprise has outgrown its humble civic roots to become market strategy. Yet, inequality in opportunity, in the workplace, in education, in social services continues to exist. Access was supposed to be the answer. We struggled to give a "head start" to those who were "behind." Today, controversy about these efforts, and the degree to which they succeeded or failed, constitutes such a key dilemma that we discuss it separately in this section.

These issues are coming to a head today because of the changing nature of the economy and the changing nature of work within it. The fact that the average real earnings of white men have been in steady decline over the past twenty years—their gains peaked in 1968—while during the same period most forms of job security have disappeared makes it easy to scapegoat affirmative action. Additionally, the successes of affirmative action are becoming increasingly overshadowed in the popular debate by stories, sometimes of mythic proportions, of failure and abuse. At the same time, the socio-economic condition of groups that this legislation was created to assist has declined substantially, to the point where, for example, some social commentators speak of a "permanent" black underclass and of the "feminization of poverty" and, less frequently, of a "poor white" class.

There is political capital to be gained (and mud to be slung) by playing off against one another segments of a population that are suffering by using affirmative action legislation as a rallying point. We fear that too many voters and citizens will not recognize that the affirmative action debate is a symptom of the present socio-economic situation, not its cause. How much will political campaigns exacerbate our already fragile racial and gender relationships? We fear that they will paint iodine on wounds that require stitches—causing yet more pain without healing.

Because the debate on affirmative action and related issues is symptomatic of deeper problems and malaise over the future, a number of our contributors deal in detail with class as a critical issue in the first section of the book. Now they give attention not only to the affirmative action debate itself, but also to related dynamics that in the present economic situation are symptomatic as well as causal.

What other issues—e.g., the educational system, the exportation of jobs, and the importation of workers—contribute to this malaise? What alternatives to present practices and symtoms exist? How do we feel about wealth, about earning it, about the dynamics of perpetuating it and passing it on? Our contributors argue all sides of the affirmative action debate and give us insights into these underlying dynamics.

100 • The Battle Over Affirmative Action

JOHN BUNZEL (SAN FRANCISCO EXAMINER)

Sometimes the worst way to get an answer is to ask a simple question. That's the case with the current debate over affirmative action. Ask people whether they favor or oppose it, and a majority often say they favor it.

But on this subject (as on so many others), simple questions are inadequate. They tell us too little about the complex ideas implicit in the term "affirmative action."

The same is true with the recent history of equality. It is not always easy to determine which principles of equality most Americans uphold or defend and what they believe should (and should not) be done to fulfill the promise of equality in our society.

Thus sociology professor Seymour Martin Lipset has written extensively about the contradiction between the two core values in the American Creed, individualism and egalitarianism.

The American people believe in both. Throughout our history, we have shifted back and forth between (1) equality and social reform, and (2) individual freedom, hard work and competitive achievement.

The tension between these fundamental values has consistently been reflected in the attitude of Americans on equality and affirmative action. But the public's feelings cannot be reduced to "yes" or "no" categorization. For example, the majority of whites favor affirmative action programs to further black employment. They make an important distinction, however, between affirmative

(i) Michael Kinsley critically examines the historical roots and current case against affirmative action in "The Spoils of Victimhood," *The New Yorker*, March 27, 1995, pp. 62-69. For an even more extensive historical analysis, see "Taking Affirmative Action Apart," by Nicholas Lehmann, *The New York Times Magazine*, June 11, 1995, pp. 36-66.

action and quotas, which they strongly oppose, especially when these are presented as alternatives to individual merit or ability.

Nor do national attitudes about affirmative action rise or fall on the single issue of quotas. Most whites are opposed to affirmative action if and when it means race-specific preferential treatment, or if businesses are required to hire a specific number of blacks.

Joseph L. Rauh, a liberal Democrat, said, "You have to have preferences for blacks if you really want affirmative action."

Most Americans firmly disagree.

Answers to survey questions illustrate what most Americans support and oppose in the name of affirmative action:

1. Most whites and most blacks support affirmative action when it means compensatory or "catch-up" assistance (special aid and training programs) that enables all who are disadvantaged to have equal opportunities in employment and education.
2. Most whites and most blacks favor the federal government's offering special education or vocational courses, free of charge, to enable members of minority groups to do better on tests.
3. Three out of four Americans say they oppose affirmative action programs that give preference to minorities or women to make up for past discrimination.
4. Nearly half of all African Americans say they oppose affirmative action programs giving preferences for minorities.
5. Two out of three women oppose affirmative action preference programs for women, compared to three out of four men.
6. In California, large majorities of citizens oppose giving women special preferences in hiring and promotion in the work place, by a 68 percent to 28 percent margin. They also oppose granting blacks special job preferences by a 75 percent to 22 percent margin.
7. The margin of opposition to preferential treatment in college and university admissions range from 71 percent against preferences for blacks or women to 72 percent against preferences for Hispanics and 77 percent against preferences for Asians or new immigrants from Eastern Europe.

The message is clear. Most Americans draw the line at predetermining the results by doing away with fair and nondiscriminatory competition. This is why they are against "special advantages" for one group over another, or dual standards whereby whites and blacks are judged differently.

Thus, as Lispet has stressed, the stiff line of public resistance "is not between nondiscrimination and compensatory action but between compensatory action and preferential treatment."

It is frequently charged that those who would seek to end race-specific affirmative action programs are engaging in racism. Leave aside the fact that this would include some 75 percent of Americans who oppose granting special job preferences to groups based solely on race or ethnicity. Those who make this charge also refuse to acknowledge that opposition to race-based targets or statistical goal-setting in the workplace may be founded on as strong a commitment to equality as that of their opponents and is, in fact, more a reflection of general principle than of racism.

Public opposition to the direction affirmative action has taken is shaped by a particular view of equal rights rooted in certain procedural guarantees—basic American principles, it should be noted, that for too long were denied to blacks and other minorities.

Properly understood, this view of equality is built on a sequence of ideas that runs from equality before the law to equality of opportunity, and only then to an equality of results. It is significantly different from the assumption, implicit in many of the preferential policies of affirmative action, that an equality of results is a precondition of equality and opportunity.

White Americans are far from agreed on what should be done about the problem of race.

Some are more likely than others to favor the use of government to remedy past and present inequalities. Some policies, like anti-discrimination laws, enjoy wide support. Other policies, such as welfare reform or fair housing, command different levels of popular support.

Race-conscious policies, however, have provoked broad opposition and resentment. As social scientists Paul Sniderman and Thomas Piazza have shown in "The Scar of Race," affirmative action is so intensely disliked because it has widened the "divide of race" rather than helping to put it behind us.

As the writers' findings make clear, white Americans believe that policies proposing to "privilege some groups rather than others, on the basis of characteristics they were born with, violates a nearly universal sense of fairness."

What gives the race-conscious agenda its distinctive character, "what makes the agenda unfair and open to challenge morally," is that the principle of preferential treatment runs against the American promise of equal rights and equal treatment.

The Remedy: Class, Race, and Affirmative Action, by Richard D. Kahlenberg (New York: Basic Books, P.O. Box 588, Dunmore, PA 18512-0588, $25, ISBN 0-465-09823-1). 1-800-331-3761. In this provocative and paradigm-shifting book, Richard D. Kahlenberg argues that affirmative action programs ought to be based not on race but on class. America's exclusive focus on race in determining how to allocate economic and educational

(i) For a cogent articulation of other perspectives on the AA debate, see the November 1995 edition of *Black Enterprise*. (For copies, contact *Black Enterprise*, 212-242-8000, ext. 568. Subscription available from 1-800-727-7777 or e-mail BEcircu@aol.com).

opportunities has served only to undermine the moral legitmacy for affirmative action, with the results clearly visible in the movement to abolish race and gender preferences in the state of California and elsewhere.

Kahlenberg shows that it is time to return to affirmative action's roots so that it works to the benefit of the truly disadvantaged—regardless of race. In a sweeping and damning analysis, Kahlenberg examines how the rationale for affirmative action has moved inexorably away from its original commitment to remedy past discrimination and instead has become a means to achieve racial diversity, even if that means giving preference to upper-middle-class blacks over poor whites. He outlines how a class-based system of affirmative action would work, why all Americans must embrace it, and how the African-American community in particular would continue to reap the benefits it needs without engendering resentment.

The drive for "affirmative action" is a phenomenon in need of further and more candid explanation than it has so far received. How can adoption of a policy that is virtually a formula for escalating racial consciousness and tension be thought a desirable course of action?

A more plausible explanation for at least some of the demand for "affirmative action" is that it supports an extensive "civil rights" bureaucracy that grew up in the long fight to end racial discrimination and that is now prospering and expanding in the movement to reinstate it. Every college and school, if not every department, must now have an "affirmative action" officer and specialists in racial- and ethnic-group liaison. The more racial tension increases on campus, the greater the need will be for their services.

—Lino A. Graglia, "Other Agendas," *The National Review*, July 5, 1993.

(i) From *The Imperiled Academy*, edited by Howard Dickman (New Brunswick, N.J.: Transaction, 1993).

101 • A Vision Betrayed: Discrimination Is No Answer to Discrimination

DOUG BANDOW (BOOKS & CULTURE)

*A*merican presidential politics is heating up, which means that serious debate, never in abundance in Washington, will soon disappear altogether. Among the nastiest policy brawls is likely to be the battle over affirmative action. On June 1, [1995], California Gov. Pete Wilson signed an executive order eliminating many of that state's race-conscious programs. Activist Jesse Jackson is demanding that Democrats resist any retrenchment. President Clinton is attempting to steer a middle course, agreeing with everyone simultaneously.

That affirmative action will be a political football is unfortunate. Nevertheless, it is a legitimate issue. There is broad support for creating a colorblind society—a vision articulated most eloquently by Martin Luther King, Jr., who told the nation that he dreamed of a time when "little black boys and black girls will be able to join hands with little white boys and white girls and walk together as sisters and brothers." Yet affirmative action, originally established to redress past discrimination against minorities, has become a vehicle for discrimination against whites and disfavored minorities, such as Asian Americans. Moreover, as affirmative action has turned into a racial spoils system, it has stoked rather than eased racial passions, driving us further from King's ideal. We must reject the invidious politics of race, whatever the justification, and focus on creating a society where people are judged on individual merit rather than group membership.

Although Christians have struggled mightily with their attitudes toward race and slavery over time, few today would disagree that Christ's command to love one's neighbors applied irrespective of a person's color or ethnicity. All people are made in the image of God and should be treated with corresponding dignity.

This standard of racial impartiality and fairness also applies to government. Scripture requires rulers to be just, while exhibiting particular concern for the most vulnerable members of society. However, extra sensitivity toward the disadvantaged does not warrant prejudice in their favor. God commanded: "Do not pervert justice; do not show partiality to the poor or favoritism to the great, but judge your neighbor fairly" (Lev. 19:15, NIV). Government should not discriminate, even in favor of a disadvantaged minority.

Of course, affirmative action was originally intended to take into account the barriers faced by members of minority groups without turning race into the primary decision-making variable. And this strategy—evaluating a person's accomplishments in the light of his or her background—seems both just and sensible. The same 1400 SAT score means different things when earned by someone growing up in a single-parent home in the inner city and by someone with a wealthy, intact family and a prep-school education. This form of affirmative action, based on individual rather than group characteristics, is entirely appropriate.

However, within a decade of passage of the 1964 Civil Rights Act, both the federal government and state governments were routinely transforming affirmative action into quotas and set-asides, establishing a multifaceted racial spoils system in which economic opportunity became an entitlement based on skin color. Arbitrary

Why isn't there more public challenge to the legitimacy of standardized tests, whether it's the Scholastic Achievement Test, the comparable tests for professional schools, the Civil Service exams with their incredibly important social and economic consequences, or I.Q. tests themselves, which continue to be given to children as a legitimate measure of their "intelligence"?

As far as I can tell, the answer is that the vast majority of people actually believe that these tests are measures of intelligence, ability, aptitude, and merit, while being secretly humiliated by their own test scores. We have created a society where we are addicted to feeling dumb, inadequate, and like failures, no matter how inaccurate and even childish the "measures" which create and reinforce this impression.

The S.A.T. does not measure how smart you are or your aptitude or your merit. It measures your capacity to think like a machine—by which I mean to think without employing the faculty of human understanding (or more accurately, while suppressing the faculty of human understanding)—under highly abusive competitive and authoritarian social conditions.

—Peter Gabel

preferences for government contracts and other benefits, such as television licenses, spawned an industry of black front men for white corporate interests and enriched a well-connected elite, symbolized by Commerce Secretary Ron Brown. These programs have been continually and grossly abused—as evidenced by the embarrassing Wedtech scandal of the Reagan years.

Even uglier has been the growing number of cases where affirmative action for qualified minorities has turned into affirmative discrimination against qualified majorities and minorities. Asian Americans are denied entrance to the University of California system because of their ethnicity; white males face an almost impossible job market in academia. People with one-eighth Indian blood seek favored treatment as disadvantaged Native Americans. The misnamed Equal Employment Opportunity Commission fined a Chicago firm for hiring too many Hispanics and too few blacks. A high school in Piscataway, New Jersey, fired one teacher because she was white in order to make room for a black teacher. And on it goes.

This perversion of affirmative action has caused more than a flood of individual injustices. It has poisoned race relations across the country and thereby threatens to set back efforts to achieve genuine equality. Citizens resent preferences granted recent immigrants who have never suffered from discrimination. College admission officials complain about pressure to abandon standards in order to attract minorities. Many whites see any black professional as a token. Businessmen privately admit that they are reluctant to hire minorities because they fear a lawsuit if the person doesn't work out. Racial tension—in schools, communities, professions, and politics—is growing, with blacks believing that they remain victims of discrimination and whites objecting to being discriminated against in the name of affirmative action. Gary Orfield of Harvard warns, "The civil rights impulse from the 1960s is dead in the water and the ship is floating backward toward the shoals of racial segregation." This problem will only grow more serious if race-conscious policies continue to spread.

After 30 years of affirmative action, it should be clear that discrimination is no answer to discrimination. Instead, we need to return to the ideal of Martin Luther King, who hoped for a time when people would be judged by their character rather than the color of their skin. To do otherwise is unjust and, as we have painfully discovered, socially destructive.

"Affirmative action has ceased to be a public policy; it's become an ideology. Still, nobody ever seems to accomplish much by pointing out this ideology's ugly antecedents and implications. Forgive the vulgar comparison, but 'abolishing' affirmative action—as Republicans like California Governor Peter Wilson have proposed to do—will prove as easy as scraping wax off broadloom. No single enactment or statute created affirmative action. Race and sex preferences are the product of literally thousands of mutually reinforcing federal executive orders, bureaucratic enforcement actions, private lawsuits, state and local laws and ordinances, and individual policies of corporations and universities.

More: it's become the livelihood of an entire industry—litigators, consultants, bureaucrats, college administrators, corporate vice presidents. The affirmative action regime won't be ended with the stroke of a pen, but only after a long, arduous struggle."—David Frum in *The American Spectator*, October 1995, p. 54.

(i) FAIRTEST, a national not-for-profit advocacy and research firm, conducts ongoing research and public policy initiatives that examine gender and race bias in standardized testing. Contact Dr. Pamela Zappardino, 342 Broadway, Cambridge, MA 02139, 617-864-4810, Fax 617-497-2224.

102 • Who Gets the Job: A Case Study

ANITA ROWE AND LEE GARDENSWARTZ

A medium-sized company located in the Midwest is looking for a manager to oversee the accounting department that consists of 14 bookkeepers, controllers and accountants and 4 secretaries.

The current manager, who has been in the job for 5 years, has been promoted and is recommending one of the accountants currently employed. While the company does have a history of promoting from within, it is also interested in creating a more diverse work environment. To that end, it is willing to consider outsiders. Four candidates have shown interest in the job. All have the technical skill and experience to handle the job.

John Conners is the one who has been recommended by the outgoing manager. He is a very skilled accountant, but more to the point he has been with this company for 7 years. He is involved in community activities, graduated from the local State University, and coaches his sons in Little League. He has good interpersonal relationships both inside and outside the company, and while he has his college degree, he continues to update his education and skills. If he does not get this promotion, he will consider leaving the company. John's biggest handicap is that he's a white male in a company looking for diversity.

Becky Cho is a co-worker of John's who has been at the company for 5 years. In fact, she and the outgoing manager started their employment at the same time. Becky, a CPA, has exceptional accounting skills and is viewed as the real expert when work related issues or questions come up. Her work relationships are mostly good, but some people are uncomfortable with the fact that she's a lesbian. While her sexual orientation is never demonstrated at work, she does bring her same-sex partner to holiday parties and company picnics. Her behavior is very circumspect,

---

Page 218

(i) On October 17, 1995, the European Court of Justice ruled that governments could not impose affirmative action programs that give women absolute priority for jobs and promotions, striking down a German state law requiring public agencies to give preference to female candidates with the same qualifications as male applicants for posts where women are unrepresented. ("European Union Court Ruling Sets Affirmative Action Limits," *The New York Times International*, October 18, 1995).

but she doesn't deny her relationship, which is a problem for some people in the department. They think she is immoral and deviant.

Ferdinand Aguilar is an outsider who heard about this opening through some of his fellow Filipinos at a recent church meeting. He ran his own business in Manila and since coming to the United States 12 years ago, he has practiced accounting in several different jobs. Currently, he is a manager of accounting at the city's water and power department overseeing 22 accountants and bookkeepers. He has depth of experience and a good track record. He is extremely involved in his ethnic community and recently joined the Rotary Club to expand his contacts. The biggest concern about Ferdinand is that most recent hires in the department are Filipino, and if he favors his fellow compatriots in future hiring, the department will be more homogeneous than diverse.

The 4th candidate, another outsider, is Malcolm Washington, Jr., an African-American who is new to the area. He graduated with honors from Amherst where he got his B.S., and Wharton, where he earned his M.B.A. He was a rising star at his former company, but left to relocate with his wife who got a once-in-a-lifetime job in this city. Malcolm is bright, charming, personable and capable. He is long on potential but short on practical experience. He looked like a shoe-in for the job until the vice president took him and his wife out for dinner. In a town not used to interracial marriage, there was a lot of discomfort. Malcolm's wife is Caucasian.

SUGGESTIONS FOR USING WHO GETS THE JOB? A CASE STUDY

Processing the Activity:

- The facilitator introduces the activity by explaining that competitive organizations today are trying to create more open climates where all people fit comfortably. Their ability to do so effectively depends largely on who they bring into the workplace when new promotional opportunities exist. The following case study will raise a number of salient issues about this complex and interesting subject.
- Facilitator distributes case study and divides participants into groups of 5 or 6 people.
- Facilitator gives each group a location in the room and then distributes case study, asking participants to read the case study on their own, making notes about the pros and cons of each candidate, and delineating the key issues for each.
- The groups are then directed to discuss each candidate and select their best one, detailing all the reasons for their thinking about each candidate.
- A spokesperson from each group then tells who has been chosen and why.
- On easel and flipchart, facilitator keeps a tally of who gets the job.

- Once all groups have presented their candidates, the facilitator leads a whole group discussion.
- Closure: Random comments charted by facilitator answering any of the following open-ended statements:

  ✓ The next time I hire or promote, I will _____

  ✓ The most important thing I learned from this experience is _____
  _____

  ✓ The one thing I will never do again in the hiring/promotion process is
  _____

  ✓ Future job candidates will benefit from my having this experience because _____

Questions for Discussion:

- What were the key issues . . . the decisive factors in awarding, or not awarding, the job?
- What assumptions did you make about each candidate? Were any of the assumptions invalid?
- What values and priorities underlie your choice of candidate?
- Each of these candidates is competent to do the job. Beyond the obvious job skill, what value does each add?
- What do these issues raised in the discussion suggest about the openness of your organization's culture? About the organization's relationship to the community?
- What might your company continue to gain and lose with its current thinking?
- What would need to happen in your organization to nudge people past some of their prejudices and open the climate more?
- What might be a good starting point? Facilitator should be sure to chart this answer.

Caveats, Considerations and Variations:

Groups can put the names of all 4 candidates on chart paper, post around the room and have participants mill around the room listing pros and cons of each. Have everyone read all the charts first and then start discussion, looking for common themes.

Objectives:

- To stimulate discussion about assumptions, prejudice or values and the role they all play in the hiring or promotion process so that participants may clarify their own priorities, assumptions and values in hiring and promotion.
- To apply this case study to real-life hiring and promotion decisions made every day.
- To minimize the negative impact prejudice and stereotypes have in hiring and promotion.

Time: 1¼ hours

Materials:

- Copies of *Who Gets The Job: A Case Study* for all participants
- Easel; flipchart; felt-tipped markers, pens or pencils
- Overhead for questions is optional

103 •   Alternative To Affirmative Action

(THE AMERICAN ENTERPRISE)

*F*or years, government assumed that the best way to aid minority contractors was by quotas, set-asides, and other forms of reverse discrimination. But now the Supreme Court has declared many of these programs unconstitutional.

An Austin, Texas non-profit called the National Council of Contractors Association (NCCA) may offer a healthier alternative for aiding minority business aspirants, one that involves no affirmative action crutches or coercion. The NCCA, which began its operations in 1993, provides small minority firms with expert advice about how to win contracts, with donated accounting services, and, most critically, with help obtaining bonding. Small businesses can't get construction work without completion bonds that guarantee clients their projects will be finished even if a firm defaults on its contract. But given the tight market in the bond business, most companies won't issue these bonds to unproven contractors.

In league with the NCCA, however, the Standard Group, a large bond broker, has begun offering special bonding help. Stacy Taylor, the Standard Group CEO, explains that he decided to help minority businesses not just for altruistic reasons, but because the idea made good business sense, since these new companies might be long-term customers once they became established enterprises. "We're in the business of creating independent business people," Taylor says. The accountants who offer reduced fee services through the NCCA also hope that struggling small businesses will remember their help once they become more successful.

Though there are no racial or gender restrictions in NCCA aid, most of the businesses it helps are minority- or women-owned enterprises. Between January 1994 and May 1995, NCCA helped 83 firms win 171 contracts. The Standard Group issued bonds worth $31.5 million and didn't have a default on any of them. (Only one of NCCA's clients had previously been able to obtain a bond.) Because these small businesses won contracts by underbidding larger competitors, the city of Austin saved over $1 million in public works expenses, and thus recouped the initial cost of a grant it gave to help launch the NCCA.

NCCA, P.O. Box 91837, Austin TX 78707-1837, 512-474-2627 or Fax 512-474-2770.

HOW HIRING QUOTAS REALLY WORK...

© 1993 Carol ★ Simpson Productions

"One of our black employees is retiring in six months. Could you come back then?"

The NCCA hopes to become a national organization and use its Austin experience to aid minority businesses in other cities.

Reprinted by permission from the September/October 1995 issue of *The American Enterprise*, a Washington-based magazine of politics, business and culture (1-800-562-2319).

In *Debating Affirmative Action: Race, Gender, Ethnicity, and the Politics of Inclusion*, edited by Nicholaus Mills (New York: Delta, 1994, $10.95, ISBN 0-385-31221-0), Dinesh D'Souza, Andrew Hacker, Anna Quindlen, Linda Chavez, Cornel West, Shelby Steele, Chang-Lin Tien, Stephen Carter, Ellen Goodman, and others debate the question: Is affirmative action a significant counterweight to institutional racism, or is it creating a divided America ripe for social turmoil?

104 • Affirmative Action, Family Style

JOAN STEINAU LESTER (SAN FRANCISCO EXAMINER)

*A*s we ponder the need for affirmative action and hear about "remedying the past," many of us have questions.

What do old injustices have to do with me?

I'm sorry if my great-great grandfather mistreated yours– yet isn't it time to bury history?

The past is over and done with, isn't it?

But is it? A news story recently reported the vastly unequal assets held by fifty-something whites compared to our counterparts of color.

My partner and I bought our major asset, a house, 15 years ago, with a low-interest loan from my parents—their retirement money. It suited us to have a lump sum. And they needed the income, which we sent every month in repayment installments.

That gift—a 10-year loan at 5 percent interest, no application fee, no points—got us started. How did my parents get their first down payment, in their 20s, when they had two babies and one job? It was a low-interest loan from my grandfather Ralph.

And his parents got him started, financially, when he started his teaching career. Ralph's grandfather had been a runaway, adopted at 12 by a doctor who financed his education.

Joan Lester is the Executive Director of Equity Institute, which developed *Sticks, Stones and Stereotypes (Palos, Piedras y Estereotipos)*, a video documentary/curriculum module for use in high school and 1st-year college classrooms about sexual orientation. Available from Equity Institute, 6400 Hollis St., Suite 15, Emeryville, CA 94608; 510-658-4577; Fax 510-658-5184.

And so the chain progressed. A legacy of down payments passed through the generations. We've each gotten a leg up because those in the preceding generation were enabled to create enough wealth by building on the seed money they received. And they in turn passed along a portion of that wealth for that critical first investment.

Once we own homes, all sorts of options open up. We make forced savings, take big tax write-offs, and have opportunities to borrow on the equity for other investments or to send children to college. We plan retirements with expectation of living almost rent-free at some point in our lives.

Informally surveying my friends, I notice that most who are African American are renters (those who own homes usually have parents who also did). I think about the legacy of slavery, which didn't produce assets. Instead, my friends' great-great grandparents were assets. For somebody else.

I think about my friend Donna, whose parents had their property confiscated during World War II when they went into a concentration camp for Japanese Americans. No wonder that now, at nearly 50, she's buying her first home.

I consider my friend Jeffrey back in Massachusetts, trying to reclaim a scrap of land his ancestors—Wampanoags—farmed and hunted.

As we formulate social policy, let's remember the biggest predictor of current financial worth—all those legacies.

Social change is designed to interrupt that cycle, no longer allowing the past to determine the future. We're working on it. But right now where we came from still matters.

105 ·   The Color Of Money

(BOOK REVIEW)

Black Wealth, White Wealth: A New Perspective on Racial Equality, by Melvin L. Oliver and Thomas M. Shapiro (New York: Routledge Press, $22.95).

Home ownership is one of the traditional investments that an American family could leverage into other investments or pass on to the children. *Black Wealth, White Wealth* by Oliver & Shapiro documents the many obstacles black Americans have historically faced in their efforts to buy land and houses. For example, when land became available in the West after the Homestead Act of 1862, "African Americans couldn't enforce their land claims in court" and "were largely barred from taking advantage of the nineteenth century federal land-grant program." The Federal Housing Authority, created in 1934 to boost the economy and shore up the flagging construction industry, would finance only exclusively white neighborhoods. The FHA's official handbook "even went so far as to provide a model 'restrictive covenant' that would pass court scrutiny to prospective white home buyers."

And in the 1980s, the practices of "redlining" (refusing to finance mortgages in inner-city neighborhoods) denied many qualified black families the opportunity to own homes. Even when they could get loans, they "often could only get mortgages at much higher rates than whites," the authors write.

A Conservative perspective: "Writing in *Forbes* about a Boston Federal Reserve study, Peter Brimelow and Leslie Spencer showed that the default rate on loans by blacks and whites was nearly identical. This seems to mean that bankers were making correct decisions. If they had been using more stringent standards for blacks, blacks should have had lower default rates than whites." From "Discreditable Reports," by Llewellyn H. Rockwell Jr. (*National Review*, 7/19/93, pp. 45-48) in an article that asserts that bankers *do not let* racism interfere with profits.

"Doing good" from a government mandate has always two sides. On one hand we want to achieve goals such as 'pay equity' and provide livable wages to people who work. But the conservative position, taken by Nobel laureate Milton Friedman expresses another perspective, also valid. How do you feel about the role of government? How do your values and beliefs cause you to support (or resent) certain public policies?

"Many well-meaning people favor legal minimum wage rates in the mistaken belief that they help the poor. It has always been a mystery to me why a youngster is better off unemployed at $4.75 an hour than employed at $4.25."

—Milton Friedman
National Review, May 1, 1995, p. 72.

Conservatives also believe that much of our society's current ills stem from bureaucratic interventions of all kinds. For example, widespread homelessness is seen as a consequence of severe building and health codes. The "free-market" philosophers would claim that if it were permitted to build low-cost economy housing (with say, no hot water), then it would be done (and be profitable) and everybody could afford some sort of housing. Does homelessness really stem from over-regulation? What do you think? [The conservative position is expressed in "Opening the Door to Low Cost Housing" by Randall K. Filer in *The City Journal* (Summer, 1992, Manhattan Institute, New York) or *Scarcity by Design* by Peter D. Salins and Jerard C. S. Mildner (Cambridge: Harvard, 1992). See also "Who goes homeless?" by Ernest Van Den Haag in *National Review*, March 1, 1993, pp. 49–50.

106 • Black Progress: A Conservative View

THOMAS SOWELL *(EDITORS' REVIEW OF OPINIONS)*

*T*homas Sowell, an economist cited elsewhere in this volume (pp. 113, 195), acknowledges the significant contributions of the civil rights movement for significant contributions to black progress. But he cites historical statistics in his book, *The Vision of the Anointed* which call into question the assumption that the civil rights movement in general (and "affirmative action" in particular) are *really* the major cause of economic advancement of blacks.

> ". . . the economic advancement of blacks, both absolutely and relative to whites, began long before the civil rights movement of the 1960s, and was due to the individual efforts of millions of black people trying to better their own lives. Hard statistics show that this advancement did not begin in the 1960s, was not even accelerated during the 1960s—and actually began to stall during the 1970s when "affirmative action" started. Affirmative action has [only] produced benefits for the elite."

•

> "The era of affirmative action . . . has been precisely . . . when the historic economic advancement of working-class blacks had begun to fizzle out, and when an underclass seems to have become an enduring part of the inner-city life."

Has affirmative action caused a decline in black economic achievement? Sowell presumes a cause-and-effect relationship. What do you think?

Sowell believes that huge legal liabilities created by affirmative action policies (particularly those that make statistical "under-representation" equivalent to discrimination) encourage employers to locate away from minority communities. Therefore, more may be lost in opportunities than is gained from quotas. Furthermore, he cites mounting evidence that quotas continue to engender hostility and resentment from whites.

What evidence can you cite that would support or refute Sowell's assertions? One thing we have noticed is that advocates of diversity (as practiced thru the 1990s) are often disparaging of, or downright hostile to, ideological diversity. This is especially true if that ideological diversity includes traditionally conservative values or beliefs.

Quoted passages copyright © 1995 Thomas Sowell. From *Is Reality Optimal?*, Hoover Institution Press, p. 106, 175. All rights reserved.

ⓘ See *The Vision of the Anointed*, by Thomas Sowell (New York: HarperCollins, 1995, ISBN 0-465-08994-1)

107 •   "White" Losers

D. NICO SWAAN

*B*oth terms, "black" and "white", cover an unbelievably rich and culturally diverse spectrum, and are therefore equally destructive in terms of creating an understanding of anything. Does a "white" person ever think to identify himself as "white"—other than when being attacked as such by a person of color? Does a "black" person ever identify himself as such other than when he feels the need to distinguish himself from the "white" community he lives alongside? Probably, in both cases, the answer is "no." Perhaps the "white" community started the vicious cycle of stereotyping and generalizing; perhaps the "white" person therefore carries a responsibility to put an end to it. But he is unlikely to be able to do that when he lives in a more or less constant fear that everything he has taken for granted in his culture and society is under threat.

Threat from whom? Certainly not in the first instance from people of color, at least not in Europe. I am talking about an average citizen of a small European state. He feels "one-down" vis á vis many groups within his own country: the wealthy bankers and industrialists who publish staggering profit figures one day, and on the next day announce yet more lay-offs, closures, and "rationalizations"; various levels of government, which grow more distant and unresponsive by the day, which announce constant cuts in the social net, and which seem to take an ever-greater percentage of earnings to cover the costs.

The Dutch, the Belgians, the Danes fear being marginalized by the French and the Germans in a "Greater Europe". They experience no connection whatsoever with the Spanish, Italian, and Swedish parliamentarians and bureaucrats in Strasbourg and Brussels who design EU Directives and pass on European legislation. The average citizen feels increasingly disempowered and disenfranchised in a complex and incomprehensible political web. The average citizen feels threatened and powerless . . . among other "whites." The result is apathy . . . or anger.

On the fringe the anger manifests itself in various vicious and violent forms. Two thousand neo-nazis from across Europe caused mayhem this past weekend in a small Belgian town. Racist attacks, especially in Germany and France, are well-documented.

The fringe remains a fringe; the danger to the fabric of society could be greater in the form of a general "back-lash" . . .

A secure, confident citizen with a sense of worth and power (meaning "able to make things happen") can easily subscribe to and support programs to help

Affirmative Action initiatives are now underway in a number of European Union countries. This reflection of a "white" European living in Holland (and discussing the dimensions of race in Europe) adds perspective to the debate in the U.S.

Swaan suggests even more strongly that issues of class underlie much of the racial debate.

those with less power and less security: tax-funded foreign aid, tax-funded programs to assist the "less-privileged," the under-dog. It is easy to buy into any form of "affirmative action" to create greater equality when I feel "equal." If, however, I feel insecure, undermined, less-than-equal, disenfranchised, powerless, then I am likely to respond less than charitably to affirmative action programs directed towards other disenfranchised and powerless groups, in whatever guise or form.

The average "white" citizen is feeling like a loser. Losers tend to lash out. Losers create a "back-lash." Losers are not strong enough or ready to invite difference to the table.

Unpublished correspondence from D. Nico Swaan, September 1995. Used with permission.

108 · Hiring and Retention Goals for Men and Women

JULIE O'MARA AND LYNDA WHITE (THE DIVERSITY FACTOR)

(i) First appeared in "Closing the Gender Gap: The Royal Bank Experience," *The Diversity Factor*, Fall, 1995. All rights reserved.

The Diversity Factor is a quarterly journal devoted exclusively to diversity issues, produced by the Elsie Y. Cross Associates, Inc. (Subscriptions are available from The Diversity Factor, P.O. Box 3188, Teaneck, NJ 07666, 201-833-0011, Fax 201-833-4184, e-mail: mbwhite@mail.att.net).

*a*t Royal Bank, the "Closing the Gender Gap" process is concerned with both men and women. While men are over-represented at the top of the organization, women dominate entry-level jobs at a rate of over 70%. This imbalance means that the bank may not be getting the best talent in all its jobs.

One senior vice president tells how each time she buys coffee at a nearby coffee shop, she tries to sell the server—usually a young man—on a career in banking. "Many of those young men are great at customer service," she notes. "We need them in banking."

Young men who take jobs in coffee shops, hardware stores, autoshops, health clubs, and the like do not think of careers in banking—which they considered "women's work." "But we can offer them a future," the senior vice president believes. "We need their talent. It's very frustrating that we have not been successful in reaching them."

While most strategies related to gender issues have focused only on increasing the number of women at the top, Royal Bank has initiated actions to increase the number of men in entry-level jobs. Managers are being held accountable for hiring and retaining men in entry-level positions. Currently, men in entry-level positions tend to leave the bank in greater numbers than women do, or move on to increased responsibilities more quickly.

A specific strategy was implemented when a new telephone banking center was established in Moncton, New Brunswick. Since call centers are traditionally staffed almost exclusively (about 90%) by women, the standard Employment Equity language used in recruiting ads to encourage applications from the four Canadian-designated groups was expanded to include men. An Interactive Voice Response System, designed to eliminate gender bias in screening, was implemented. As a result, 19 men and 31 woman were hired in the staffing process for Moncton. Inspired by the results, Moncton is committed to continuing the strategy in its efforts to achieve gender equity.

109 • Job Accommodations— Situations & Solutions

PRESIDENT'S COMMITTEE ON EMPLOYMENT OF PEOPLE WITH DISABILITIES

*I*n December 1994 the President's Committee's Job Accommodation Network (JAN) reported that 68% of job accommodations made cost less than $500, and further, that employers report that for every dollar spent on accommodations, the company received $28 in benefits.

Accommodations, which are modifications or alterations, often make it possible for a qualified person with a disability to do the same job as everyone else but in a slightly different way. Some accommodations are simple adaptations; others require technically sophisticated equipment. The essential functions of the job and the functional limitations of the individual are what the employer and the employee want to match up.

An employer should analyze the job tasks, basic qualifications needed to do those tasks, and the kinds of adjustments that can be made to ensure that performance standards will be met. The way the worker does the job is far less important than the outcome.

The following examples are a small sampling of real situations that businesses have reported, along with the solutions used. What is common to all these situations is that accommodations are always made on an individual basis. To find solutions to your own situations, call JAN toll-free at 1-800-526-7234.

Situation: A greenhouse worker with mental retardation has difficulty staying on task and knowing when to take breaks.

Solution: At no cost to the employer, a job coach gave initial training. The worker then carried a tape recorder that provided periodic reminders to stay on task and indicated break time. The worker also carried a set of laminated cards which showed the basic list of tasks to be completed. Cost: $50.

Situation: A radio broadcaster/announcer who is blind needs to read the AP wire news desk material.

Solution: The employer connected a Braille printer to the incoming news service and installed a switch to move from regular printed material to Braille. Cost: $1,700.

Situation: An administrative assistant in a social service agency has a psychiatric disability that causes concentration and memory problems related to word processing, filing, and telephone work.

Solution: Accommodations included using soothing music in one earphone to block distractions and taped instructions to augment written material. Cost: $150.

Situation: A police officer has a learning disability that makes it difficult to take standard civil service tests.

Solution: Officer was permitted 50% more time to take the test and was allowed to use a dictionary during the examination. Cost: $0.

Situation: A laboratory technician has a permanent restriction on mobility of head and neck and must use a microscope on the job.

Solution: A periscope was attached to the microscope so the worker does not need to lower her head and bend her neck to perform the job. Cost: $2,400.

Situation: A chef who is paraplegic needs a way to move around the various work stations in the kitchen.

Solution: The chef was provided with a stand-up wheelchair that allowed flexibility and mobility, thereby eliminating the need to change the worksite itself: Cost; Approximately $3,000.

Situation: A highly skilled electronics company technician who has AIDS was taking large amounts of annual and sick leave.

Solution: The employer provided a flexible work schedule and redistributed portions of the workload. The company also instituted AIDS awareness training for employees. Cost: $0.

Situation: A bakery worker with mental retardation had trouble placing cookie dough by precise numbers and patterns on sheets due to visual perception problems.

Solution: A plastic template was made for the cookie sheet, with holes cut to indicate the precise placing pattern. Cost: Under $50.

Public domain material available through the President's Committee on Employment of People with Disabilities, 1331 F St., NW, Washington, D.C. 20004. 202-376-6200, 202-376-6205 TDD/TTY.

Diversity Equals Inclusion: Twelve-minute video highlights the contributions that people with disabilities are making in our schools, workplaces, and communities when disability becomes an integral part of what we seek as diversity. Presents three key premises: First, that the most common definition of diversity as including people with multicultural, ethnic, and religious backgrounds needs to be expanded to include people with disabilities; next, that inclusion means increased productivity because it allows everyone to participate, not only as students, employees, and volunteers, but as customers as well; last, that to make this happen, attitudes must change.

Civic and religious organizations will find that *Diversity Equals Inclusion* speaks to the social benefits that disabled persons give back to their communities and their unique perspective on what it takes to achieve and be successful in any community. (Available for $50 from the National Easter Seal Society, 230 West Monroe, Suite 1800, Chicago, IL 60606, 312-726-6200, TDD 312-726-4258, Fax 312-726-1494. A catalog of excellent publications and products is available: 708-238-4202, Fax 708-238-4135, TDD 312-726-4258.)

110 • Education: Doing Bad and Feeling Good

CHARLES KRAUTHAMMER *(TIME)*

A standardized math test was given to 13-year-olds in six countries last year. Koreans did the best. Americans did the worst, coming in behind Spain, Britain, Ireland and Canada. Now the bad news. Besides being shown triangles and equations, the kids were shown the statement "I am good at mathematics." Koreans came last in this category. Only 23% answered yes. Americans were No. 1, with an impressive 68% in agreement.

American students may not know their math, but they have evidently absorbed the lessons of the newly fashionable self-esteem curriculum wherein kids are taught to feel good about themselves. Of course, it is not just educators who are convinced that feeling good is the key to success. The Governor of Maryland recently announced the formation of a task force on self-esteem, "a 23-member panel created on the theory," explains the Baltimore *Sun*, "that drug abuse, teen pregnancy, failure in school and most other social ills can be reduced by making people feel good about themselves." Judging by the international math test, such task forces may be superfluous. Kids already feel exceedingly good about doing bad.

Happily, some educators are starting to feel bad about doing bad. Early voice to the feel-bad movement was given by the 1983 *Nation at Risk* study, which found the nation's schools deteriorating toward crisis. And Bush's "education summit" did promise national standards in math and science. The commitment remains vague but does recognize that results objectively measured, not feelings, should be the focus of educational reform.

Now the really bad news. While the trend toward standards and testing goes on at the national level, quite the opposite is going on in the field, where the fixation on feeling is leading to the Balkanization of American education.

The battle cry is "inclusion" in the teaching curriculum for every politically situated minority. In California, for example, it is required by law that textbooks not just exclude "adverse reflection" of any group but include "equal portrayal" of women, minorities and the handicapped. In texts on "history or current events, or achievements in art, science or any other field, the contributions of women and men should be represented in approximately equal numbers."

Says a respected female historian: "I'm beginning to think that in the future it will become impossible to write a history textbook and satisfy these kinds of demands. After all, how do you write a history of the Bill of Rights giving equal time to the contribution of women?"

In New York State, a report from the Task Force on Minorities (*A Curriculum of Inclusion*) has launched a fierce attack on "Eurocentrism" in the schools. It begins, "African Americans, Asian Americans, Puerto Rican/Latinos and Native Americans have all been the victims of an intellectual and educational oppression that has characterized the culture and institutions of the United States and the European-American world for centuries." Result: "Terribly damaging" to

the "psyche" of minority youth. Recommendation: Prepare all curricular materials "on the basis of multicultured contributions to the development of all aspects of our society."

This is ideology masquerading as education and aspiring to psychotherapy. It demands outright lying. Not all groups in America have contributed "to the development of all aspects of our society." There is little to be said, for example, about the Asian-American contribution to basketball, about the Jewish-American contribution to the Pequot War or about the contribution of women to the Bill of Rights. Some connection could, of course, be found—manufactured—if one pushed it.

But pushing it would be entirely in the service of ideology, not truth. American history has not been smoothly and proportionately multicultural from the beginning. Honesty requires saying so.

But honesty is not the object of the inclusion movement. Psychic healing is. The fixation on inclusionary curricula is based on the widespread assumption that the pathologies afflicting many minorities, from teen pregnancy to drug abuse to high dropout rates, come from a lack of self-esteem. Which, in turn, comes from their absorbing (as the New York task force puts it) "negative characterizations" of themselves in school books.

This argument is wrong on its face. This is the era of Cosby and affirmative action. If today's high dropout rates, drug abuse and teen pregnancy stem from negative characterizations of minorities, then 40 years ago—the era of *Amos 'n' Andy* and parks with NO DOGS OR NEGROES signs—self-esteem should have been lower and social pathology worse. Of course, the opposite is true. In 40 years negative characterizations have decreased and social pathologies have increased.

The real tragedy of this obsessive preoccupation with Eurocentrism is that it is a trap and a diversion. Of all the reasons for the difficulties encountered by the minority kids in and out of school, curricular Eurocentrism ranks, if at all, at the bottom. That New York State, in the midst of an education crisis, should be devoting its attention to cleansing the grade school curriculum of Eurocentrism is a waste, a willful turning away from real problems.

The attack on Eurocentrism did not start in the New York public schools. It started at the elite universities. Last year Stanford University changed its course on Western civilization into a curriculum of inclusion by imposing a kind of ethnic and gender quota system for Great Books.

Stanford can afford such educational indulgences. Its graduates will get jobs even if their education is mildly distorted by this inclusionary passion. Not so inner-city third-graders, whose margin of error in life is tragically smaller. And for whom any dilution or diversion of education to satisfy the demands of ideology can be devastating.

The pursuit of good feeling in education is a dead end. The way to true self-esteem is through real achievement and real learning. Politically Balkanized

curricula will only ensure that our schools continue to do bad, for which feeling good, no matter how relentlessly taught, is no antidote.

111 •   What's Fair?

KAREN BURSTEIN INTERVIEWS LANI GUINIER (MS. MAGAZINE)

*W*ith the fate of affirmative action hanging in the balance, Ms. asked Lani Guinier, a professor of law at the University of Pennsylvania and author of *The Tyranny of the Majority*, and Karen Burstein, a former family court judge in Brooklyn New York and practicing New York City attorney, to think aloud about the prospects for this 30-year-old initiative designed to provide equal opportunity for women and "minorities."

KAREN BURSTEIN: The thesis of your work has been that the majority—in order not to be tyrannical—must allow the minority to win some of the time so that there's a stake in continuing to play the game. Is that a fair expression of your beliefs?

LANI GUINIER: Yes.

BURSTEIN: Now it seems to me that one of the arguments against affirmative action has been that in allowing minorities to win, members of the majority lose. If you look at it from a great distance there may not be a win/lose result, but in any individual circumstance there may be. Can affirmative action be implemented so that no one loses?

GUINIER: If you look at the big picture you can see a fundamental fairness, but if you're looking at the small picture, you see unfairness. But, the conventional approach has excluded women as well as underrepresented members of some minority groups. For example, the New York City Police Department used to have a height requirement that effectively excluded women and many men who are minorities. Successful challenges to the rule opened the force to women as well as Asian, Latino, and short white men. The women who came onto the force are often considered more effective at defusing domestic violence incidents. So it's not just that we're going to hire a woman instead of a man. It's that we're looking to hire a range of people because we need different skills in order to have an effective department.

Lani Guinier

BURSTEIN: While diversity allows us new ways of seeing how human beings respond to one another and new ways of solving problems, Lani, it also underlines the most terrifying nature of affirmative action: the fear that if society were to say discrimination is wrong, major changes would occur in who would have power.

GUINIER: But those with power are not being asked to give it up. People who feel insecure about their ability to provide for their families are the ones most threatened.

BURSTEIN: But my point is that the discourse does not allow us to talk about the big picture the way we did a minute ago. How, for example, can we get white men who are frightened about their jobs to say, "Wait, we need a larger pie so there's more for all of us"?

GUINIER: By not polarizing the debate. For example, Lowell High School is this magnet school in San Francisco that is under a federal court order to desegregate. To maintain diversity, the school combined students' averages with their performance on a test and established a ceiling on the number of any one group attending. Asian American kids had to score higher than African American, white, or Latino students. A group of Chinese American parents charged that the order was discriminatory. A group of African Americans and the NAACP defended the order, saying that without it Lowell would not be diverse. So, in a course I teach on race and gender, I asked the class to think of a new paradigm in which Lowell could admit students and be respectful of the legitimate concerns on both sides of the debate. The students proposed that Lowell admit applicants through a lottery. There would be a floor for admissions for everyone. However, if they needed trombone players, for example, and you played the trombone, this talent could be rewarded by your name being put in the lottery twice, thus enhancing your chances.

BURSTEIN: But part of our politics has been to set one group against another as opposed to finding points of intersection. One of the values of affirmative action is that you've got a bunch of people from all over, and you can imagine solutions, and you can't be so dishonest. So how do you overcome the fundamental dishonesty of a system that frames the issue as a conflict?

GUINIER: I coauthored a study of women at the Penn Law School that found that many women who come in with the same entry-level credentials as men are not doing as well once they get here. The culture of the law school is affirming of the ways men (and I'm generalizing) have been socialized. One way of looking at this is that we need to teach women how to play the game. But women are saying that instead of demonizing your opponent, there could also be more collaborative forms of problem solving, and it may be that the litigation model is not always effective.

BURSTEIN: Yes, my work as a family court judge has shown me that the adversary system is absolutely inappropriate in resolving family disputes. Even when you make a decision, people don't accept it. And even though people are

(i) In *The Tyranny of the Majority: Fundamental Fairness in Representative Democracy*, by Lani Guinier (New York: The Free Press, 1994, $24.95, ISBN 0-02-913172-3) a collection of her law journal articles, she calls for a more representative democratic system that relies on "majority rule" rather than on "majority tyranny." Guinier argues that we may need an alternative to "winner-take-all majoritarianism"—something that relies on what she calls the "principle of taking turns." She covers such issues as the history and enforcement of the Voting Rights Act, race-conscious redistricting, and the representation of various group interests.

speaking about new paradigms, there still is a world out there framed by the old ones. So, that brings us back to this issue of how we get people talking about affirmative action in terms of a more diverse society instead of where they currently are, which is, "I lost a job 'cause a black person wanted it" or "I'm a man and they need a woman for the job."

GUINIER: The great tragedy of the current debate is that it takes place in a win/lose context. Both the terms and substance of the debate need to be changed so that there are no inevitable losers. Even those who feel as if they are being denied a job unfairly have to be heard. People need to tell their stories, and then recommendations need to be made to accommodate these collective stories . . .

BURSTEIN: Opponents of affirmative action have seized on the notion that its beneficiaries are less competent than those who have not benefited from it. That's rooted both in this idea that there's such a thing as an objective standard of excellence and in an absolute denial of the persistence of pure prejudice in our society. Racism is like a sore that will fester if not opened to the light.

GUINIER: The TV news magazine *Day One* went to three schools and talked to nine- and ten-year-olds because we are told that that's the age when kids get a sense of race. Every kid was asked to complete the statement, "Black people are best at . . ." And most answered "sports." The kids said white people are good at math or management. And most did not have friends from other races. We limit racism and sexism to intentional discrimination, when in fact the phenomenon is structural and institutional. We need to acknowledge the way these ideas have penetrated down to our children.

BURSTEIN: [There was a] female reporter who couldn't say out loud, "Look, I was offered positions I might not have gotten if people weren't sensitive to the fact that women had been excluded from the process." In this country the myth is that you pull yourself up by your bootstraps. Another myth is that our society is colorblind. Maybe our language needs to be more precise. When I'm talking about a white person, maybe I should say she's a white person.

GUINIER: On some level we all have a group identity and we should be explicit about that. And, as you say, Karen, if we don't acknowledge racism, it's going to fester like a wound. Diverse workforces make for more humane and inventive problem-solving, and so the beneficiaries of affirmative action who have transformed the workplace need to tell their stories.

(i) *One by One from the Inside Out: Essays and Reviews on Race and Responsibility in America*, by Glen C. Loury (New York: The Free Press, $24.95).

Numerous large U.S. companies have gotten the message that "diversity is a business imperative, rather than just a government edict." The diversity encouraged by affirmative action is a powerful tool for marketing and recruiting successfully. Many firms see it as a critical edge in fierce global competition. See "Affirmative Action's Corporate Converts," by Jonathan Glater and Martha M. Hamilton, *The Washington Post*, March 19, 1995.

At the same time, corporate executives seem reluctant to engage in the Affirmative Action debate. While hiring practices that promote diversity seem successful, the "glass ceiling" seems hard to break. The successful retention and advancement of women and minorities is still a challenge, as is the effort to make employees realize the potential of diversity in a global market. See "Some Action, Little Talk," by Judith H. Dobrzynski, *The New York Times*, April 20, 1995.

Our Common Future—Shaping 21st-Century Pluralism

10

What will the future North America look like? Culturally speaking, on the eve of the twenty-first century, we might expect one of three scenarios to further unfold: 1) that almost everyone will become assimilated to a "mainline culture;" 2) that we will become increasingly balkanized into warring factions and, at best, politically unstable coalitions will be sustained; or 3) that a composite, new "melting pot" culture will emerge shaped partly by the existing cultures and partly by what each successive wave of immigrants has brought with them.

Such projections are, of course, only projections. They are scenarios based on what we know about the past as if it were to follow some linear continuity into the future. More likely, the economic revolution already under way will continue to disrupt the culture more radically. For the vast majority of the population the myth of prosperity in a "promised land" could easily disappear, if it has not already. The United States will disappear as a place of opportunity where individuals succeed, free from the oppression of past histories. Rather it may more and more resemble those histories. The vast divide between rich and poor may remind some of us with immigrant pasts of what we or many of our ancestors fled in coming here. It may feel like the reestablishment of slavery to those of us, supposedly freed, whose ancestors were brought here as slaves. It may signal continued exploitation and marginalization for those of us whose Native American world was occupied by strangers.

In the town of Santa Cruz, California, which has 900 homeless children of high-school age in a population of about 50,000, part of this future generation, the "gutter tribe," sits on the sidewalks and curbs of Pacific Avenue and Cathcart Street. This crossroads, described by some observers as "the corner of Carmel and Beirut," has a lot left vacant by the earthquake of 1989. It has become a "camp-out" for panhandling, youthful anger, and homeless activism. It divides the affluent, rebuilt downtown from the damaged and rundown end of the main street.

Today, one might say that North America itself stands at "the corner of Carmel and Beirut." In this section our contributors explore the utopia and the hell of today's North America and that to come. They detail much of our unfinished business. How we handle this will send us careening in one direction or another. They discuss the nature of the decisions and the thinking, the responsibility and the leadership, required to shape our future together—or apart. Their visions and fears echo our own, so we can examine and discuss them more wisely.

112 · Diversity Is a Business Issue

BOB ABRAMMS INTERVIEWS ROOSEVELT THOMAS

BOB ABRAMMS: You approach diversity by going to the deepest cultural assumption within the organization, but it isn't always possible to get people to that level. Many initiatives I've seen just aren't maintained. Do the client systems you work with maintain momentum?

ROOSEVELT THOMAS: Peaks and valleys come from the magnitude of the change involved. You are fundamentally asking for a major individual mind shift or a major organizational culture shift. That doesn't typically take place in a straightforward way. You take five steps forward and three backward, but you still net two steps.

The clearer you are about the business rationale and the positive impact your efforts will have on business, the more sustainable your efforts. The challenge is convincing managers that people are strategic. This is not to say that they're mistreating people. It means that if you ask the source of competitive advantage, few managers in their gut believe it's how they deal with and what they get from people. That's a major barrier.

ABRAMMS: Well, the business rationale may motivate people, but it might not get them to grapple with achieving justice or reducing bias.

THOMAS: Most people see diversity as a legal, moral, or social responsibility. As such, it can feel like a burden. To think about this as a business issue, and seriously see it facilitating initiatives that are already under way—that's a challenge. The diversity piece, as well as the managing piece presents significant challenges for the typical manager. In our experience, the biggest barrier to managing diversity has not been racism, sexism, or any -ism, or even lack of motivation. It's been poor management, or no management, or inadequate management . . .

ABRAMMS: An inability to change?

THOMAS: To cope with change and complexity. When we say "managing diversity" we mean empowerment. In most organizations that we've dealt with, however, empowerment management has been *talked about*, but it's not a legitimate activity.

One reason for this is because empowerment management demands the willingness and ability to differentiate between the organization's absolute business requirements, and its preferences, conveniences, and traditions. Few organizations are doing this.

ABRAMMS: Do you see the political spectrum as a form of diversity?

THOMAS: Yes. And right now, I see us asking how much diversity we, as a nation, want or can stand. Part of the problem is that people want to act like diversity is synonymous with differences. They talk about diversity fracturing the country, fracturing the organization. For me, diversity refers to both differences and similarities. So diversity, as opposed to fracturing, becomes the context within which you can talk about the ties that bind and also the differences that make us unique. If you think about diversity that way it becomes less frightening. In fact, it opens up possibilities for creative problem solving.

To me diversity is a kind of multiculturalism where one culture reflects multiple individual cultures. A multicultural nation is one that reflects multiple cultures within its borders. A "multiculture" in an organization reflects the cultures of the individuals in the organization. But there's only one culture. You're not talking about multiple cultures.

ABRAMMS: Why do you think Americans are having difficulty accepting diversity?

THOMAS: In this country we have never said that we wanted diversity. What we have said is that we want to include people who are different—as long as they leave their differences at the door . . .

ABRAMMS: Right.

THOMAS:—and fit in. Diversity sort of sneaked in the back door. When the people we went after got in and said, "I'm not willing to fit in," or "I cannot fit in," we ended up with uninvited diversity. That's been our major challenge.

We can be different and still united. Having different sets of values doesn't mean that we are divided; it means we are different. Now, it remains to be seen if we come together and move forward in a united way around similarities and still be very different. We like to disguise or deny differences. When something peels back the curtain and reveals those differences, we profess to be surprised. Then we say we're divided and have to close the gap. That means we've got to make everybody the same.

ABRAMMS: We have an entry point for change in corporations where there is a strong commitment, a willingness to be vulnerable, and the energy, time, and resources to support the work that you're doing. In society as a whole, we don't have an institution to pull us toward a common good. Can our nation create the kind of breakthrough that you facilitate on a corporate basis?

THOMAS: In the civil-rights movement, the country stimulated change in organizations. I think, with respect to diversity and managing diversity, corporations will lead society. I often get the question, "How can I practice managing diversity when the environment we are located in is not anywhere near doing so?" My response is, "You are managing diversity or practicing diversity because if you don't, it will have a negative impact on your bottom line. To continue to thrive, you're going to have to exercise leadership in the general society."

ABRAMMS: So, as the government ratchets back its commitment toward access and opportunity, believers from corporate ranks will lead this change in consciousness.

THOMAS: Yes, but—I want to be clear—I think that most corporations are nowhere near being ready to lead. Most corporations still have not dealt with diversity. They are calling what they used to do under affirmative action "diversity." What's going to get them to that point is economic reality. It's the environment saying you can ill afford not to take the diversity of your workers into consideration as you seek to fully utilize them, and you've got to be concerned about the diversity of your customers as you talk about being customer focused.

This interview is included with the permission of R. Roosevelt Thomas, Jr., President and Founder of the American Institute for Managing Diversity. Copyright © 1996.

"Diversity: Business Rationale and Strategies, A Research Report," which was released by the Conference Board in November 1995, highlights ten key areas in which organizations are taking steps to integrate diversity into business units and functions: 1) mission statements incorporating diversity; 2) annual reports that highlight diversity; 3)employee and management handbooks; 4) diversity action plans; 5) accountability in individual business objectives; 6) employee involvement from all levels and functions; 7) community involvement and outreach; 8) career development and planning; 9) creation of a position to lead diversity objectives; and 10) culture change. Copies of the report (Report Number 1130-95-RR) are available from the Conference Board, Publication and Sales Department, 212-759-0900, Fax 212-980-7014.

For many organizations, sponsorship of a Multicultural or Diversity Awareness Day is an effective way of increasing the cultural sensitivity and awareness of their workforce. AT&T Interntional in Orlando, Florida, provides an example. The four-year program evolved from what we popularly known as "Food Day," which focused on the savoring of different ethnic cuisines, to a "Multicultural Awareness Day" that emphasizes awareness of beliefs and traditions, artifacts, textiles, and crafts. Events in the day include a parade of participants in native costumes giving the assembled group greetings in their native language, followed by a short narrative about their cultures and traditions. Over the course of the program's growth participants were surveyed for suggestions on how to improve the day. Employees appreciated the company's dedication to cultural awareness and offered helpful critiques which enabled the program to get beyond stereotypes of cultural groups.

While some diversity experts disparage such multicultural "show and tell" events, AT&T perceives the increased participation level and more employees' active involvement on the day itself as an indication of success. For more information, contact Dolly Ali, AT&T International Billing Control Office, 7700 Southland Blvd., Orlando, FL, at 407-850-2932, Fax 407-850-3724.

Jeremy Rifkin's scenario in "Choosing Our Future" is one futuristic vision of the "Post-Market Era." A quite different future was envisioned by Kurt Vonnegut, Jr. in *Player Piano* (Delacourt Press). In this 1952 novel, Vonnegut prophetically describes a highly automated world where most workers have been made redundant and are relegated to a pitiful existence of welfare and make-work "jobs." The class differences between the managers/professionals and the "rest of society" are deeply disturbing. We are nearly fifty years beyond the time in which he created this work, and it is more than a bit eerie that our culture is in many ways growing to resemble the apartheid society of *Player Piano*.

113 · Choosing our Future
"The good life in the Post-Market Age"

JEREMY RIFKIN (UTNE READER)

*T*he year is 2045.

Life for most Americans is quite different today from what it was half a century ago. Perhaps the greatest visible change is the diminishing role of the economic marketplace in day-to-day affairs. Now that we are deep into the Information Age, most of the world's goods and services are produced in nearly workerless factories and marketed by virtual companies run by a small team of entrepreneurs and highly trained professionals. Sophisticated computers, robots, and state-of-the-art telecommunications technologies have replaced the "worker" of the industrial era. Less than 20 percent of the adult population works full time.

Most Americans receive their economic livelihood, in the form of voucher payments, from their local governing body in return for community service work in non-profit organizations. The vouchers are financed by the imposition of a value-added tax on high-tech goods and services.

Their projects run the gamut from helping take care of children and the elderly to working in preventive health programs, local art galleries, park maintenance, history projects, adult education, community gardens, and neighborhood sports teams as well as religious and political activities. Interestingly enough, the kind of nurturing and community-building skills that characterize work in the volunteer sector are the least vulnerable to replacement by computers, robots, and telecommunications technology. While market-oriented tasks–even highly technical and professional jobs—are often reducible to digitization and computerization, caring tasks that require intimate relationships between people are far too complex and difficult to be attended to by high-tech software. In the Post-Market Era, these are the high-status jobs. Because the productivity gains resulting from technological advances have been broadly distributed among all Americans, people's work—whether in community service or private business— takes up fewer than five hours a day, leaving more time for family, friends, personal projects, and relaxation. Some of the wealth from the high-tech revolution is also being shared with people in developing nations.

The values of the market economy that so dominated the industrial era have steadily given way to a new ethos based on personal transformation, community participation, and global responsibility. The older market system reinforced a materialist vision glorifying production and efficiency as the chief means of advancing happiness. As long as people's primary identification was with the market economy, the vision of unlimited personal consumption continued to influence most people's behavior. Americans thought of themselves first and foremost as "consumers," not as neighbors or citizens.

As more and more human beings were freed up from formal work in the market economy and began doing community service in the social economy, the values of community began to gain dominance across America and around the world. In preparation for a career in the social economy, children learn at home and in schools the value of helping others and of strengthening neighborhood and community bonds. While children spend part of their school time deep in cyberspace and virtual reality, they are expected to spend the remainder of their school experience in "real time," meeting people in their communities, helping create a more humane and ecologically sustainable society. Hands-on community service has become an integral part of the school experience. Youngsters help out in senior centers, animal shelters, environmental cleanup projects, and countless other neighborhood programs. They are prepared for a full life, not simply for a job. The emphasis on personal participation with others in the community is seen as a necessary antidote to the increasingly impersonal interaction generated by new computer and telecommunication technologies.

The transition to a Post-Market Era has not been easy. Corporate leaders and other vested interests fought the shift to a social economy every step of the way, particularly in the first decades of the 21st century. Nonetheless, support for postmarket social policies continued to grow as more and more people were marginalized by the workings of the market economy. Although some opposition continues to this day from critics clinging to the values of the 20th-century market ethos, most Americans have adjusted well to the new Post-Market Era, enjoying the freedom that comes with less work in the marketplace.

This material is drawn from *The End of Work* by Jeremy Rifkin (New York: Putnam Publishing, $24.95, ISBN 0-87427-779-8, 350 pages). 1-800-847-5515.

114 • Beyond the Tortilla Curtain: Welcome to the Borderless Society

GUILLERMO GÓMEZ-PEÑA
(GRANTMAKERS IN THE ARTS)

From 1978 to 1991, I lived and worked in and among the cities of Tijuana, San Diego, and Los Angeles. Like hundreds of thousands of Mexicans, I was a binational commuter. I crossed that dangerous border regularly, by plane, by car, and by foot. The border became my home, my base of operations,

Good-bye White Majority

In a society as thoroughly and violently racialized as the United States, White-Black relations have defined racism for centuries. Today the composition and culture of the U.S. are changing rapidly. We need to consider seriously whether we can afford to maintain an exclusively White/Black model of racism when the population will be 32 percent Latino, Asian/Pacific American and Native American—in short, neither Black nor White—by the year 2050. We are challenged to recognize that multi-colored racism is mushrooming, and then strategize how to resist it. We are challenged to move beyond a dualism comprised of two white supremacist inventions: Blackness and Whiteness.

—Elizabeth Martinez

and my laboratory of social and artistic experimentation. My art, my dreams, my family and friends, and my psyche were literally and conceptually divided by the border. But the border was not a straight line; it was more like a Möbius strip. No matter where I was, I was always on "the other side," feeling ruptured and incomplete, ever longing for my other selves, my other home and tribe.

Thanks to my Chicano colleagues, I learned to perceive California as an extension of Mexico and the city of Los Angeles as the northernmost barrio of Mexico City. And in spite of many California residents' denial of the state's Mexican past and their bittersweet relationship with contemporary Mexicans, I never quite felt like an immigrant. As a mestizo with a thick accent and an even thicker moustache, I knew I wasn't exactly welcome; but I also knew that millions of Latinos, "legal" and "illegal," shared that border experience with me.

Then in 1991 I moved to New York City, and my umbilical cord finally snapped. For the first time in my life, I felt like a true immigrant. From my Brooklyn apartment, Mexico and Chicanolandia seemed a million light years away.

I decided to return to Southern Califas in 1993. Since the riots, Los Angeles had become the epicenter of America's social, racial, and cultural crisis. It was, unwillingly, the capital of a growing "Third World" within the shrinking "First World." I wanted to be both a witness and a chronicler of this wonderful madness.

I found a city at war with itself, a city gravely punished by natural and social forces; a city that is experiencing in a more concentrated manner what the rest of the country is undergoing. Its political structures are dysfunctional and its economy is in shambles; cutbacks in the defense budget have resulted in increased unemployment; and racial tensions are the focus of daily news reports. Crime rates and poverty levels can be compared to those of a Third World city. All this coincides with an acute crisis of national identity. Post-Cold War America is having a very hard time shedding its imperial nostalgia, embracing its multiracial soul, and accepting its new status as the first "developed" country to become a member of the Third World.

Perhaps what scared me more than anything was to realize who was being blamed for all the turmoil. The Mexican/Latino immigrant community was the scapegoat and was being singled out by both Republican and Democratic politicians, fanatic citizen groups like SOS (Save Our State), and sectors of the mainstream media as the main cause of our social ills. The racist Proposition 187, which denies nonemergency medical services and education to illegal aliens, passed with 60 percent of the vote on November 8, 1994, and turns every doctor, nurse, pharmacist, police officer, schoolteacher, and "concerned citizen" into a de facto border patrolman. Furthermore, the very same people who supported Prop 187 [now held up in court] also opposed women's and gay rights, affirmative action, bilingual education, freedom of expression, and the existence of the National Endowment for the Arts. Why? What does this mean? What are we all losing?

Despite the fact that the United States has always been a nation of immigrants and border crossers, nativism has periodically reared its head. American identity has historically depended on opposing an "other," be it cultural, racial, or ideological. Americans need enemies against whom to define their personal and national boundaries. From the original indigenous inhabitants of this land to the former Soviets, an evil "other" has always been stalking and ready to strike.

Fear is at the core of xenophobia. This fear is particularly disturbing when it is directed at the most vulnerable victims: migrant workers. They become the "invaders" from the south, the human incarnation of the Mexican fly, the subhuman "wetbacks," the "aliens" from another (cultural) planet. They are always suspected of stealing "our jobs," of shrinking "our budget," of taking advantage of the welfare system, of not paying taxes, and of bringing disease, drugs, street violence, foreign thoughts, pagan rites, primitive customs, and alien sounds. Their indigenous features and rough clothes remind uninformed citizens of an unpleasant pre-European American past and of mythical lands to the south immersed in poverty and political turmoil, where innocent gringos could be attacked for no apparent reason. Yet these invaders no longer inhabit the remote past, a banana republic, or a Hollywood film. They actually live down the block, and their children go to the same schools as do the Anglo kids.

Nothing is scarier than the blurring of the border between them and us; between the Dantesque South and the prosperous North; between paganism and Christianity. For many Americans, the border has failed to stop chaos and crisis from creeping in (the origin of crisis and chaos is strangely always located outside). Their worst nightmare is finally coming true: The United States is no longer a fictional extension of Europe, or the wholesome suburb imagined by the screenwriter of *Lassie*. It is rapidly becoming a huge border zone, a hybrid society, a mestizo race, and, worst of all, this process seems to be irreversible. America shrinks day by day, as the pungent smell of enchiladas and the volume of *quebradita* music rise.

It is time to face the facts: Anglos won't go back to Europe, and Mexicans and Latinos (legal or illegal) won't go back to Latin America. We all are here to stay. For better or for worse, our destinies and aspirations are in one another's hands.

For me, the only solution lies in a paradigm shift: the recognition that we all are protagonists in the creation of a new cultural topography and a new social order, one in which we all are "others" and we need the other "others" to exist. Hybridity is no longer up for discussion. It is a demographic, racial, social, and cultural fact. The real tasks ahead of us are to embrace more fluid and tolerant notions of personal and national identity and to develop models of peaceful coexistence and multilateral cooperation across boundaries of nationality, race, gender, and religion. To this end, rather than more border patrols, border walls,

and punitive laws, we need more and better information about one another. Culture and education are at the core of the solution. We need to learn each others' languages, histories, art, and cultural traditions. We need to educate our children and teenagers about the dangers of racism and the complexities of living in a multiracial borderless society, the inevitable society of the next century.

115 • My American Journey

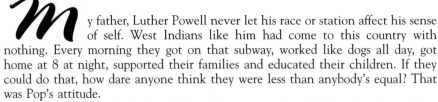

COLIN POWELL

y father, Luther Powell never let his race or station affect his sense of self. West Indians like him had come to this country with nothing. Every morning they got on that subway, worked like dogs all day, got home at 8 at night, supported their families and educated their children. If they could do that, how dare anyone think they were less than anybody's equal? That was Pop's attitude.

I have been asked when I first felt a sense of racial identity, when I first understood that I belonged to a minority. In those early years, I had no such sense, because on Banana Kelly (a slightly curved part of Kelly Street in the Hunt's Point section of the South Bronx) there was no majority. Everybody was either a Jew, an Italian, a Pole, a Greek, a Puerto Rican or, as we said in those days, a Negro. Racial epithets were hurled around and sometimes led to fist-fights. But it was not "You're inferior—I'm better." The fighting was more like avenging an insult to your team. Among my boyhood friends were Victor Ramirez, Walter Schwartz, Manny Garcia, Melvin Klein. The Kleins were the first family in our building to have a television set. Every Tuesday night we crowded into Mel's living room to watch Milton Berle. On Thursdays we watched Amos 'n' Andy. We thought the show was marvelous, the best thing on television. It was another age, and we did not know that we were not supposed to like Amos 'n Andy.

[After graduation from high school in 1954] I frequently found myself asked to play or coach basketball, apparently out of a racial preconception that I must be good at it. As soon as I was old enough to be convincing, I feigned a chronic "back problem" to stay off the court.

Colin Powell

Graduating from college in 1958, Powell underwent basic training at Fort Benning, Georgia. The segregated South was a revelation for Powell as he quickly discovered he could buy what he wanted at the local Woolworth so long as he didn't try to eat there or use the men's room.

Racism was still relatively new to me, and I had to find a way to cope psychologically. I began by identifying my priorities; I wanted, above all, to succeed at my Army career. I did not intend to give way to self-destructive rage, no matter how provoked. If people in the South insisted on living by crazy rules, then I would play the hand dealt me for now. If I was to be confined to one end of the playing field, then I was going to be a star on that part of the field. I was not going to let myself become emotionally crippled because I could not play on the whole field. I was not going to allow someone else's feeling about me to become my feelings about myself. I occasionally felt hurt: I felt anger; but most of all I felt challenged. I'll show you!

When his required three-year stint in the Army was up in 1961, Powell opted to stay, much to the bewilderment of his parents. "I did not know anything but soldiering," he recalls. "I was in a profession that would allow me to go as far as my talents would take me. And for a black, no other avenue in American society offered so much opportunity."

To sum up my political philosophy, I am a fiscal conservative with a social conscience. Neither of the two major parties, however, fits me comfortably in its present state. Granted, politics is the art of the compromise, but for now I prefer not to compromise just so that I can say I belong to this or that party. I am troubled by the political passion of those on the extreme right who seem to claim divine wisdom an political as well as spiritual matters. God provides us with guidance and inspiration, not a legislative agenda. I am disturbed by the class and racial undertones beneath the surface of their rhetoric. On the other side of the spectrum, I am put off by patronizing liberals who claim to know what is best for society but devote little thought to who will eventually pay the bills. I question the priorities of those liberals who lavish so much attention on individual license and entitlements that little concern is left for the good of the community at large. I distrust rigid ideology from any direction, and I am discovering that many Americans feel just as I do. The time may be at hand for a third major party to emerge to represent this sensible center of the American political spectrum.

Frankly, the present atmosphere does not make entering public service especially attractive. I find that civility is being driven from our political discourse. Attack ads and negative campaigns produce destructive, not constructive, debate. Democracy has always been noisy, but now, on television and radio talk shows, you will hear endless whining and not much constructive advice for our country. Any public figure espousing a controversial idea can expect to have not just the idea attacked, but his or her integrity. And Lord help anyone who strays from accepted ideas of political correctness. The slightest suggestion of offense toward any group,

In his recent book on the current cultural landscape *Postethnic America: Beyond Multiculturalism* (Pennsylvania: Basic Books, $21, ISBN 0-465-01990-0, 1-800-331-3761). David Hollinger argues that the conventional liberal toleration of all established ethnic groups no longer works because it leaves unchallenged the prevailing imbalance of power. Yet the multiculturalist alternative does nothing to stop the fragmenting of American society into competing ethnic enclaves, each concerned with its own well-being. He urges in place of this an appreciation of multiple identities based not on the biologically given but on consent. Hollinger calls for a new nationalism which would help bridge the gap between our common fellowship as human beings and the great variety of ethnic and racial groups represented within the United States.

however innocently made, and even when made merely to illustrate a historical point, will be met with cries that the offender be fired or coerced to undergo sensitivity training, or threats of legal action.

Ironically, for all the present sensitivity over correctness, we seem to have lost our sense of shame as a society. Nothing seems to embarrass us; nothing shocks us anymore. Spend time switching channels on daytime television, and you will find a parade of talk shows serving up dysfunctional people whose morally vacant behavior offers the worst possible models for others. None of this mass voyeurism is more offensive to me than the use of black "guests" by talk-show producers, reinforcing the most demeaning racial stereotypes. At least in the old days of Amos 'n' Andy, Amos was happily married and hardworking, and he and his wife together were raising sweet little Arabella, who said her prayers every night.

We have to start thinking of America as a family. We have to stop screeching at each other, stop hurting each other, and instead start caring for, sacrificing for and sharing with each other. We have to stop constantly criticizing, which is the way of the malcontent, and instead get back to the can-do attitude that made America. We have to keep trying, and risk failing, in order to solve this country's problems. We cannot move forward if cynics and critics swoop down and pick apart anything that goes wrong to a point where we lose sight of what is right, decent and uniquely good about America.

Jefferson once wrote, "There is a debt of service due from every man to his country, proportioned to the bounties which nature and fortune have measured to him." As one who has received so much from his country, I feel that debt heavily, and I can never be entirely free of it. My responsibility, our responsibility as lucky Americans, is to try to give back to this country as much as it has given to us, as we continue our American journey together.

116 · Beyond Black and White

MANNING MARABLE

Ethnic pride and group awareness constitute a beginning stage, not an end in itself, for a richer understanding of the essential diversity and pluralism that constitute our America. That awareness of diversity must point toward the restructuring of the elaborate systems of ownership and power that perpetuate the unequal status of these ethnic groups and oppressed social classes. This leap of awareness depends on our willingness to define our political, educational, and social goals in a way that is truly majoritarian.

Many people from divergent ethnic backgrounds, speaking various languages and possessing different cultures, now share a common experience of inequality in the USA—poor housing, homelessness, inadequate health care, underrepresentation within government, lagging incomes and high rates of unemployment, discrimination in capital markets, and police brutality on the streets. Yet there is an absence of unity between these constituencies, in part because their leaders are imprisoned ideologically and theoretically by the assumptions and realities of the past. The rhetoric of racial solidarity, for instance, can be used to mask class contradictions and divisions within the black Latino and Asian American communities. Symbolic representation can be manipulated to promote the narrow interest of minority elected officials who may have little commitment to advancing the material concerns of the most oppressed sectors of multicultural America.

Beyond Black and White: Transforming African-American Politics, Manning Marable, (New York and London: Verso Books) $24.95, ISBN 1-85984-924-5. 1-800-634-7064, Fax 1-800-248-4724.

117 · To Save Our Children

MARIAN WRIGHT EDELMAN

*W*hen the new century dawns with new global economic and military challenges, America will be ready to compete economically and lead morally only if we:

1. Stop cheating and neglecting our children for selfish, short-sighted, personal, and political gain;
2. Stop clinging to our racial past and recognize that America's ideals, future, and fate are as inextricably intertwined with the fate of its poor and nonwhite children as with its privileged and white ones;
3. Love our children more than we fear each other and our perceived or real external enemies;
4. Acquire the discipline to invest preventively and systematically in all of our children now in order to reap a better trained work force and more stable future tomorrow;

(i) "To Save Our Children" is excerpted from Edelman's *The Measure of Our Success: A Letter to My Children and Yours.* Available from Beacon Press, 25 Beacon Street, Boston, MA 02108-2892. ISBN 0-8070-3102-X.

For more thoughts on the rights and obligations we have to chidren within society see Marion Wright Edelman's *Guide My Feet, Mediations and Prayers on Working and Loving.* (Boston: Beacon Press, 1995, ISBN 0-8070-2308-6).

5. Curb the desires of the overprivileged so that the survival needs of the less privileged may be met, and spend less on weapons of death and more on lifelines of constructive development for our citizens;
6. Set clear, national, state, city, community, and personal goals for child survival and development, and invest whatever leadership, commitment, time, money, and sustained effort are needed to achieve them;
7. Struggle to begin to live our lives in less selfish and more purposeful ways, redefining success by national and individual character and service rather than by national consumption and the superficial barriers of race and class.

Copyright © 1992, Marian Wright Edelman.

Rick Reinhard, Impact Visuals.

Marian Wright Edelman

118 • People on the Move

PHILIP HARRIS

*I*n only 10 percent of the world's 191 nations are the people ethnically or racially homogeneous.

Never before in humanity's history have there been so many people traveling beyond their homelands, either to seek work abroad or simply as tourists. In the host countries, the social fabric is being reconfigured and strained by massive waves of immigrants, whether legally or illegally, who come to live and work, permanently or temporarily.

In 1994, 10,000 respondents to an *AARP Bulletin* questionnaire indicated they left their jobs because of pressures to nudge or push them out the door. By a 2-to-1 margin, readers replied that their dismissals violated in some way the Age Discrimination Act (ADA). In addition to the high toll on older workers, they noted that the traditional employer-employee compact that rewarded performance and loyalty with job security, no longer exists. While some of these displaced, experienced workers go into business for themselves, the majority find it a struggle to get back into the workplace, often settling for less pay, part-time and/or temporary work.

Today job security is only to be found within the individual worker who has marketable skills and the ability to learn new ones.

119 • Vanishing Jobs

JEREMY RIFKIN (MOTHER JONES)

Some business leaders are concerned, but politicians seem strangely deaf to what is likely to be the most explosive issues of the decade.

"Will there be a job for me in the new Information Age?"

This is the question that most worries American voters—and the question that American politicians seem most determined to sidestep. President Bill Clinton warns workers that they will have to be retrained six or seven times during their work lives to match the dizzying speed of technological change. Speaker of the House Newt Gingrich talks about the "end of the traditional job" and advises every American worker to become his or her own independent contractor.

But does the president really think 124 million Americans can reinvent themselves every five years to keep up with a high-tech marketplace? Does Gingrich honestly believe every American can become a freelance entrepreneur, continually hustling contracts for short-term work assignments?

Buffeted by these unrealistic employment expectations, American workers are increasingly sullen and pessimistic. Most Americans have yet to recover from the recovery of 1993-1995, which was essentially a "jobless" recovery. While corporate profits are heading through the roof, average families struggle to keep a roof over their heads. More than one-fifth of the workforce is trapped in temporary assignments or works only part time. Millions of others have slipped quietly out of the economy and into an underclass no longer counted in the official unemployment figures. A staggering 15 percent of the population now lives below the official poverty line.

Both Clinton and Gingrich have asked American workers to remain patient. They explain that declining incomes represent only short-term adjustments.

Ben Cohen Interviewed in *Utne Reader* September/October 1993

Do I believe that business can solve social and environmental problems?

You bet. In fact, business is the only institution capable of solving social and environmental problems. Business is the most powerful force in the country: business controls the country. It's business and businessmen's money that finance political campaigns and pay for most of the lobbyists in Congress. It's businesses that do most of what goes on in the country. Most of our daily interactions involve businesses. Business have created most of our social and environmental problems. If business were instead trying to solve these problems, they would be solved in short order.

The Information Age may present difficulties for the captains of industry as well. By replacing more and more workers with machines, employers will eventually come up against the two economic Achilles' heels of the Information Age. The first is a simple problem of supply and demand: If mass numbers of people are underemployed or unemployed, who's going to buy the flood of products and services being churned out?

The second Achilles' heel for business—and one never talked about—is the effect on capital accumulation when vast numbers of employees are let go or hired on a temporary basis so that employers can avoid paying out benefits—especially pension fund benefits. As it turns out, pension funds, now worth more than $5 trillion in the United States alone, keep much of the capitalist system afloat. For nearly 25 years, the pension funds of millions of workers have served as a forced savings pool that has financed capital investments.

Pension funds account for 74 percent of net individual savings, more than one-third of all corporate equities, and nearly 40 percent of all corporate bonds. Pension assets exceed the assets of commercial banks and make up nearly one-third of the total financial assets of the U.S. economy. In 1993 alone, pension funds made new investments of

Democrats and Republicans alike beseech the faithful to place their trust in the high-tech future—to journey with them into cyberspace and become pioneers on the new electronic frontier. Their enthusiasm for technological marvels has an almost camp ring to it. If you didn't know better, you might suspect Mickey and Pluto were taking you on a guided tour through the Epcot Center.

Jittery and genuinely confused over the yawning gap between the official optimism of the politicians and their own personal plight, middle- and working-class American families seem to be holding on to a tiny thread of hope that the vast productivity gains of the high-tech revolution will somehow "trickle down" to them in the form of better jobs, wages, and benefits. That thread is likely to break if, as I anticipate, the economy skids right by the soft landing predicted by the Federal Reserve Board and crashes headlong into a deep recession.

The Labor Department reported that payrolls sank by 101,000 workers in May 1995 alone—the largest drop in payrolls since April 1991, when the U.S. economy was deep in a recession. In June, overall unemployment remained virtually unchanged, but manufacturing jobs declined by an additional 40,000. At the same time, inventories are up and consumer spending and confidence are down—sure signs of bad economic times ahead.

Used with permission. Huck/Konopacki Labor Cartoons.

The psychological impact of a serious downturn coming so quickly upon the heels of the last one would be devastating. It is likely to set the framework for a politically wild roller-coaster ride for the rest of the decade, opening the door not only to new parties but to extralegal forms of politics.

Meanwhile, few politicians and economists are paying attention to the underlying causes of—dare we say it?—the new "malaise" gripping the country. Throughout the current welfare reform debate, for example, members of both parties have trotted onto the House and Senate floors to urge an end to welfare and demand that all able-bodied men and women find jobs. Maverick Sen. Paul Simon (D.-Ill.) has been virtually alone in raising the troubling question: "What jobs?"

The hard reality is that the global economy is in the midst of a transformation as significant as the Industrial Revolution. We are in the early stages of a shift from "mass labor" to highly skilled "elite labor," accompanied by increasing automation in the production of goods and the delivery of services. Sophisticated computers, robots, telecommunications, and other Information Age technologies are replacing human beings in nearly every sector. Factory workers, secretaries, receptionists, clerical workers, salesclerks, bank tellers, telephone operators, librarians, wholesalers, and middle managers are just a few of the many occupations destined for virtual extinction. In the United States alone, as many as 90 million jobs in a labor force of 124 million are potentially vulnerable to displacement by automation.

A few mainstream economists pin their hopes on increasing job opportunities in the knowledge sector. Secretary of Labor Robert Reich, for example, talks incessantly of the need for more highly skilled technicians, computer programmers, engineers, and professional workers. He barnstorms the country urging workers to retrain, retool, and reinvent themselves in time to gain a coveted place on the high-tech express.

The secretary ought to know better. Even if the entire workforce could be retrained for very skilled, high-tech jobs—which, of course, it can't—there will never be enough positions in the elite knowledge sector to absorb the millions let go as automation penetrates into every aspect of the production process.

It's not as if this is a revelation. For years the Tofflers and the Naisbitts of the world have lectured the rest of us that the end of the industrial age also means the end of "mass production" and "mass labor." What they never mention is what "the masses" should do after they become redundant.

This steady decline of mass labor threatens to undermine the very foundations of the modern American state. For nearly 200 years, the heart of the social contract and the measure of individual human worth have centered on the value of each person's labor. How does society even begin to adjust to a new era in which labor is devalued or even rendered worthless?

between $1 trillion and $1.5 trillion.

If too many workers are let go or marginalized into jobs without pension benefits, the capitalist system is likely to collapse slowly in on itself as employers drain it of the workers' funds necessary for new capital investments. In the final analysis, sharing the vast productivity gains of the Information Age is absolutely essential to guarantee the well-being of management, stockholders, labor, and the economy as a whole.

—Jeremy Rifkin

ⓘ "Vanishing Jobs" is from *The End of Work* by Jeremy Rifkin (New York: Putnam Publishing, 1995, $24.95, ISBN 0-87477-779-8), 1-800-847-5515.

Rodney Curtis, Impact Visuals

More than 1,000 people line up for jobs at Cabletron's New Hampshire facility.

This is not the first time the issue of devalued human labor has arisen in the history of the United States. The first group of Americans to be marginalized by the automation revolution was black men, more than 40 years ago. Their story is a bellwether.

In the mid-1950s, automation began to take a toll on the nation's factories. Hardest hit were unskilled jobs in the industries where black workers concentrated. Between 1953 and 1962, 1.6 million blue-collar manufacturing jobs were lost. In an essay, "Problems of the Negro Movement," published in 1964, civil rights activist Tom Kahn quipped, "It's as if racism, having put the Negro in his economic place, stepped aside to watch technology destroy that 'place.'"

Millions of African-American workers and their families became part of a perpetually unemployed "underclass" whose unskilled labor was no longer required in the mainstream economy. Vanquished and forgotten, many urban blacks vented their frustration and anger by taking to the streets. The rioting began in Watts in 1965 and spread east to Detroit and other Northern cities.

Today the same technological and economic forces are beginning to affect large numbers of white male workers. Many of the disaffected white men who make up ultraright-wing organizations are high school or community college graduates with limited skills who are forced to compete for a diminishing number of agricultural, manufacturing, and service jobs. While they blame affirmative action programs, immigrant groups, and illegal aliens for their woes, these men miss the real cause of their plight—technological innovations that devalue their labor. Like African-American men in the 1960s, the new militants view the government and law enforcement agencies as the enemy. They see a grand conspiracy to deny them their basic freedoms and constitutional rights. And they are arming themselves for a revolution.

See *When Corporations Rule the World*, by David C. Korten (San Francisco: Berrett-Koehler Publishers; 1995); 1-800-929-2929.

120 • The Disharmonic Convergence: The Far Left and Far Right as Strange Bedfellows

JAY KINNEY

*I*n these days of governmental gridlock and political floundering, it seems as if conservatives and liberals alike are irrelevant to tackling the problems confronting use. This realization among increasing numbers of people leads us to the search for a new political analysis and a workable economics that transcend the old Left/Right debate.

Yet, because mass media and our political and business institutions have a vested interest in maintaining the status quo—even as it crumbles—it is nearly impossible to engage in a public discussion of alternatives. To make serious changes involves rejuggling the power relations of society, and that is the last thing that those who monopolize the public arena wish to see happen—or even discussed.

Neo-conservatism and neo-liberalism have been presented in recent years as steps toward formulating a new pragmatic politics, but neither camp in fact represents much more than the shifting of warm bodies from the vaguely left to the vaguely right and back again. The only critiques of the status quo with any bite have been those of groups so far outside the mainstream that they never get favorable mention in the mass media, i.e., the far left and far right.

As mortal enemies, these camps generally want nothing to do with each other. Yet, ironically, their worldviews have more in common than either usually cares to admit. At their worst, many proponents in both camps share a mutual fondness for sweeping solutions that all too easily slide into totalitarianism. At their best, however, they each hit political nails on the head more often than those in the center. If a new political perspective is to emerge, it will likely incorporate the insights of both of these camps rather than hover around the center.

Both the far left and far right assert that America's pluralism has not, in fact, prevented small elites from acquiring and manipulating economic and political power. These elites—labeled the ruling class in the case of left analyses and international bankers and one worlders in the case of right analyses—are identified as individuals and entities that largely operate outside of the arena of public decision-making. Both worldviews challenge the prevailing myths that Western nations are democracies and they are commonly labeled as "conspiracy theories." However, the most sophisticated analyses of both sides are worth serious consideration.

Both left and right analyses describe the present economic order as "monopoly capitalism" though some other terms are used (on the left: late capitalism, imperialism; on the right: supercapitalism, finance capitalism). Both analyses contrast monopoly capitalism with an earlier system of free enterprise capitalism, and see monopoly capitalism as having overtaken free enterprise.

The left's analysis views this situation as the result of the evolving logic of capitalism itself, not necessarily the result of a sneaky plot by some backroom elite; rather, the system of capitalism produces monopolies and elites as natural byproducts of its own evolution.

By contrast, the right's analysis sees monopoly capitalism as having usurped free enterprise through a combination of government controls (manipulated by "insiders"), the conniving of international financiers and internationalists, and the drowning of real capital in a sea of debt and paper-based money. The right usually presumes that if the elite conspirators behind this usurption were identified and their influence and control destroyed, the U.S. economy could then be returned to a system of free enterprise.

Significantly, both analyses are primarily talking about the same phenomenon: the means by which the leadership of the Establishment have attempted to "make the system work." Because the largest (and most influential) American corporations are now multinationals with both markets and workers all over the world, they have a vested interest in expediting international economic cooperation and coordination. This coordination is characterized by the intertwining of U.S. Corporate and Government policy with their counterparts in dozens of countries (the much touted "interdependence" of the modern era).

In mirror-like fashion, the classic right analysis sees no hope for socialism, viewing it as tyrannical and stagnant due to bureaucratic waste, power-monopolizing elites, lack of freedom and incentive, and assuming that the only way out is through a return to market-driven free enterprise. Because the left is driven by a vision of a utopian future that has never materialized, and the right is driven by a romanticized concept of a past that never was, both analyses cancel each other out. However, there are parts of both the left and the right that begin to depart from this stalemate.

The question of patriotism and nationalism may be the area where the political extremes are farthest apart. Building on the principle of proletarian internationalism (i.e., that the working people of various countries have more in common with each other as a class than they do with the capitalists and governments of their own countries), the far left has usually considered nationalistic patriotism to be a reactionary delusion. the far right has generally considered the U.S. to be the greatest country in the world, one uniquely blessed with freedoms and opportunities not found elsewhere, and fears any internationalism that would compromise national sovereignty or usher in a coercive world government from which there would be no escape.

ⓘ Jay Kinney is the author of "Anarcho-Emergentist-Republicans" (*Wired* Sept. 1995, p. 90) which explores the possibility of a new politics emerging in the Net/cyberspace/digital culture.

Nevertheless there are numerous exceptions within these stances. It turns out that many on the far left do support nationalistic patriotism, in other countries at least (in the form of so-called national liberation movements and/or the struggles of indigenous peoples), while many on the far right practice a kind of internationalism in forging links with anti-socialists in other countries and, ironically, don't have much fondness for the actual U.S. government.

A common complaint about the far right's use of the terms "international bankers" or "internationalists" or "insiders" is that they are code words for Jews and indicate an anti-Semitic bias. While some writers do indulge in a reductionism that says: Bankers=Jews=Zionists=Communists, the simple truth is many of the far right's assertions about manipulative elites are independent of anti-Semitic intent.

Perhaps the biggest roadblock to getting a handle on the ideas of the political extremes is the taboos surrounding reading each other's literature. If either side were to check it out they'd likely discover that both do have some valid points in their critiques. Of course, to discover coherent points of intelligence in the literature of the previously despised is to surrender some small part of one's own dogmatic purity, which is often the primary solace of the isolated extremist.

What this means in practical terms is that though a political convergence may be on the horizon (most likely with the label "populist," I'll wager) it will probably not involve leftists as leftists sitting down to cooperate with rightists as rightists. Rather it will probably be birthed by people fed up with both ideologies who scavenge for truths wherever they may be found and who are not scared off by obsolete stereotypes and ad hominem attacks.

Projecting into the future, what are some areas of concern where those coming from both left and right backgrounds are likely to come together?

- Regionalism (Fourth World/indigenous autonomy). The defense of native peoples and their cultures against encroachments from both multinational corporations and racist governments cuts across political lines.
- Community (Ethnic Traditions/cooperation). The celebration of ethnicity, be it Afro-American or Hispanic or Anglo-Saxon, should be something that everyone can support without having to be stigmatized as racist or, conversely, claiming that one's own heritage is superior. (See the article by Bo Sears on pages 162, which describes some of the new rules for making these coalitions.)
- Spirituality (Anti-materialism/non-mainstream religion). Many people share a disgust with the worship of "success" as the goal of one's life. Outside of the ranks of the fundamentalists (both religious and atheist) who have little tolerance for anyone who doesn't agree with them, large numbers of people have been responding to the spiritual barrenness in their lives by investigating and participating in non-mainstream religions.
- Populism (Anti-Big Business/Anti-Banks/new monetary policies). No one likes to be yanked around by giant structures and bureaucracies, private or

(i) See *Race Traitor* (no. 5, Winter 1996, pp.17–48) for just such a conversation between a National Socialist (commonly called the "American Nazi Party") and Noel Ignatiev, the founder of the "magazine of the new abolitionism."

"The most dangerous thing to me is when we ask the President what he is going to do for us. We have to do things for ourselves. It always makes me think of Franklin Roosevelt, who was reputed to have said to some constitutency group, 'O.K., you've convinced me. Now go out and force me to do it.' I don't believe that change happens from the top down. That has not been my experience. Change happens from the bottom up. Even if it happens from the top down, it is not real. People don't use it unless they've fought for it. So I hope we don't fall into the trap of looking for rescue, which is disempowering."

—Gloria Steinem, Interviewed in *The Progressive*, (June, 1995) by L. A. Winokur. Reprinted with permission by L. A. Winokur.

public. This goes for the farmer in Iowa losing his farm to the bank or the city dweller forced out of her neighborhood by gentrification.

- Health/Environment (Alternative medicine/anti-pollution). Increasing numbers of people want the FDA and the AMA to quit breathing down their necks. In recent years, the far right and the far left have been increasingly likely to join forces at the vitamin counter. Three Mile Island and Chernobyl helped drive home the value of a decent environment to everyone.

- Foreign Policy (Non-interventionist/Isolationist). Both political extremes question U.S. involvement in other regions, especially if shooting wars are likely.

Freedom is the mutually stated goal of both the far left and far right; if weary veterans of both camps can just reach an agreement regarding freedom from what and freedom to do what, then a truly "third way" may develop unlike any seen before. That would be a convergence worth celebrating!

MAKING THE FIELDBOOK CONTINUE TO WORK FOR YOU

*W*e think of the *Cultural Diversity Fieldbook* not simply as a book but as a network of people and a process of continuous learning in which we share knowledge, resources, and advice. For that reason we have tried to make it as user friendly as possible, giving you information on how to find resources and contact the people who are of interest to you.

But this is only a starting point. The network continues, and you may become an ongoing part of it for the asking. If you mail, fax, or e-mail to us the information requested in the "Make me part of the CDF Network" form on page 273, you can stay connected and receive a number of benefits as well:

- A **Resource Kit** describing some of the newest and best resources in the diversity field. You may also contact us for help in finding or using any of the resources in this book. New resource materials will be sent as they develop.
- Information on how to use our **900** number for diversity resources which is under development as this book goes to press.
- Information on how to use our **Web Page** www.hrpress-diversity.com and NetServe Mailing List most effectively.
- The Web page features: articles on a wide range of workplace diversity issues from some of the nation's most respected experts; links to other diversity related web sites; a Diversity Book Store and Training Library with on-line ordering; and a Directory of Diversity Consultants. It will be of special interest to corporate and government trainers, educators, consultants, or anyone with an interest in workforce diversity.
- **The chance to publish** work that you would like to see published or reviewed in the literature of the field, including future versions of, or supplements to, the *Cultural Diversity Fieldbook*. Send us your contribution, preferably by e-mail, on a floppy disk in any standard word-processing format, Mac or PC, or typed double-spaced—with information about how to reach you by e-mail, fax, or phone. Contributions will not be returned unless specifically requested.

- A chance to air your own views and give the editors **Feedback.** Tell us what you liked and didn't like about the book, its philosophy, its contents. Tell us what was missing for you. Share your thoughts about its format, ease or difficulty of use.
- And, a **bonus.** Send us a "Make me part of the CDF Network" form and you will receive a trial Subscription to **Cultural Diversity at Work.** The 8-year old newsletter/journal highlights organizational and personal change strategies emerging out of diversity and cross-cultural initiatives. In this special four-month, no-obligation, trial offer for *Fieldbook* readers, you receive:

  1. *Cultural Diversity at Work*, two issues (20 pages)
  2. *The Diversity Training Bulletin*, four issues (a monthly calendar of workshops, conferences, new programs and resources, announcements, etc)
  3. A copy of *An Annotated Bibliography: Recent Diversity Research Reports.*

Send your "Make me part of the CDF Network" form (see last page of the book) and other queries and comments to:

The Cultural Diversity Fieldbook Project
P.O. Box 134
Amherst, MA 01004 USA
Toll-free U.S. and Canada: 1-800-736-1293
413-549-1293
Fax: 413-549-3503

Bob Abramms e-mail: 0003475157@mcimail.com

George F. Simons e-mail: gsimons@euronet.nl
    voice mail and fax from the USA: 888-215-3117
    voice mail and fax in Europe: +31-(0)20 524 1439
    Website: htpp://www.intl-partners.com

CONTRIBUTORS

Niels Agger-Gupta is a consultant in diversity and organizational effectiveness with the Alberta Department of Community Development, Alberta Multiculturalism Commission in Canada. Reach him at Alberta Community Development, #301 - 525 11 Ave. S.W., Calgary, Alberta, T2R 0C9 Canada; 403-297-8407, Fax 403-297-2785, e-mail 75224.1001@Compuserve.com.

Robert L. Allen is a member of the board of directors of the Oakland Men's Project and senior editor of the journal *The Black Scholar*.

Margaret L. Andersen is professor of sociology and women's studies at the University of Delaware. She currently serves as editor of *Gender and Society*.

Doug Bandow is a senior fellow at the Cato Institute and nationally syndicated columnist with Copley News Service. He has written for periodicals (*Christianity Today, Harper's*, and *The New Republic*) and leading newspapers. Bandow has written and edited several books, including *The Politics of Envy: Statism as Theology* (Transaction).

Karen Grigsby Bates writes on issues of race and culture and is a regular contributor to the *Los Angeles Times'* Op-Ed page, and a frequent commentator on National Public Radio's "All Things Considered." She is, with Karen E. Hudson, coauthor of *Basic Black: Home Training for Modern Times* (Doubleday).

David S. Bernstein is an associate editor at The Free Press, and a commentator for National Public Radio's "All Things Considered." He is a co-founder of Third Millennium, a nation-wide youth advocacy and education organization.

Ellen Hofheimer Bettmann is Director of Research and Development for the ADL A WORLD OF DIFFERENCE Institute, a national education and diversity training program of the Anti-Defamation League. Reach her at the Anti-Defamation League, 823 United Nations Plaza, New York, NY 10017; 212-885-7700, e-mail Ellen.Bettmann@Dartmouth.edu

Joy Bodzioch, Ph.D., is a staff development psychologist, professional speaker and president of The Diversity Advantage. Reach her at 14662A Big Basin Way, Saratoga, CA 95070; 408-867-2585.

James M. Bradley is a freelance writer and collaborator with The Kaleel Jamison Consulting Group, Inc. He also creates business and educational videos and is an english instructor at Hudson Valley Community College.

Keith Bradsher is the Bureau Chief for *The New York Times* in Detroit.

John H. Bunzel is past president of San Jose University, a former member of the U.S. Commission on Civil Rights, and currently a senior research fellow at Stanford's Hoover Institution.

Karen Burstein is a practicing New York City attorney. As Commissioner of the New York State Department of Civil Service in the mid-1980s, she oversaw the state's affirmative action policy.

Danielle Cécile is director-sector development at the Co-operative Housing Federation of Canada, 311-225 Metcalfe St., Ottawa, Canada K2P 1P9; 614-230-2201, Fax 613-230-2231.

Patricia Hill Collins is professor of african-american studies and sociology at the University of Cincinnati. She is the author of *Black Feminist Thought: Knowledge, Consciousness and the Politics of Empowerment.*

Ben Cohen is a cofounder and chairman of the board of Ben & Jerry's Homemade, Inc. Mr. Cohen is active in the Social Venture Network, and speaks extensively throughout the world on the topic of socially responsible business.

Missy Daniel is a writer for *U.S. News & World Report.*

Ron Daniels' weekly column "Vantage Point" appears in more than one hundred african american and progressive newspapers. He is national chairperson of Campaign for a New Tomorrow, a Black and people-of-color led, multi-racial, independent political organization and eExecutive director of the Center for Constitutional Rights in New York.

Barbara Deane is editor-in-chief of *Cultural Diversity at Work* newsletter. She designs and conducts workshops on cross-cultural topics, especially involving U.S.-Mexico relations. Ms. Deane speaks on diversity issues and intercultural communication. Reach her at The GilDeane Group, 13751 Lake City Way N.E. #106, Seattle, WA 98125-3615; 206-362-0336, Fax 206-363-5028, e-mail 75364.2356@Compuserve.com.

Ronnie Dugger, founding editor of *The Texas Observer*, now lives in New York City and is at work on books about electronic vote-counting and new social-policy ideas.

Marian Wright Edelman, founder and president of the Children's Defense Fund, has been an advocate for disadvantaged Americans for her entire professional career. She was the first black woman admitted to the Mississippi Bar, moved to Washington as counsel to the Poor People's March, and founded the Washington Research Project.

Mark R. Edwards, Ph.D., CEO of TEAMS, Inc. (4450 S. Rural Road S. A200, Tempe, AZ 85282; 602-413-9773, Fax 602-413-9701), serves as the director of the Laboratory for Innovation and Decision Research and as a professor in the College of Engineering at Arizona State University. He has built multisource feedback systems for over 200 organizations.

Barbara Ehrenreich is the author of *The Worst Years of Our Lives: Irreverent Notes from a Decade of Greed* (Pantheon, 1990). In addition to her work for *Time Magazine*, Ehrenreich writes a biweekly column for The Guardian in the U.K. Her latest book is a collection of essays entitled *The Snarling Citizen* (Farrar, Straus & Giroux).

Sybil Evans of New York City-based Sybil Evans Associates provides consulting and training in the field of diversity and workplace dispute resolution. Ms. Evans is a recognized authority having more than 20 years experience solving conflicts. She can be reached at 244 Madison Ave., New York, NY 10016; 212-697-0974, Fax 212-697-9104.

Ann J. Ewen, Ph.D., serves as president of TEAMS, Inc. (4450 S. Rural Road S. A200, Tempe, AZ 85282; 602-413-9773, Fax 602-413-9701). She has industrial experience in marketing, strategic planning, organizational development and process management. She has supported MSA projects with Intel, AlliedSignal, American Airlines, Bellcore, and the Department of Energy.

Born in Ireland, raised in Alberta, **Helgi Eyford** is currently a program manager with the Canadian Bureau for International Education and the managing editor of Intercultural and Community Development Resources (ICDR), a company that publishes and distributes books and brokers training in multiculturalism and community development. He can be reached at 9815-45th Ave., Edmonton, Alberta, T6E 5C8; 403-437-8013, Fax 403-439-6879.

Warren Farrell is the author of two award-winning best-sellers: *Why Men Are The Way They Are* and *The Myth of Male Power*. In his workshops, both sexes emotionally experience "walking a mile in each other's moccasins." His clients include AT&T, IBM, NASA, Bell Atlantic, and Toyota. Reach him at 103 North Highway 101, Box #220, Encinitas, CA 92024; 619-753-5000, Fax 619-753-2436.

H. Vincent Ford is the president and founder of VISTAR Corporation (446 Penn Estates, East Stroudsburg, PA 18301; 717-476-0895, Fax 717-476-0893) a management consulting firm specializing in workforce diversity, global relationship management, and total quality management. He is the author of a national benchmarking study on the topic of workforce diversity.

Matthew Fox, a former Catholic and now an Episcopal priest, is the director of the Institute in Culture and Creation Spirituality at Holy Names College in Oakland, California. He has authored *The Reinvention of Work* (HarperCollins), which received the 1996 Body Mind Spirit Book Award.

Reach him at the institute, 3500 Mountain Blvd., Oakland, CA; 510-436-1046, Fax 510-436-1188.

William H. Frey teaches at the University of Michigan.

Since publication of his first bestselling book *All I really Need to Know I Learned in Kindergarten,* philosopher and essayist **Robert Fulghum** has had more than 14 million copies of his books printed and published in 27 languages and 93 countries. His books reflect on the wonders of the commonplace, encouraging us to find the extraordinary within the ordinary.

Peter Gabel is president of the New College of California and associate editor of *TIKKUN* Magazine: A bimonthly jewish critique of politics, culture, and society.

Donna L. Goldstein, Ed.D. has taught management, human resources and education at several South Florida universities. She is the managing director of Development Associates International. She speaks, writes, and conducts training on diversity issues. Contact her at Development Associates International, 3389 Sheridan St., #309, Hollywood, FL 33021; 954-926-7822, Fax 954-926-6280.

Guillermo Gómez-Peña is a writer and performance artist living in Los Angeles, California. His book *Warrior for Gringostroika*, was published in 1994. He received a MacArthur Fellowship in 1991.

Jack Gordon is editor of *TRAINING* magazine, a monthly publication covering corporate training and management issues. Subscriptions to *TRAINING* are available from 1-800-707-7749. Contact Gordon at Lakewood Publications, 50 S. 9th Street, Minneapolis MN 55402; Phone 612-333-0471; Fax: 612-333-6526, E-mail: TrainMag@aol.com.

Lino A. Graglia is A. Dalton Cross Professor of Law at the University of Texas at Austin.

Paulette Gerkovich Griffith is vice president of research and project development of Advanced Research Management Consultants (ARMC). She is currently a doctoral candidate at the University of Maryland. Reach her at Advanced Research Management Consultants, Inc., 1014 South Second St., Philadelphia, PA 19147; 215-551-5340, Fax 215-551-3710.

Lani Guinier is professor of law at the University of Pennsylvania and author of *The Tyranny of the Majority*.

Philip R. Harris is president of Harris International (2702 Costebelle Dr., La Jolla, CA 92037; 619-453-2271, Fax 619-454-4712). With Robert Moran, he is the author of *Managing Cultural Differences*, (Gulf Publications, 1995). He is a leading expert on space psychology and author of *Living and Working in Space* (NY: Wiley/Praxis, 1996).

Rabia Terri Harris is coordinator of the Muslim Peace Fellowship and the translator of *Ibn 'Arabi's [Journey to the Lord of Power]* (Rochester, Vermont: Inner Traditions International, 1981, 1989) and other works of medieval Arabic spirituality. For further information, contact: Muslim Peace Fellowship, FOR, P.O. Box 271, Nyack, NY 10960; 914-358-4601, Fax 914-358-4924.

Paul G. Hawken is the author of the highly acclaimed book, *The Ecology of Commerce* (New York: HarperCollins, 1-800-237-5534), published in 10 languages. George Gendron, editor-in-chief of *Inc.* magazine, says, "*The Ecology of Commerce* is nothing less than a masterpiece by the poet laureate of American Capitalism." Hawken is also the cofounder of Smith & Hawken.

Nat Hentoff is the author of *Free Speech for Me—But Not for Thee: How the American Left and Right Relentlessly Censor Each Other*.

bell hooks, Distinguished Professor of English at City College in New York City, is one of America's leading black intellectuals. She is the author of many books, most recently *Teaching to Transgress: Education as the Practice of Freedom*, available from Routledge, 29 W. 35th St., New York, NY 10001; 212-244-3336.

Yu-Liang Huang (Sally Nissen), M.A. is an independent diversity specialist. Sally implemented three diversity initiatives: diversity dialogue groups, cross-cultural mentoring, and Asian career development. Reach her at Huang-Nissen & Associates, P.O. Box 748, Livermore, CA 94550; 510-449-4208, Fax 510-606-5486 e-mail SHNissen@aol.com.

Noel Ignatiev worked for over twenty years in steel mills, farm equipment plants, and machine-tool and electrical parts factories. He is cofounder and coeditor of *Race Traitor: A Journal of the New Abolitionism*. His latest book, *How the Irish Became White* is published by Routledge (ISBN 0-415-91384-5). He can be reached at 30 Elm St., Somerville MA 02143; 617-628-8019.

Intercultural Press is a publisher and distributor of cross-cultural and multicultural resources for both domestic and international business. They carry books, videos, and training simulations. A free catalog is available from P.O. Box 700, Yarmouth, ME 04096; 207-846-5168, Fax 207-846-5181, e-mail: http://www.bookmasters.com/interclt.htm.

Herbert Jacob is professor of political philosophy at Northwestern University.

Rita Henley Jensen is a prizewinning investigative journalist based in New York City. She often writes for *The New York Times*, the *Washington Post*, and the American Bar Association's *ABA Journal*.

As former director of product development at ODT, Inc., **Diane Johns** contributed content and editorial guidance to many of ODT's resources on diversity and employee empowerment. She is currently pursuing her personal growth, professional development, and spiritual awareness in urban and suburban health-care settings in the Boston area.

Natasha Josefowitz writes a weekly newspaper column on management issues. She is the best-selling author of three management books and an award-winning writer of eight books of humorous verse and a book for children. She is a well-known, international keynote speaker and a frequent guest on talk shows. Reach her at 2235 Calle Guaymas, La Jolla, CA 92037; 619-456-2366.

Ward L. Kaiser lectures and leads workshops on maps and the stories behind them. He has been a publisher—as such he introduced the Peters map to the English-speaking world—a college teacher, author, clergyperson and consultant with special interest in publishing and education. He presently lives at 5018 Pinegrove Crescent, Beamsville, Ontario L0R 1B2 Canada; 905-563-7642.

Jon Katz, a former newspaper reporter and editor, encourages computer-driven news media to foster dialogue between reporters and readers. He has written for *Rolling Stone*, New York, and is the media critic for *WIRED* magazine. He can be e-mailed at jdkatz@aol.com.

Marjorie Kelly is the founding editor and current publisher of *Business Ethics*, a national magazine focusing on corporate responsibility. The magazine serves both businesspeople trying to run their businesses in a responsible way, and the increasing number of people involved in socially responsible investing. Subscriptions (6 issues a year) are $19.95 and are available from 612-962-4702.

Jay Kinney is publisher and editor-in-chief of *Gnosis: A Journal of the Western Inner Traditions*. An earlier and more extensive version of his article appeared in *Critique and Whole Earth Review*. It can be found on his web page at http://www.well.com/user/jay/.

Paul Kivel is a cofounder of the Oakland Men's Project and author of *Men's Work: How To Stop the Violence That Tears Our Lives Apart* (Ballantine). For more information, write to the Oakland Men's Project, 440 Grand Ave., Suite 320, Oakland, CA 94610; 510-835-2433, e-mail pkivel@netcom.com.

Thomas Kochman, Ph.D. is a nationally recognized leader in the field of cultural diversity, research, and management and author of *Black and White Styles in Conflict*. Kochman is president of Kochman Communication Consultants, Ltd. He can be reached at 120 North Oak Park Ave., Suite 206, Oak Park, IL 60301; 1-800-723-7640.

Charles Krauthammer is a psychiatrist, educator, journalist, and author. He has been a contributor to *The New Republic*, *Time*, and the *Washington Post*.

Andrew Lam, an editor for Pacific News Service, was born in Vietnam and came to the United States in the mid-1970s. He is working on his first short story collection.

265

Dianne M. LaMountain is a Senior Associate with ODT, Inc. She is the author of a number of award-winning training modules, and regularly gives speeches and conducts seminars on managing cultural diversity for both the public sector and for Fortune 500 corporations. Contact her at ODT, Inc., P.O. Box 134, Amherst MA 01004; 1-800-736-1293. She works out of the ODT office in Richmond, VA.

Ginger Lapid-Bogda is a Los Angeles-based organization development (O.D.) consultant in large scale change management for Fortune 500 companies. Dr. Lapid-Bogda has been a speaker at numerous O.D. conferences. She has written for the *Wall Street Journal* and *Across the Board*. Reach her at Bogda & Associates, 2396 Nalin Dr., Los Angeles, CA 90077; 310-440-9772, Fax 310-472-2381).

Dr. Joan Steinau Lester, a television, radio, and print commentator is author of *The Future of White Men and Other Diversity Dilemmas* and executive director of Equity Institute, Inc. She speaks on diversity and is author of a new book on women's empowerment. For further information contact The Equity Institute, 6400 Hollis St., Suite 15, Emeryville, CA 94608; 510-658-4577, Fax 510-658-5184.

Deena Levine is a cross-cultural consultant who specializes in communication training, including speaking and writing skills for U.S. and foreign-born professionals. Contact her at Deena R. Levine & Associates, P.O. Box 582, Alamo, CA 94507; 510-947-5627, Fax 510-947-5628.

During twenty years in the United States Army specializing in Latin American Affairs, **Leonard Loomis** helped break color lines in Panama (1962) and gender lines in Army Intelligence (1978). He consults and trains for L.A. County and industry. Reach him at Portll Enterprises, 208 Somerset Circle, Thousand Oaks, CA 91360; 805-373-1448, e-mail Seislls@aol.com, Web page http://www.adnetsol.com/portll/portll.html.

Manning Marable, perhaps the most widely-read black intellectual in the United States, is professor of history and director for research in African-American studies at Columbia University. His most recent book, *Beyond Black and White*, will be followed by *Speaking the Truth to Power, and Affirmative Action and the Politics of Race*.

Elizabeth "Betita" Martinez is the author of 5 books and many articles on social movements in the United States and Latin America. Her new video, *Viva La Causa: 500 Years of Chicano History*, is available from the Southwest Organizing Project in Albuquerque New Mexico; 505-247-8832, Fax 505-247-9972.

Russell Means is an American Indian movement activist who participated in an armed occupation of Wounded Knee, South Dakota in 1973. He has starred in four movies. His autobiography, *Where White Men Fear to Tread* (1995), was published by St Martin's Press (800-221-7945). He has been an assistant golf pro, a ballroom dance instructor, a rodeo bullrider, and a computer programmer.

Frederick A. Miller is president and CEO of The Kaleel Jamison Consulting Group, Inc. (KJCG). His work has included groundbreaking work in many large systems change initiatives within Fortune 100 companies. He can be contacted at The Kaleel Jamison Consulting Group, Inc., 1731 Robinway Dr., Cincinnati, OH 45230-2236; 513-231-1007, Fax 513-231-0890

Richard Moran is a professor of sociology & criminology at Mount Holyoke College, South Hadley, Mass.

Lance Morrow, journalist and author, is a senior writer at *Time* magazine. He is author of *The Chiefs: A Memoir of Fathers and Sons* (Random House, 1984).

Kevin O'Kelly first interviewed Arun Gandhi while a history student at Mississippi State University. Kevin has a master's degree in English from the University of North Carolina at Chapel Hill. He has written for *The Sun, Southern Exposure* and the *Austin American-Statesman*. He is working on a series of articles about Arun Gandhi.

Julie O'Mara is president of O'Mara Associates, 5979 Greenridge Rd., Castro Valley, CA 94552-1817; 510-582-7744, Fax 510-582-4826.

Céline-Marie Pascale is a freelance writer living in Santa Cruz, California.

James L. Payne taught at Yale, Wesleyan, Johns Hopkins, and Texas A & M University. His books include a study of Congress and spending, *The Culture of Spending*, and an examination of the social, moral, and economic burdens of the U. S. tax system, *Costly Returns*. He is now director of Lytton Research and Analysis, 335 Lavina Ave., Sandpoint, ID 83864; 208-263-3564.

Lydia Phillips is education services officer at the Co-operative Housing Federation of Canada, 311-225 Metcalfe St, Ottawa, Canada K2P 1P9; 613-230-2201, Fax 613-230-2231.

Benjamin Pimental is a staff writer for the *San Francisco Chronicle*.

Adrian Piper wrote a 14,000 word article entitled "Passing for White, Passing for Black" by which originally appeared in *Transition* (58: 4-34; 1992). At that time she was a professor of philosophy at Wellesley College in Wellesley, Mass.

Katha Pollitt is the author of *Reasonable Creatures: Essays on Women and Feminism* (Vintage). She writes a bimonthly column for *The Nation*.

Merlin G. Pope is adjunct professor at the Graduate School of Community Planning of the University of Cincinnati. He is an authority on the subject of "Personnel Diversity and its Impact on Organizational Productivity." He has been the keynote speaker on this and other related topics for many annual EEO conferences, professional organizations, and civic groups.

General **Colin Powell**, former Chairman of the Joint Chiefs of Staff, served both Republican and Democratic administrations.

Elizabeth Power, President of E. Power & Associates, is a management consultant and author. She may be reached at P.O. Box 2346, Brentwood, TN 37024-2346; 615-371-1320, e-mail PowerE@AOL.com.

Dr. Tony Rey helps build communities to prevent alcohol, tobacco, and other drug abuse. Every January until he finished high school he took his unmarried mother's and his grandmother's alien registration cards to the post office. Reach him at Executive Consulting, P.O. Box 167973, Irving, TX 75016; 214-550-1231, Fax 214-580-8992, e-mail TreyTX@aol.com.

Elayna Reyna, in partnership with her husband Juan Jose (Sonne) Reyna, is an indigenous author, lecturer, artist. Together they are Native American activists and members of San Juan American Indian Council in San Juan Bautista, CA, and cofounders of One Earth One People Peace Vision, Inc. (P.O. Box 1388, San Juan Bautista, CA 95045; 408-623-2379, Fax 408-623-2108).

Alan Richter, Ph.D. is a cofounder of Quality Educational Development, Inc. He developes innovative curricula for corporations and organizations that utilize games, videos, software, case studies, and graphic and written presentations. Reach him at QED, 41 Central Park West, New York, NY 10023; 1-800-724-2215 or 212-724-3335, Fax 212-724-4913, e-mail richterqed@aol.com.

Jeremy Rifkin is the author of thirteen books on the impact of technological changes on the economy, the workforce, society, and the environment. His most recent book is *The End of Work* (Putnam Publishing). He is the founder and president of the Foundation on Economic Trends in Washington, D.C. Rifkin has been a resident scholar at more than three hundred universities in some ten countries.

Karen Ritchie is executive vice president/managing director at General Motors Mediaworks.

Roberto Rodriguez and Patrisia Gonzalez write a weekly syndicated column for Chronicle Features. They are married and live in El Paso, Texas.

Anita Rowe and Lee Gardenswartz are partners in the consulting firm of Gardenswartz & Rowe of Los Angeles. Since 1980, they have specialized in the "human side of management" for a variety of regional and national clients, helping them manage change, handles stress, build productive and cohesive work teams, and create intercultural understanding and harmony in the workplace. Together they have authored numerous books and articles. Their *Managing Diversity: A Complete Desk Reference and Planning Guide* (Business-One Irwin) won the book-of-the-year award from the Society for Human Resource Managers. Reach them at Gardenswartz & Rowe, 12658 West Washington Blvd. #105, Los Angeles, CA 90066; 310-823-2466, Fax 310-823-2932.

Mevlana Jelaluddin Rumi in the islamic world is held in the highest esteem not only as a literary figure, but as a saint whose personal example inspired the founding of a major religious order, and as a philosopher whose elaboration of the cosmic sense of Love has had a significant cultural impact. A figure of almost prophetic dimensions, he became for some Muslims almost a second Muhammed, for Christians a second Christ, and for Jews a second Moses. Although following the details of the Islamic faith, Rumi expounded a religion of love. His works have been translated into English by John Moyne and Coleman Barks and are available from Threshold Books; 802-254-8300, Fax 802-257-2779.

Suzanne Salimbene, Ph.D., president of Inter-Face International, has more than twenty years' experience in language and cross-cultural communication experience in health care. She has worked in over twenty-two countries. **Jacek W. Graczykowski, M.D.** a Fellow in Reproductive Endocrinology at USC School of Medicine and graduate of the School of Medicine in Gdansk, Poland, works extensively in multicultural environments. Contact Inter-Face International at 19201 Santa Rita Street, Tarzana CA 91356; 818-342-4354, e-mail IFI4you@aol.com.

Chris Sandoval is the director of the Multicultural AIDS Resource Center of California (MARCC) at Polaris Research and Development, Inc. (China Basin Landing, Suite 4300, 185 Berry St., San Francisco, CA 94107; 415-777-3229, Fax 415-512-9625). He has an international reputation as an expert in the field of managing diversity and cross-cultural communication.

Professor Arthur M. Schlesinger Jr. is the author of fourteen books, including *The Age of Jackson* and *The Disuniting of America.*

Beauregard "Bo" Sears interests include working with Resisting Defamation to reduce abrasive and derogatory public discourse against any member of any ethnic or religious group. Reach him at Resisting Defamation, 2530 Berryessa Rd., #616, San Jose, CA 95132; 408-995-0570, Fax 408-995-5124, e-mail ResistDef@aol.com.

Share the Wealth is a national, nonprofit organization working to focus action and attention on the growing economic inequality in the United States and its impact on our quality of life. They publish a newsletter, *Too Much: A Quarterly Commentary on Capping Excessive Income and Wealth.* Membership which includes a subscription is $25 per year available from Share the Wealth, 37 Temple Pl., 3rd. Floor, Boston, MA 02111; 617-423-2148.

Ralph G.H. Siu is a retired executive who devotes his intellectual energy to the synthesis of East-West psycho-philosophical thought. He is the author of *The Tao of Science; The Portable Dragon: The Western Man's Guide to the I Ching,* and *Transcending the Power Game: The Guide to Executive Serenity.* He can be reached at 4428 Albermarle Street, NW, Washington D.C. 20016; 202-362-3710.

Thomas Sowell, a senior fellow at the Hoover Institution at Stanford University, has written extensively on economics, social decision-making and ethnicity. Since 1991 he has been a columnist for *Forbes* magazine. He has authored *Race and Culture: A World View* (New York: Basic Books, 1994) and *The Vision of the Anointed* (New York: Basic Books, 1995).

Study Circles Resource Center promotes using "Study circles," small-group, democratic, highly participatory discussions which are helping public officials and others to engage citizens in public dialogue and problem-solving on issues such as crime, race, and education. Contact them at P.O. Box 203, Pomfret, CT 06258; 860-928-2616, Fax 928-3713, e-mail scrc@neca.com.

Nico Swaan, a Dutch-Canadian consultant and trainer with expertise in cross-cultural communications, multi-cultural team building, and diversity issues, has worked in the Middle and Far East, in North America, and throughout Europe. He may be reached at Pastorielaan 1, 8441 AA Heerenveen, The Netherlands; +31-513-626609, Fax +31-513-623619, e-mail D.N.Swaan@inter.nl.net

Toy-Ping Taira is a consultant and proprietor of Potomac Change Management in Potomac, Maryland. Concurrently, she is an adjunct faculty member in the master's program of applied behavioral sciences at Johns Hopkins University. She has worked for numerous years in high-level management and evaluation positions in both the executive and legislative branches of the U.S. government.

R. Roosevelt Thomas Jr., one of America's most respected authorities on diversity issues, is a consultant to numerous Fortune 500 companies and a frequent speaker at national conferences and industry seminars. Dr. Thomas is the author of *Beyond Race and Gender, Differences Do Make a Difference,* and *Redefining Diversity* (AMACOM). He is president of The American Institute for Managing Diversity, Inc., based in Atlanta, Georgia.

Jonathan Tilove writes about race relations for Newhouse News Service.

Judith C. Tingley, Ph.D., is a psychologist, corporate consultant, and author of *Genderflex™: Men & Women Speaking Each Other's Language at Work.* Her clients have included Motorola, Sierra Pacific Power Company, BMW, and the U.S. Forest Service. Reach her at Performance Improvement Pros, Inc., 7601 N. Central Avenue, #10, Phoenix, AZ 85020; 602-371-1652, Fax 602-371-3432, e-mail: genderjudy@aol.com.

Lindsy Van Gelder is a coauthor of *The Girls Next Door* (New York: Simon and Schuster).

Tim Vanderpool is a reporter for the Nogales International. He can be reached at 520-281-9706, Fax: 520-761-3115.

With twenty years' experiene as a consultant and trainer on human resource management issues, **Carmen Vazquez** provides services in cross-cultural and diversity issues both domestically and internationally in both English and Spanish. Reach her at Paradigm, Inc., 404 New Mark Esplanade, Rockville, MD 20850; 301-424-3675, Fax 301-424-2664.

Alan Weiss, Ph.D. is the founder and president of Summit Consulting Group, Inc. (Box 1009, East Greenwich, RI 02814-0964; 401-884-2778, Fax 401-884-5068), a firm specializing in management and organization development. He has published

over 300 articles in the fields of strategy, innovation, leadership, ethics, diversity, and interpersonal relations.

Lynda White is in corporate human resources, employment equity & diversity managment, Royal Bank,123 Front St. West, 7th Fl., Toronto, Ont. M5J 2M2, Canada.

Rosemarie White-Starr is executive director of the YWCA of Jamestown, New York. She as over fifteen years experience with design and implementation of programs for women, children, and families including administration of two teenage pregnancy prevention and education programs. Reach her at YWCA, 401 North Main St., Jamestown, NY 14701; 716-488-2237, Fax 716-484-1752, e-mail RMW1445@aol.com.

John Edgar Wideman is a professor of English at the University of Massachusetts in Amherst, Massachusetts, and the author of more than a dozen books and numerous articles. A two-time PEN/Faulkner Award-winner, his most recent book is *Fatheralong: A Meditation on Fathers and Sons, Race and Society* (Pantheon Books, 1994). His forthcoming book *Cattle Killing* will be published in the fall of 1996 by Houghton Mifflin.

Professor Walter E. Williams is a nationally syndicated columnist as well as the chairman of the economics department at George Mason University, Fairfax, VA. He is the author of *Do the Right Thing* (Hoover Press Publications, ISBN 0-8179-9382-7; 415-723-3373, Fax: 415-723-1687).

Robert Worth is a freelance writer based in New York. His work has appeared in *The Atlantic Monthly, Commonwealth,* the *London Guardian,* the *Philadelphia Inquirer,* and other publications.

Felice Yeskel, Ed.D. is one of the founders and currently the co-director of Diversity Works, Inc. (P.O. Box 2335 Amherst, MA 01004; 413-256-1868). She has been providing training and consulting for social service agencies, universities, religious organizations, and other non-profit groups across the U.S. for over 15 years. She also serves as the co-director of Share the Wealth (see page 269).

Amy J. Zuckerman is general manager of George Simons Internationsl. She trains organizations on cultural awareness and competency. She is a coauthor of *Sexual Orientation in the Workplace: Gay Men, Lesbians, Bisexuals and Heterosexuals Working Together* (Sage, 1995). Reach her at 1647 McAllister Street #6, San Francisco, CA 95115 415-931-4194.

ABOUT THE AUTHORS

*D*R. GEORGE F. SIMONS is President of George Simons International, an organization specializing in gender and cultural diversity management, and a Senior Associate with ODT Inc. As an educator, counselor, and writer he helps organizations know and achieve their purposes, working with both corporate culture and individual skills.

George is a Doctor of Psychology & Theology (Claremont 1977) and Diplomate of the Gestalt Center, San Diego. He did master's work in the history and psychology of human rituals at Notre Dame and in anthropology at Oberlin. He has authored: *Working Together: How to Become More Effective in a Multicultural Organization*, *Men & Women: Partners at Work* (with Deborah G. Weissman), *Transcultural Leadership* (with Carmen Vázquez and Phil Harris) and *Sexual Orientation in the Workplace* with Amy Zuckerman. He is principal designer of the DIVERSOPHY training game.

He has worked as a clergyman and adult education consultant, creating and editing multimedia training materials. In 1975, while teaching at Oberlin College, he was named an Underwood Fellow for outstanding work in Human Development. For many years, Dr. Simons also directed Hidden Valley Center for Men, an organization whose purpose is to educate men to meet the stresses of contemporary living.

Speaking English, German, Spanish, and French, he has worked in over thirty countries, serving such clients as: The Bank of Montreal (Canada), Chase Manhattan Bank, Colgate (Latin America), The Department of National Defense (Canada), Management Centre Europe (Belgium), Mobil Plastics (Luxembourg) Procter & Gamble (USA, Switzerland and the Rep. of the Philippines), PT Arun (Indonesia), Shell Canada, Silicon Graphics, The Universities of Warsaw and Cracow (Poland), Varian Associates, Whirlpool Corporation, and the General Services Administration of the United States government.

*D*R. BOB ABRAMMS is an international expert on designing, conducting, and evaluating management training and executive development programs. Bob's background includes a B.S. in industrial engineering, Master's degrees in both business administration and counseling, and a doctorate in applied behavioral science. He has published over fifty articles on leadership, motivation, human relations training, prejudice, stereotyping, and cultural differences.

He is currently Chair of the Board of ODT, Inc., an employee-owned Massachusetts-based management consulting and publishing company. Bob is a certified Human Relations Trainer and Consultant and has been a registered Organizational Development Professional Consultant. He has conducted his seminar on "Managing Cultural Differences" for a wide variety of corporate and association clients.

In 1990, he edited and produced ODT's Complete Cultural Diversity Library which won an award as one of the year's "20 hottest Human Resource products." He has pioneered the use of the Peters Projection Map materials in large corporations and been involved in a variety of diversity diagnostic projects. He co-authored (with Dianne LaMountain) *Cultural Diversity: A Workshop for Trainers*, a best-selling module for empowering organizations to initiate their own in-house diversity efforts. He also is the co-editor, with Dr. Simons, of the *Questions of Diversity*, a collection of diversity diagnostic assessment tools, currently in its 6th edition (and 16th printing). He co-authored with George Simons, the *Cultural Diversity Sourcebook* which won the Outstanding Book Award for 1997, presented by the Gustavus Myers Center for the Study for Human Rights in North America.

Avocationally, he is a Contact Improvisation (CI) dancer, who has worked with mixed dance companies (and classes) of able-bodied dancers and dancers with physical disabilities. This work has enhanced and enriched his perspective as a diversity consultant.

Bob Abramms at a mixed-ability dance workshop. Abramms borrowed a wheelchair to explore patterns of movement that can be created with the rolling effect of the chair.

273

ANN HOPKINS is a former university instructor who has spent several decades simultaneously in the academic and business worlds. During and following her graduate degree from the University of Pennsylvania she taught at several colleges and universities, choosing classes of nontraditional students and emphasizing the need for communication among diverse groups. While a resident abroad for some years, first in India, then in Australia and Hong Kong, she developed a program in conversational English as a Second Language, trained volunteers in the program, taught the program herself, and tutored other students from a variety of cultural and language backgrounds, including Yugoslav, Senegalese, Indian, and Indonesian. Additionally she edited articles for publication in English in local scientific journals.

As a small business owner in the US, she developed market strategies, wrote advertising, trained staff, and mounted exhibits—all of which contributed to communication training programs she developed and taught in such companies as Champion International and Avon Corporation. These resources found their way into her speeches to corporate groups on the communication needs of the changing workplace.

Since 1986 she has been associated with ODT, Inc. in a variety of editorial and developmental roles. She is currently a psychometrist at the University of Massachusetts working with diverse student populations, both traditional and nontraditional and including those with physical and learning disabilities. She trains staff to administer tests, prepares and edits outreach materials for her department, and independently edits manuscripts, particularly in philosophy and economics. She finds inspiration in singing with a Symphony Chorus, debating issues with her two daughters, and creating her own designs for knitting projects.

Ann Hopkins (6th from left) has been a member of mixed choruses since the age of 14. She rehearses here with the Pioneer Valley Symphony Chorus in Deerfield, Massachusetts.

*D*IANE J. JOHNSON is President of Mmapeu Consulting, a national consulting firm that specializes in organizational development, program planning, and diversity initiatives. The title for the firm comes from a South African word *mmapeu*, meaning "woman who carries ideas." This name was given as a gift to Diane during her travels and work in South Africa in the early 1990s. The name, mmapeu, was the ideal representation of the work she hoped to share.

Ms. Johnson received her M.A. from The New School for Social Research at the Graduate School of Management and Urban Policy. Her undergraduate work was executed at the University of Pennsylvania in the Annenberg School of Communications and the Wharton School. She is also certified in conflict mediation from the Institute for Mediation and Conflict Resolution in New York City.

Her decade of work with both for-profit and not-for-profit organizations provides her with an integrated perspective of organizational diversity work. The diversity trainings and workshops created by Diane evolved out of a personal commitment to assist organizations and individuals to create honest dialogues around race, class, gender, and other social identities.

Her clients include: Oxfam America, Tufts University, International Fellowship of Reconciliation, Brown University, Amherst College, Dept of Housing and Urban Development, MA Dept. of Education, MA Dept. of Public Health, Oberlin College, and the Lincoln Center for the Arts. She is author of *Proud Sisters, The Wisdom and Wit of African-American Women*, currently in its third printing and *Mama Love*. She holds an M.A. in Non-Profit Management and is pursuing a doctorate in Organizational Behavior.

Make Me Part of the CDF Network

CULTURAL DIVERSITY FIELDBOOK

ODT, Inc.
P.O. BOX 134
Amherst, MA 01004
or fax the form to: 413-549-3503
or call: 1-800-736-1273

Use this "Make me part
of the CDF Network
Form" as a way to stay
connected with new
developments, tools, and
resources as they emerge.

❏ Send me the Free Resource Kit.

❏ Send me information on your 900 number.

❏ Send me information on how to access resources on the Net
(or find us at www.hrpress-diversity.com).

❏ Send me a free trial subscription to *Cultural Diversity at Work*.

Name _____

Title _____

Organization _____ # of employees _____

Address _____

City _____

State/Prov. _____ Zip/Postal Code _____ Country _____

Phone # _____ Fax # _____